Lessons in Machine Piecing

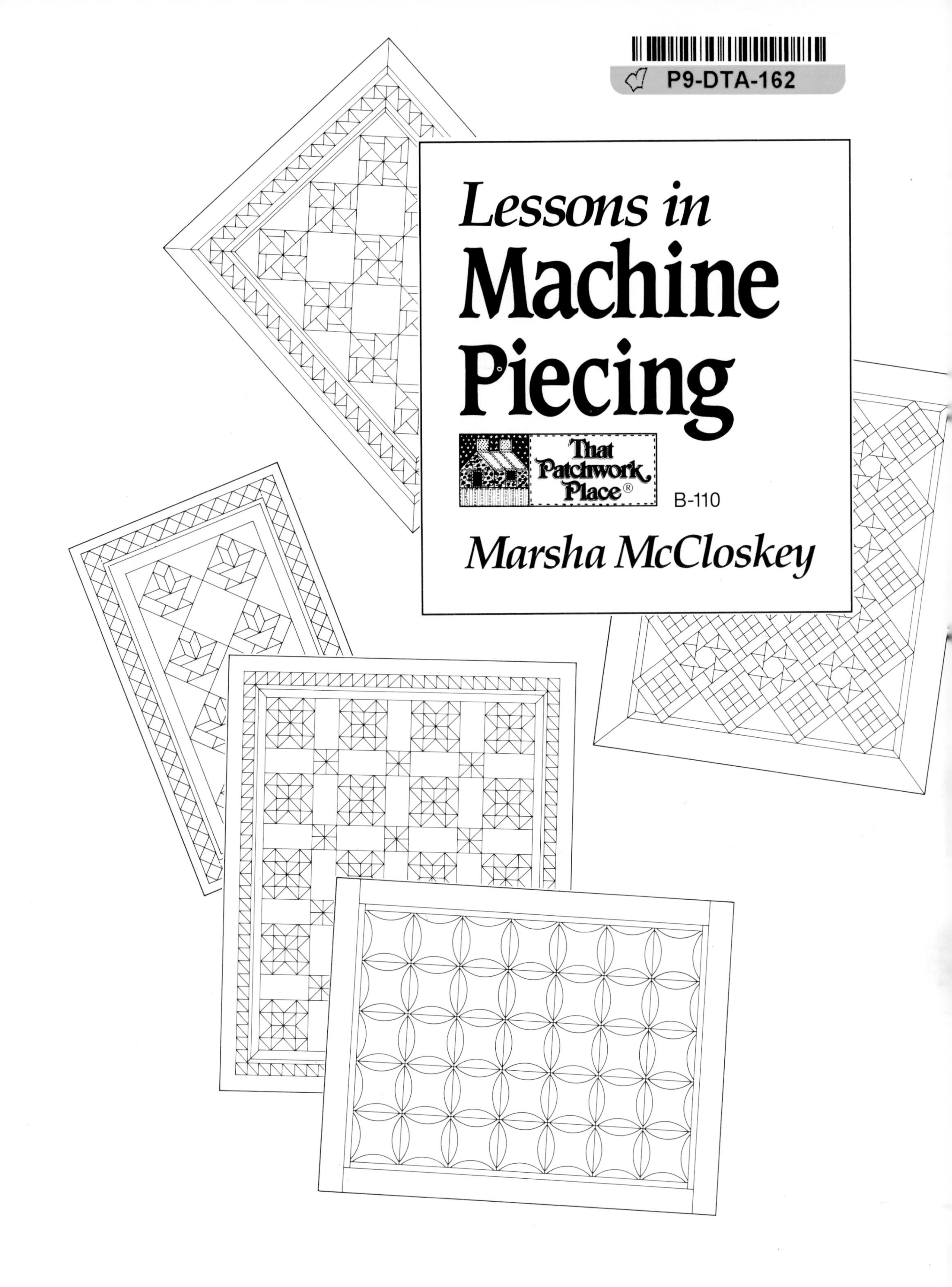

B-110

Marsha McCloskey

Acknowledgments

Sincere thanks are extended to the editorial and design staff at That Patchwork Place for their hard work in preparing this manuscript for publication. Thanks, too, to Freda Smith and Virginia Lauth for all their fine hand quilting; to Judy Martin, Nancy Martin, and Glendora Hutson for sharing their piecing expertise; and to my husband, David, for his patience and understanding.

Lessons in Machine Piecing is a distillation of years of teaching machine piecing classes. My students are largely responsible for much of the content because they came, asked questions, and demanded solutions. I owe them a great deal. So, here is the book on machine piecing that I have been promising for so long; it is dedicated to you, my students, because of all we have learned together.

Credits

Photography .... Brent Kane
Cover Photo .... Fred Milkie
Graphic Art and Illustration .... Stephanie Benson
Text and Cover Design .... Judy Petry
Editor .... Liz McGehee

Printed in the Republic of Korea
97 96 95 94 93 92 6 5 4

Library of Congress Cataloging-in-Publication Data

McCloskey, Marsha.
Lessons in machine piecing.

1. Machine quilting —Patterns. 2. Patchwork—Patterns. I. Title.
TT835.M3965 1990 746.9'7 89-20597
ISBN 0-943574-63-3

Contents

Introduction

For many years I offered a one-day, hands-on workshop called Basic Machine Piecing. I thought it was a great class. It gave students the opportunity to learn how to draft patterns on graph paper and how to make their own templates. They cut and sewed a series of increasingly complex patchwork blocks and learned about different piecing situations, seam allowances, pressing, pinning, and so on. But I couldn't get many students to take the class. I learned that quilters felt they "basically" already knew how to piece their designs on the sewing machine, but what they really wanted to know was how to do it "precisely." I thought about it and decided to change the name of the workshop to Precision Machine Piecing. Now, even though I haven't changed the content of the class one iota, it fills every time I offer it, and the students seem happy with what they learn there.

My point is: Good, basic skills in drafting, cutting, and machine sewing are what produce accurate patchwork. Precision piecing is not hard and is a natural result of doing all the steps accurately and with care.

The basics of quilt construction, the cutting and the sewing, have not changed since the first pieced quilts were made hundreds of years ago. Today, we still cut out pieces and sew them together to make designs, but how we cut and how we sew has changed with the technology available to us. What quiltmaker two hundred years ago could have imagined plastic rulers, rotary cutters, and electronic sewing machines? How our methods for performing the basic tasks of quiltmaking have changed! With the new tools, quilters have developed new techniques to make quilts that look like Grandma's but that take a lot less time and are more durable.

Lessons in Machine Piecing is a guide to piecing quilts, using the sewing machine. It covers the whole process of making a quilt top, from drafting the pattern to adding the borders. A series of lessons designed to build concepts and skills cover drafting, making templates, cutting, piecing blocks, pressing, setting the blocks together, and adding plain and pieced borders.

Throughout this book, **General Rules** will be highlighted to guide you in each process being described. **General Rules** for patchwork are just that—general. Adhering to them unfailingly, without critical attention to each new piecing situation, can get your piecing into trouble. Most **General Rules** will have exceptions. Watch for them and be open to breaking a few rules in the interest of better piecing.

Tools and Supplies

Graph Paper: Use the most accurate graph paper you can find. Check to make sure it is true. Some papers will be accurate in one direction but not the other. Find a store that sells supplies to drafting or engineering students. The large sheets (17" x 22") come in several grids: 1/4", 1/5", 1/6", 1/8", and 1/10". If you can, buy the kind with the heavy lines at the 1" increments—it is easier to work with. Expect to pay from 25 to 85 cents per sheet. Smaller sheets and tablets are handy for drafting blocks 8" and smaller and for quilt design and planning.

Pencils: A fine-tipped mechanical drawing pencil is ideal for drafting, but an ordinary #2 pencil and a good sharpener will do just fine. Keep your pencil sharp. Drawn lines made with a dull pencil have extra width and will make your draftings inaccurate.

Rulers: I use two rulers; both are clear plastic with a red grid of 1/8" squares. A short ruler is for drawing quilt designs on graph paper; a longer one, 2" wide and 18" long, is for drafting designs full size and making templates. Be aware that clear plastic grid rulers are not always printed accurately. Some rulers vary up to 1/16" from a true 1/4" along the long sides. Check your ruler to see if it is accurate.

Compass: A compass is used for two things: drawing circles and arcs and taking (and keeping) measurements. The dime-store variety is not good enough; it slips. A bow compass with a 7" radius and a roller stop to hold a setting is sufficient for most operations encountered while drafting patchwork patterns.

Scissors: You will need scissors for paper, a good sharp pair for cutting fabric only, and possibly a little pair for snipping threads. If your fabric scissors are dull, have them sharpened. If they are close to "dead," invest in a new pair; it's worth it.

Template Material: To make stiffened templates, you will need lightweight posterboard (manila file folders are good) or plastic (X-ray film is a good weight), and a glue stick.

Removable Tape: Most stationers and art supply stores carry this great product. Use removable tape to hold tracing paper in place while you work. This kind of tape will not harm the paper underneath when the tape is removed.

Fabric Markers: Most marking of cutting lines on fabric can be done with a regular #2 lead pencil and a white dressmaker's pencil. If you use a marking pen, test it on your fabric first to make sure the lines won't bleed.

Rotary Cutter: These generally come in two sizes. I use the larger one with the 2" diameter blade. The blades are very sharp when new, so take care not to cut yourself. They are easily nicked and dulled with use, so keep a fresh refill blade on hand.

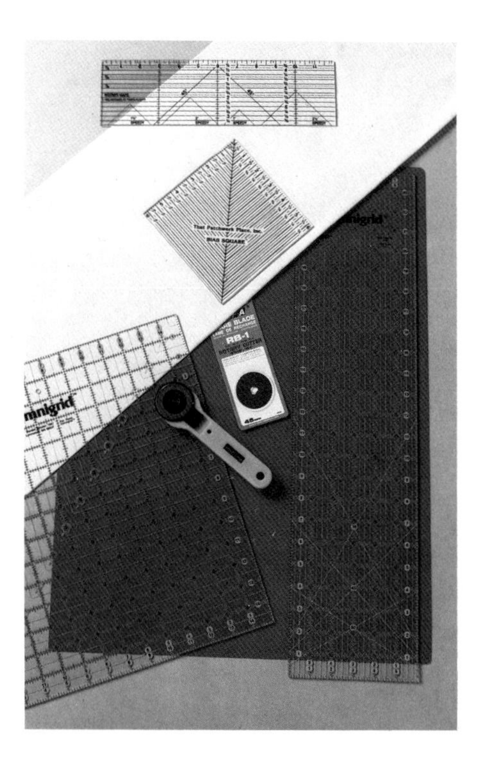

Cutting Mat: Made of various plastic materials, these mats come in several sizes and serve to protect your table and keep cutting blades sharp. My favorite mat measures 24" x 36" and covers half of my work table.

Cutting Guides: For rotary cutting, rulers are 1/8" thick transparent Plexiglass™ and come in an amazing array of sizes and markings. Of all the rulers for rotary cutting I own, these four are the ones I use the most:

1. A 6" x 24" ruler for cutting long strips. It is marked in 1", 1/4", and 1/8" increments (that's important!), with both 45°- and 60°-angle lines.
2. A 15" square for cutting large squares. It is marked in 1", 1/4", and 1/8" increments and is extremely useful for cutting quilt set pieces.
3. A 3" x 12" ruler. This one is handy for shorter cuts and medium-sized pieces, where the previous two rulers prove too cumbersome.
4. Bias Square™. This handy 6" square is marked in 1/8" increments with a 45°-angle line running diagonally corner to corner. Originally invented for rotary cutting pieced half-square triangle units like those used for Sawtooth borders, this tool can be used for cutting small squares and triangles and trimming points for easy matching.

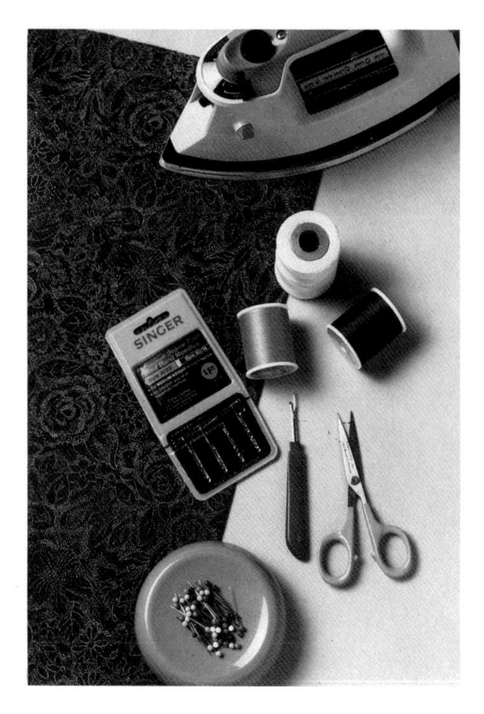

Sewing Machine: It needn't be fancy. All you need is an evenly locking straight stitch. Whatever kind of sewing machine you have, get to know it and how it runs. If it needs servicing, have it done, or get out the manual and do it yourself. See pages 21–22 for further discussion of sewing machines.

Needles: A supply of new sewing machine needles for light- to medium-weight cottons is necessary. You'll also need an assortment of hand-sewing needles, known as Sharps, and quilting needles, called Betweens (#8, #9, or #10).

Pins: Multicolored glass- or plastic-headed pins are generally longer, stronger, and easier to see and hold than regular dressmaker's pins.

Iron and Ironing Board: A shot of steam is useful.

Seam Ripper: I always keep one handy.

Getting Started

Drafting Patterns

Accurate machine piecing begins with accurate templates or pattern pieces. Although the templates in most quiltmaking books today are accurate, they are not always offered in an appropriate format for machine work. Templates for machine piecing include seam allowances and have the points trimmed for easy matching.

I have always been most comfortable drafting my own designs and making my own templates. Far from being an onerous task, it allows me to draw and color, glue and cut—activities I have enjoyed since preschool. More importantly, drafting allows me to get inside a block design and truly know it. Because I have drawn it, I know how the pieces must fit together and that helps me sew the pieces in the proper order. Because I draw the designs in full, finished sizes, I can also make scale judgments on the size of the pieces: Are they too big or too small? Is this the proper scale for the quilt I want to make?

There are thousands of patterns for patchwork quilts. The pieced designs are, for the most part, all variations on a few basic draftings. The patterns in this book are based on grids, the Le Moyne Star, or squares with curved design elements. Other groups of designs are based on circles or hexagons. If you know how to make a basic drafting in each of these categories, you can draft most any pattern you want by adding or dropping out the appropriate lines.

Patterns on a Grid

Easily half of all designs in patchwork are based on squares and subdivisions of squares. These lend themselves nicely to the graph paper approach to drafting and making templates.

A grid in patchwork is simply a set of small squares that make up a larger square. Each smaller square can be subdivided into smaller shapes to make a design. These are the steps taken in each of the draftings of patterns based on grids:

1. Study the design and determine the type of grid needed. Is this a nine-square grid design, a sixteen-square grid, a twenty-five-square grid, etc.?
2. Decide on a finished size of the block square: Divide the side of the square by the number of divisions on each side to determine the size of the grid squares and the type of graph paper to use. The resulting number is often a whole number plus a fraction. The fraction will tell you what kind of graph paper to use. For instance, if your grid square measures 1¼", use graph paper with four squares to the inch; if it measures 1⅖", use graph paper with five squares to the inch. Use 6

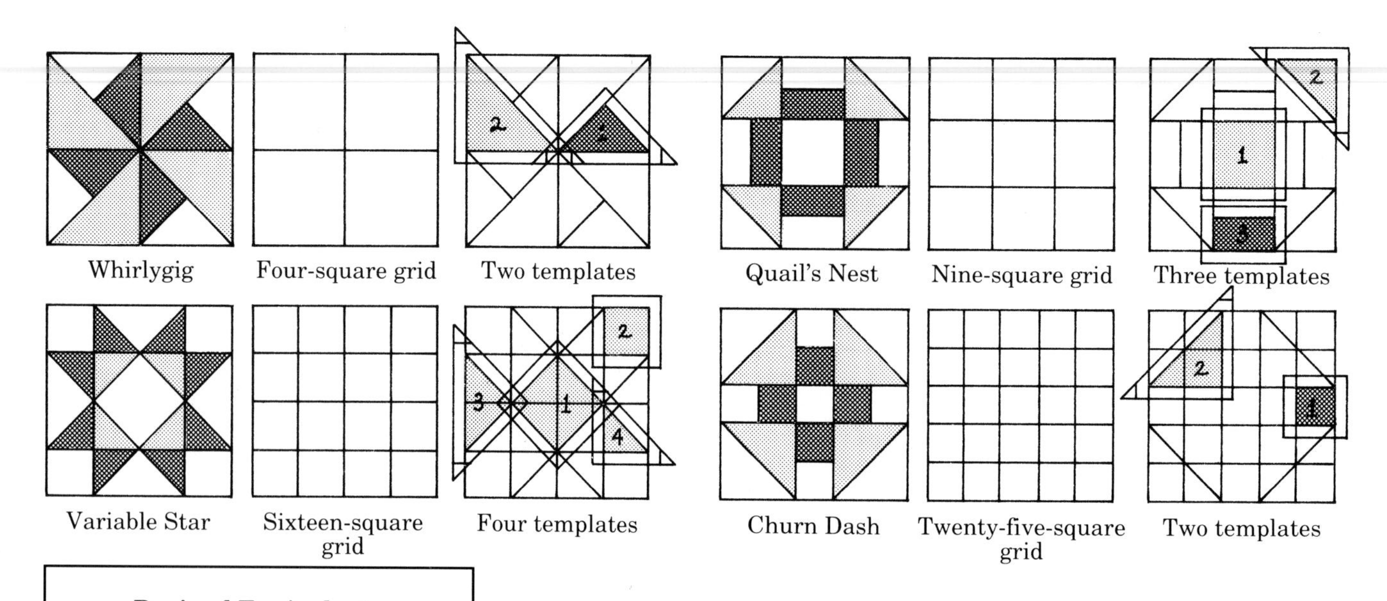

Whirlygig — Four-square grid — Two templates — Quail's Nest — Nine-square grid — Three templates

Variable Star — Sixteen-square grid — Four templates — Churn Dash — Twenty-five-square grid — Two templates

Decimal Equivalents

.1	=	1/10
.125	=	1/8
.166	=	1/6
.2	=	1/5
.25	=	1/4
.3	=	3/10
.333	=	1/3
.375	=	3/8
.4	=	2/5
.5	=	1/2
.6	=	3/5
.625	=	5/8
.666	=	2/3
.7	=	7/10
.75	=	3/4
.8	=	4/5
.833	=	5/6
.875	=	7/8

squares to the inch for measurements that end in thirds or sixths; use 8 squares to the inch for measurements in eighths, fourths, halves, and so on. If you use a calculator for this simple math, your answers will be in decimals. Use the decimal equivalent chart provided here to translate the decimals to fractions.

3. Draw a square the finished size of the design on the proper graph paper.
4. Draw the grid squares inside the larger square.
5. Subdivide the grid squares to create the design. Note that not every line in the drafting will be a seam line. Some lines need to be dropped out to simplify piecing.
6. Identify those shapes that need to be templates by coloring them in with colored pencils.

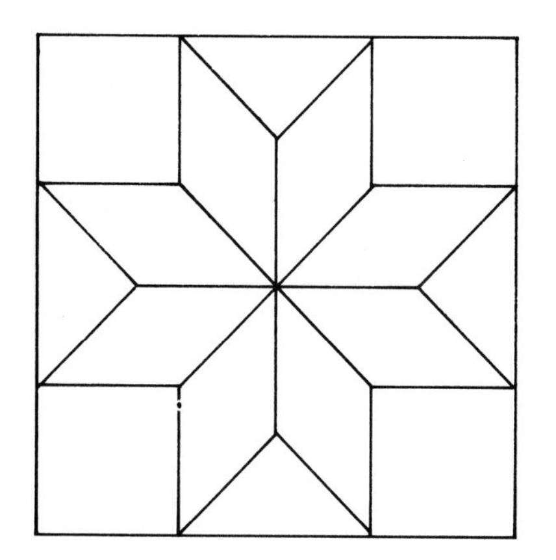

Drafting the Le Moyne Star

The Le Moyne Star is one of the most basic patterns in patchwork. An early pieced design, it was named after two brothers, Jean Baptiste and Pierre LeMoyne, who founded New Orleans in 1718. Popular in the early 1800s, the block became known in New England as the Lemon Star. It is the basis for flower designs that combine piecing with applique, like the Peony and Lily patterns, and for the many star blocks that utilize its 45° diamonds as a design base.

The Le Moyne Star is based not on equal grid squares, but on equal triangles that radiate from the center of the square. The eight star points are equidistant. It can be drafted on graph paper or plain unlined paper. The following directions apply to any size square.

1. Draw a square of any size on a sheet of paper. Graph paper lines can sometimes be distracting in this drafting, so I draw the size of square I want on graph paper first and then trace it onto an unlined sheet.

2. Draw two lines to divide the square in half vertically and horizontally, as shown; then draw two more lines from corner to opposite corner to divide the square into eight triangles.
3. With a compass, take a setting diagonally from the center of the square to one of its corners. Keeping this setting, move the point of the compass consecutively to each corner of the square, making two marks from each corner on each side of the square. These points will be the points of the star.
4. Draw four lines, joining the eight points across the square, as shown.
5. Draw four more lines joining the points diagonally across the square, as shown.
6. Identify the diamond, square, and triangle that will be templates and color them in.

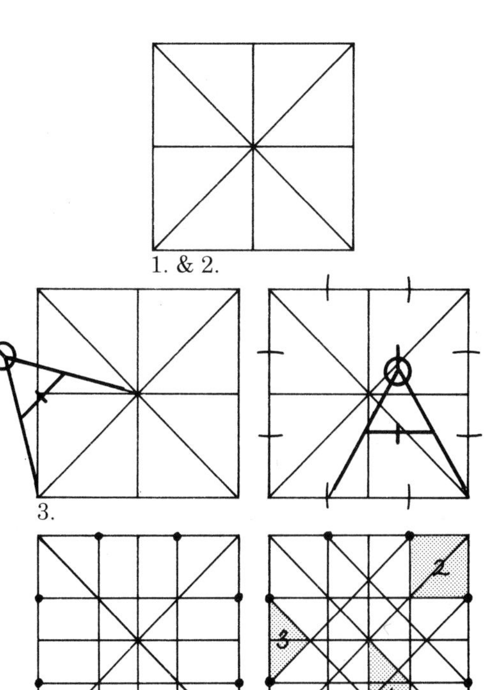

Patterns with Curves

The curved patterns in this book contain curved elements that are not based on circles. Instead, they are patterns based on squares with curves added. If you are interested in drafting truly circular patterns, I recommend two books: *Mariner's Compass* by Judy Mathieson and *Patchwork Patterns* by Jinny Beyer.

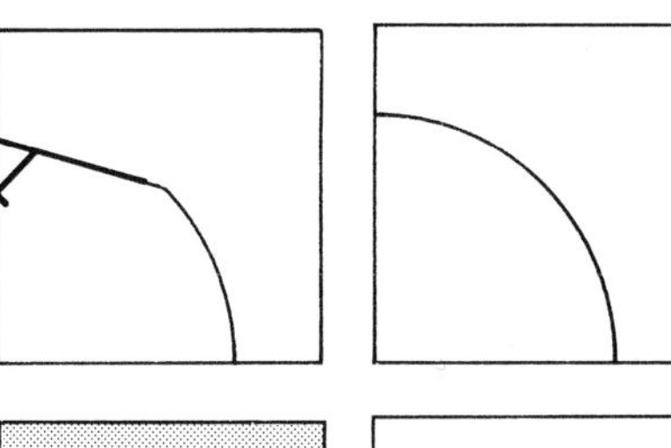

Example: Drunkard's Path, 12" block (Plate 11)

A popular traditional pattern, the Drunkard's Path is based on squares with curved elements added. It has only two templates and they are drafted as follows:

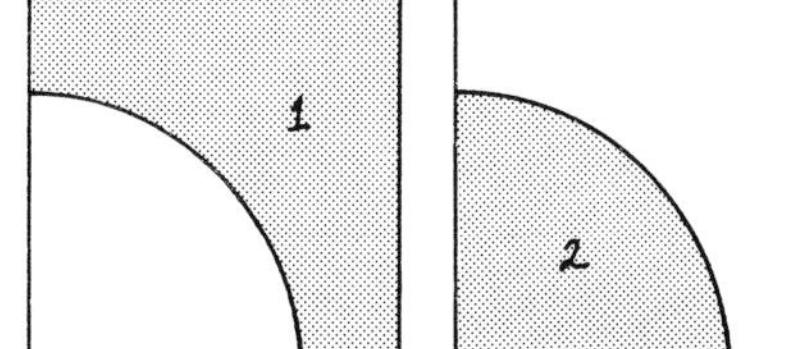

1. On $\frac{1}{4}$" graph paper, draw two 3" squares 1" apart.
2. With a compass setting of $2\frac{1}{4}$" (an arbitrary number, you can use whatever you think is attractive), draw identical quarter circles in each 3" square.
3. In each square, color in the shape that will be a template, as shown.
4. To add the $\frac{1}{4}$" seam allowance to the curve of Template #1, reduce the original setting of $2\frac{1}{4}$" by $\frac{1}{4}$". Draw a second quarter circle inside the first. Add $\frac{1}{4}$" seam allowances to the remaining four sides with a ruler.
5. To add the $\frac{1}{4}$" seam allowance to Template #2, increase the original compass setting by $\frac{1}{4}$" and draw a second quarter circle outside of the first. Add seam allowances to remaining two sides, using a ruler.

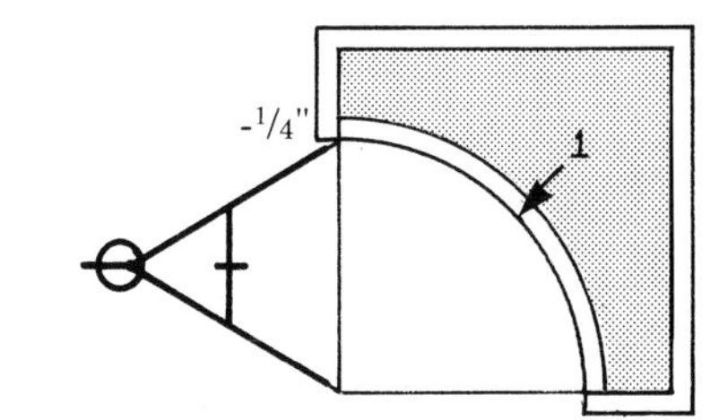

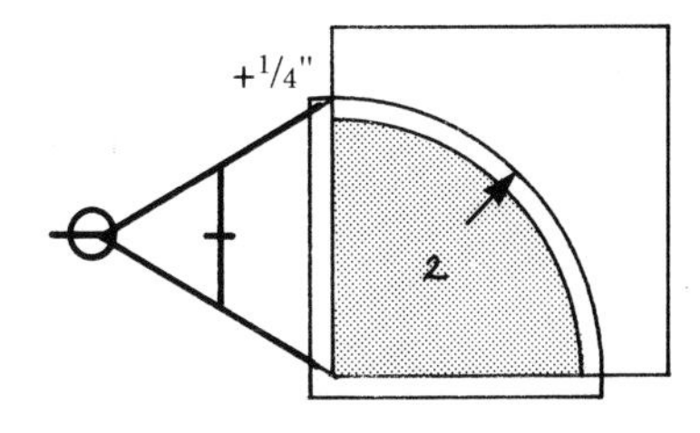

Making Templates

The **General Rule** for making templates is to be precise—there are no exceptions. Accurate templates or pattern pieces are the cornerstone of good piecing. Sloppiness in this step can only result in sloppy pieced work.

Adding Seam Allowances

Templates for machine piecing should always include 1/4" seam allowances. Therefore, fabric is marked (if your method includes marking) and cut on the cutting line. There is no marked line to guide your sewing, so it follows that by sewing exactly 1/4" in from an accurately cut edge, your sewing will be precise. See page 22 for how to find the proper 1/4" guide on your sewing machine.

Once a pattern has been drafted and the pieces that are to be templates identified, the next step is to add seam allowances. There are several ways to do this:

Method I. For simple shapes with straight sides and measurable dimensions, simply redraw the isolated shape on graph paper and then add the 1/4" seam allowances, using the 1/4" grid lines (if available) as a guide, or the 1/4" line on the transparent plastic gridded ruler.

Method II. For more complex shapes, carefully trace each shape from the drafting and use the ruler to add the seam allowances.

Tracing accurately is important and can be aided by the use of removable drafting tape to keep the tracing paper from shifting while you work. Removable tape will not harm the paper it is used on, so it also can be used in your quilt books without harming the pages.

Method III. For this method, I add seam allowances directly to the shapes on the drafting. The completed template shapes can then be traced or the dimensions used as cutting guides for no-template rotary cutting (see page 16).

It is extremely important that the 1/4" seam allowance be consistent all the way around each template in the design. It can be slightly fat or skinny, but it must be consistent. Also, I find that pieces cut with scissors and templates are slightly larger than pieces cut with a rotary cutter and ruler. Therefore, I use a slightly smaller (scant) 1/4" seam allowance for rotary cut pieces than I do for pieces cut with scissors.

Method I

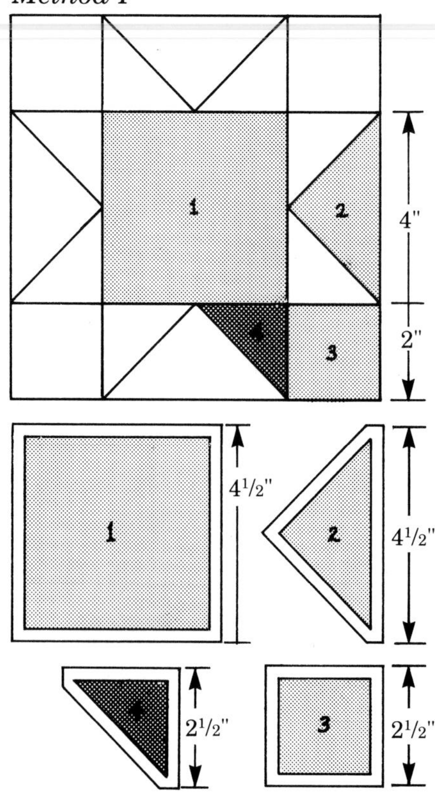

Method II

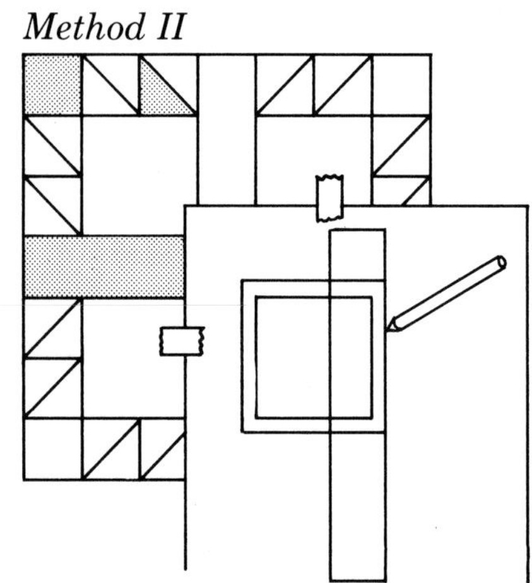

Method III

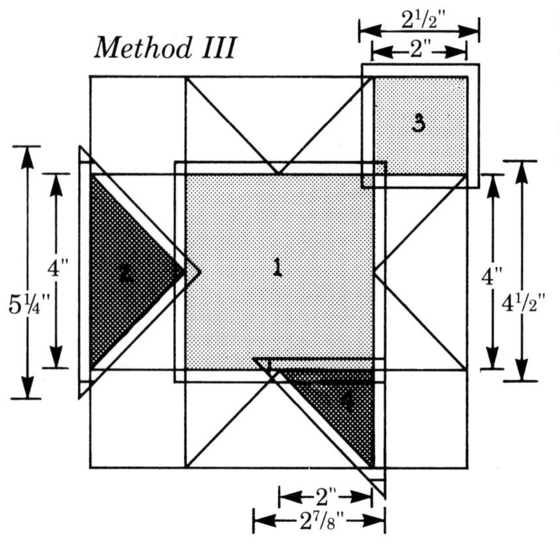

Labeling Templates

I don't know what your sewing room is like, but mine is a mess most of the time. I like to think of it as creative clutter, but occasionally things do get lost. As a result, I number each template and mark it with the name of the design, the finished size of the block, and the number of pieces to cut for one block. A notation of 4 + 4 tells me to cut four of one color, plus four of another. To help me while cutting, I mark a grain line; to help me while sewing, I trim points for easy matching. These last two items need some discussion.

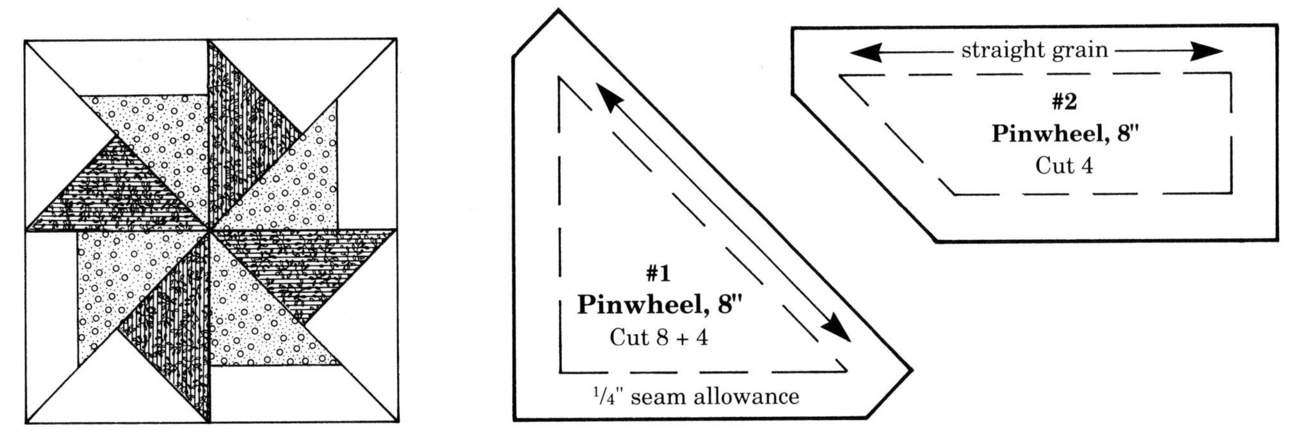

Pinwheel, 8"

Straight Grain and Bias

Fabric is made of threads woven together. Threads that run the length of the fabric, parallel to the selvage, are lengthwise grain. Threads that run across the fabric are crosswise grain. All other grains are considered bias. True bias is a grain line that runs at a 45° angle to the lengthwise and crosswise grains. For the small pieces in patchwork, both crosswise and lengthwise grain are considered straight grain.

Bias stretches and straight grain holds its shape, so fabric pieces should be cut with one or more edges aligned with the straight grain of the fabric. When you make templates, mark your drafting and each template with a grain-line arrow to guide you when placing templates on the fabric for cutting.

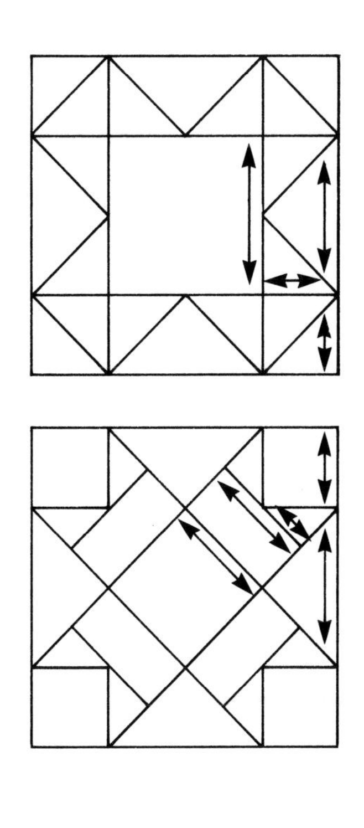

Because bias-cut edges stretch, the **General Rule** is that the straight grain should fall on the outside edge of any pieced unit. This applies to pieced units, pieced blocks, set pieces in the larger quilt, and the edge pieces in pieced borders.

The exception is that sometimes, in order to use a special print (such as a stripe) in a block the way you want to, a bias-cut edge must fall on the outside of the block. On such a piece, a line of stay stitching 1/8" from the cut bias edge will stabilize the fabric and help keep it from stretching.

Many quilters find that sewing a bias edge to a straight-grain edge creates a good, stable seam—more so than sewing bias to bias. Even so, choose first to place straight grain on the outer edges of pieced units and blocks, and then worry about bias and straight grain of interior seams.

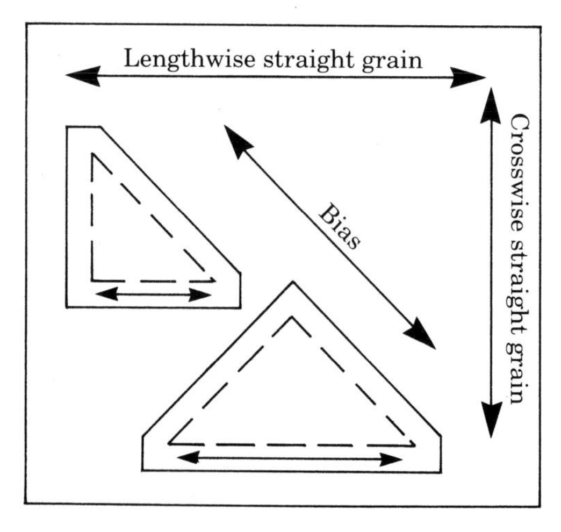

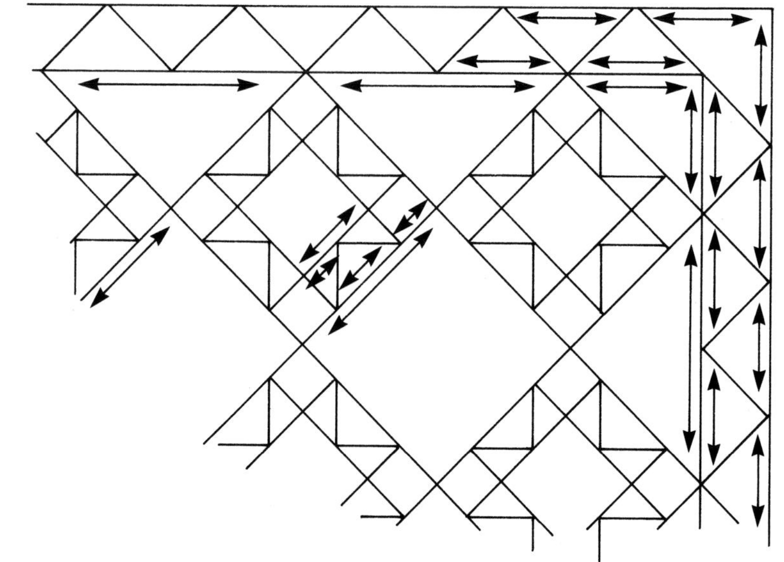

Trimming Points for Easy Matching

I think trimming the seam allowance points of templates is one of the most important elements in accurate machine piecing. Judy Martin showed me how to do it years ago, and I have been making templates this way ever since. The purpose of trimming points is to take the guesswork out of matching cut patches before sewing. Careful needlewomen trim points after stitching seams anyway, so why not cut them off in the first place and let them help you to piece precisely? If you have never used templates prepared in this manner, you are in for a pleasant surprise.

The **General Rule** is to trim points of less than 90° at the 1/4" seam allowance lines, so they match neighboring pieces. Most shapes with 45° angles can be trimmed at the 1/4" line on the graph paper. Shapes with other angles are harder. Study the examples given here; notice that each shape is trimmed to fit the piece it will be sewn to in the block design. If you are in doubt as to which points to trim where, make your templates with the points left on. Then simply match the seam lines of two pieces to be sewn together with positioning pins and trim away any points that stick out.

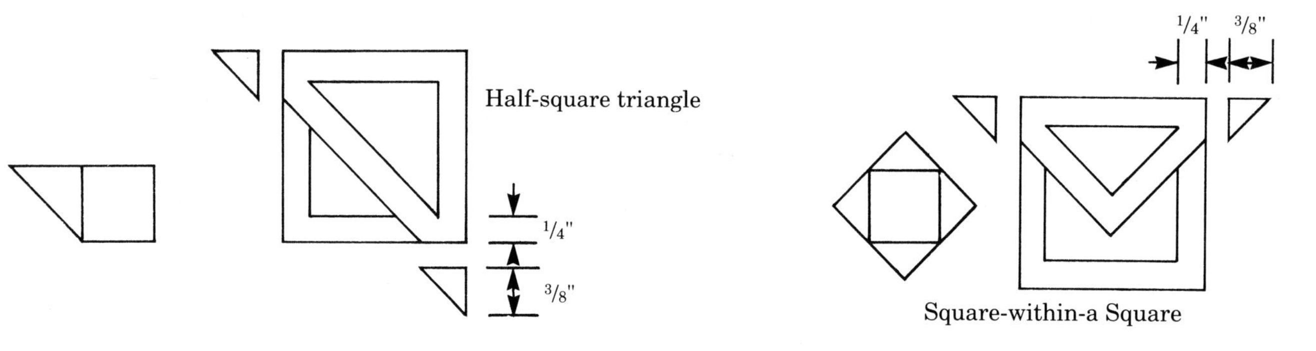

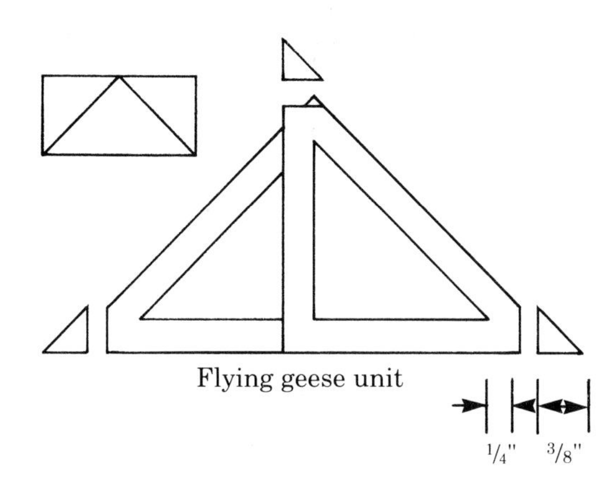

Flying geese unit

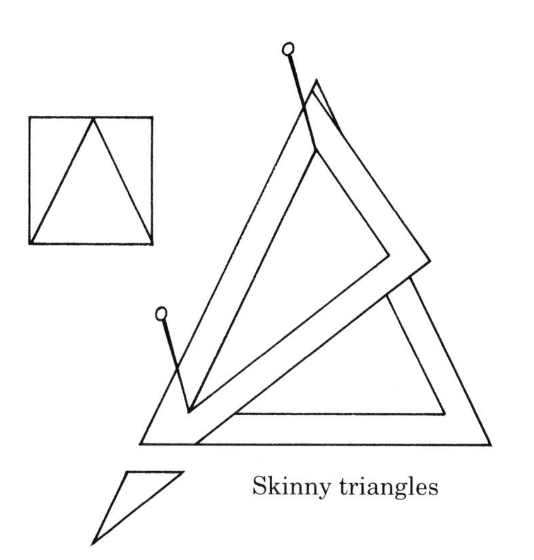
Skinny triangles

The templates provided for the quilt patterns in this book have trimming points indicated on each shape. If you choose to rotary cut your pieces without templates, you can still trim the important points to make your piecing easier. Trimming certain triangle points with a Bias Square™ is discussed on page 18. For other shapes, proceed to make templates for the design, but use them only for trimming points, not to cut the whole piece.

Types of Templates

The next step is to decide the best form of template to use for the particular project at hand. Should it be stiffened, just paper, or should you use no templates at all? What I choose depends on the kind of design I'm making, the number of pieces I need to cut, and whether I plan to use scissors or a rotary cutter.

No-Template Method. For simple, straight-sided shapes with dimensions that coincide with cutting guide markings, I use a rotary cutter and no templates. The drafting is prepared as in Method III on page 10, and pieces are cut as described on page 16. This method is great when a lot of pieces need to be cut from only a few fabrics.

Paper Templates. For more complex, straight-sided shapes with dimensions that perhaps do not coincide with cutting guide markings, I make paper templates by simply cutting the completed shapes out of graph paper. These can be taped to a cutting guide to get proper measurements for rotary cutting (see page 18), or simply held down on the fabric and cut around with scissors. Using a template this way is also suitable for scrap quilts, where only a few pieces of each of many fabrics are needed.

Stiffened Templates. For curved seam patterns, I use traditional stiffened templates, trace around them on fabric, and cut out the shapes with scissors.

To make stiffened templates, roughly cut out the pattern pieces (outside the cutting line). Glue each one to a thin piece of plastic (X-ray film is good) or lightweight posterboard. Cut out the paper pattern and the stiffening together. Be precise. Make a template for each shape in the design.

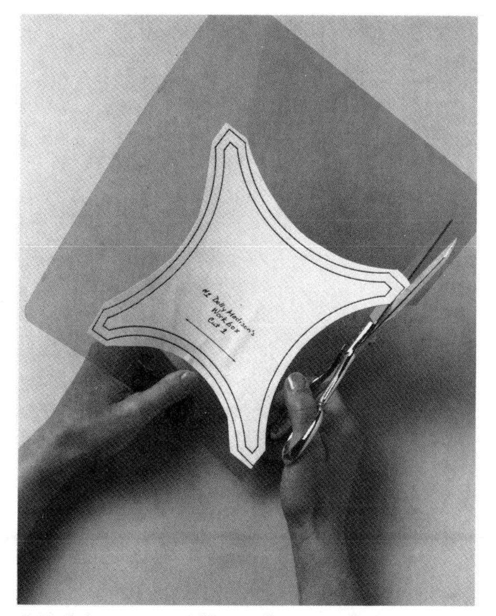
Making a stiffened template

Varying visual texture

Choosing and Preparing Fabric

Choosing just the right fabrics for your quilt project can be a long and very personal process. My main focus here is not the colors and prints you may choose, but the type of fabric. Most traditional quilters prefer lightweight, closely woven, 100% cotton fabrics for their quilts.

Lightweight means broadcloth weight, neither sheer or flimsy nor so heavy that the thickness interferes with accurate piecing. Closely woven refers to thread count—how many threads are actually woven together in a given area. Without getting into numbers, what I look for is material that feels firm, doesn't have too much give to it, and that I can't see through when I hold it up to the light.

Fabric of 100% cotton is the traditional choice for quiltmaking. Cotton feels good and behaves well during cutting, sewing, and pressing. Polyester, on the other hand, is stronger than cotton and holds color well, but I find it slippery. It skitters away from scissors, slips during sewing, tends to pucker along seam lines, and has a mind of its own when you try to iron it. A high polyester content in fabrics can make small patches difficult to cut and sew. In addition, cottons and poly-blends fade and wear at different rates, so it is best to use all of one kind of fiber in a quilt.

The fabric you buy should be preshrunk, color tested, and ironed before it is stored with your other fabrics. That way you can be confident that every piece on the shelf is ready to use.

Wash lights and darks separately with detergent and warm water. Dry them in the dryer. If you suspect the dark colors might run, rinse those fabrics repeatedly in clear water until dye loss stops. Sometimes, white vinegar in the rinse water can help set a problem dye. If the color continues to run, don't use it in your quilt. Better to waste a little fabric than a lot of work.

Cutting

For years, I have used paper pattern pieces or stiffened templates and cut with good-quality, sharp scissors. More recently, I have begun using a no-template, rotary-cutter-and-ruler method to cut pieces. I feel both template and rotary methods have their place in my quiltmaking and I sometimes combine them if it seems the best way.

In the sections that follow, I will explain how to cut with scissors and templates and discuss how to cut with a rotary cutter and ruler. It is up to you, the quiltmaker, to choose the cutting method that seems the most reasonable for your project, your resources, and your skills.

Always make one sample block of a design before embarking on a large project. After cutting the necessary number of pieces of each color and shape for one unit block, arrange the pieces on a flat surface in the desired design. This will help you determine which pieces to sew together first and to evaluate your fabric choice and arrangement.

Scissors

Study the design and templates. Determine the number of pieces of each shape and each fabric to cut. Trim the selvage from the fabric before you begin cutting. When one fabric is to be used both for borders and the unit block designs, cut the borders first; then cut the smaller pieces from what is left (see Adding Borders on pages 92–94).

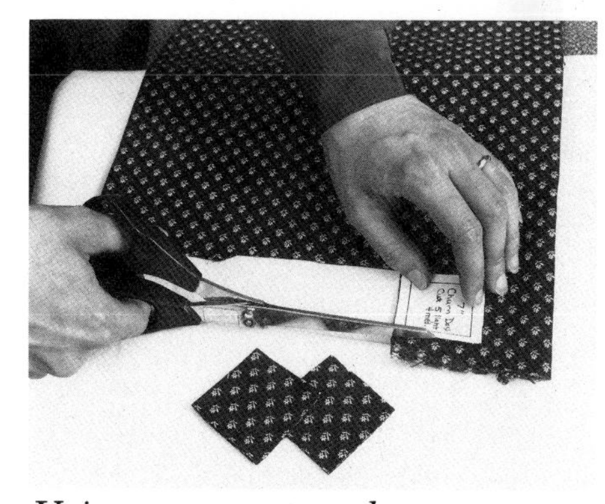

Using a paper template

At the ironing board, press and fold the fabric so that one, two, or four layers can be cut at one time. Fold the fabric so that each piece will be cut on the straight grain. Linear prints, such as stripes and checks, should be cut one at a time if you want the design to line up with the seam lines.

About the only time I use a stiffened template is for curved seam patterns. When using a stiffened template, position it on the fabric so the arrows match the straight grain of the fabric. With a sharp pencil (white for dark fabrics, lead for light ones), trace around the template on the fabric. This is the cutting line. Cut just inside this line to most accurately duplicate the template.

For most straight-sided shapes, I use a paper template. Line the template up with the straight grain of fabric, hold it in place on the fabric and cut around it. Be precise. Compare cut pieces with the template to be sure they are true.

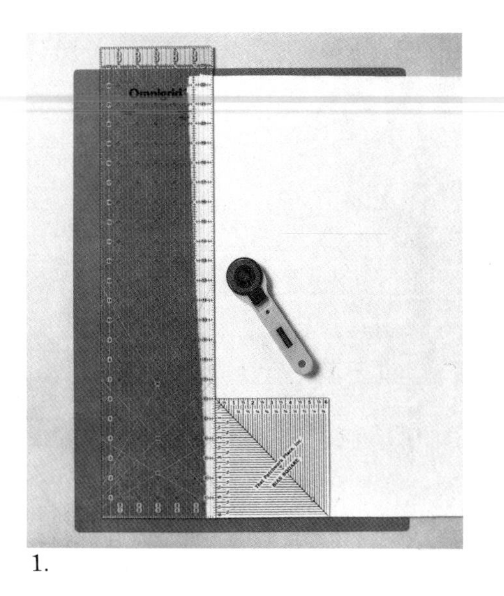

1.

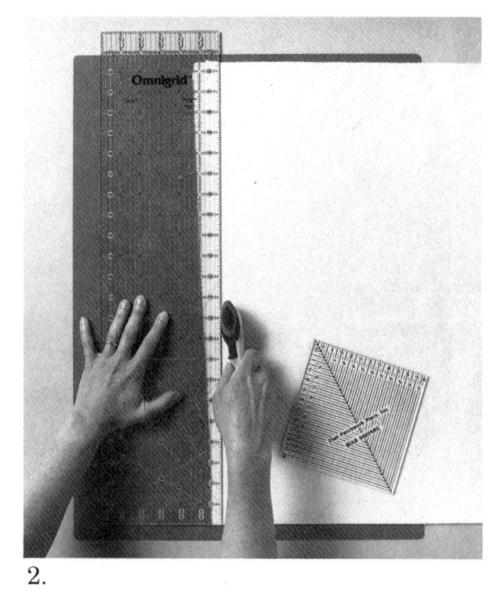

2.

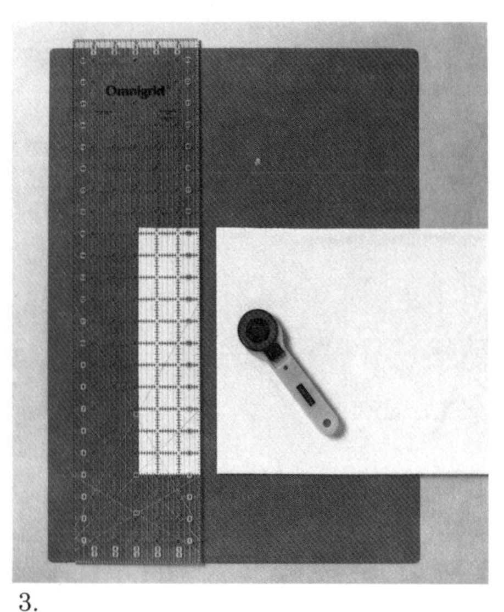

3.

Rotary Cutter

Scissors have been with us for centuries, but the rotary cutter was introduced to the quilt world in the early 1980s. It is a great tool, but with it came the need for cutting mats; special thick plastic rulers in various shapes, sizes, and markings; and plenty of refill blades.

Besides requiring a number of accessories, the rotary cutter has also changed the way quilters think about the pieces of fabric they cut. With most rotary cutting there is no marking of either cutting or sewing lines according to a template. Careful attention must be paid to measuring each dimension before making a cut. The dimensions of the cut pieces must include proper 1/4" seam allowances, and grain lines must fall in the right places. The guiding principle for grain line, as discussed on pages 11–12, is that the straight grain should fall on the outer edge of pieced units and blocks.

If fabric is badly off-grain, pull diagonally in the opposite direction to straighten. It is impossible to rotary cut exactly on the straight grain of fabric, and many fabrics are printed off-grain. In rotary cutting, straight, even cuts are made as close to the grain as possible. A slight variation from the grain will not alter your project.

Straight Strips

In quilt construction, long strips of fabric are used for borders, and shorter ones are used for lattices. Narrow strips of fabric are used to construct design blocks, and the rotary method of cutting squares and rectangles shown here begins with straight strips of fabric.

To begin, fold the fabric selvage to selvage, aligning the cross and straight grains as best you can:

1. Align the Bias Square™ with the fold of fabric and place a cutting guide to the left. When making all cuts, fabric should be placed to your right. **Note:** Reverse these techniques if you are left-handed.
2. Remove the Bias Square™ and make rotary cut along right side of ruler. Hold ruler down with left hand, placing smallest finger off the ruler. Your finger serves as an anchor and keeps ruler from moving. Move hand along ruler as you make the cut, making sure the markings remain accurate. Use a firm, even pressure as you cut. Begin rolling the cutter before you reach the fabric edge and continue across the fabric. Always roll cutter away from you; never pull rotary cutter toward yourself. The blade is necessarily very sharp, so be careful!
3. Fold fabric again so that you will be cutting four layers at a time. (This means shorter cuts.) Open and check the fabric periodically to make sure you are making straight cuts. If fabric strips are not straight, use Bias Square™ and cutting guide to realign.

Squares and Rectangles

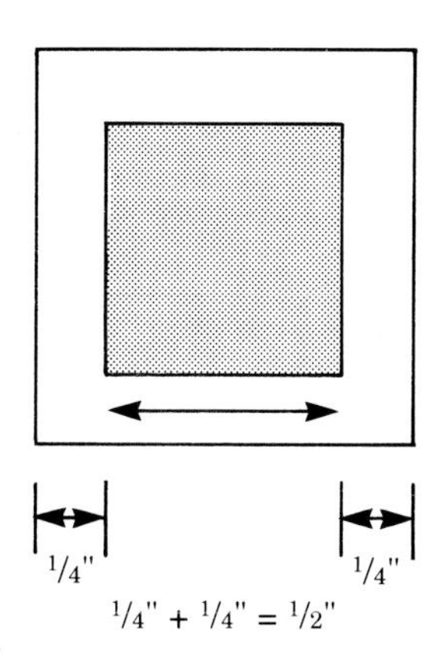

1. First cut fabric into strips the measurement of the square, plus seam allowances.
2. Using the Bias Square™, align top and bottom edge of strip and cut fabric into squares the width of the strip.
3. Cut rectangles in the same manner, first cutting into strips the length of the rectangle.

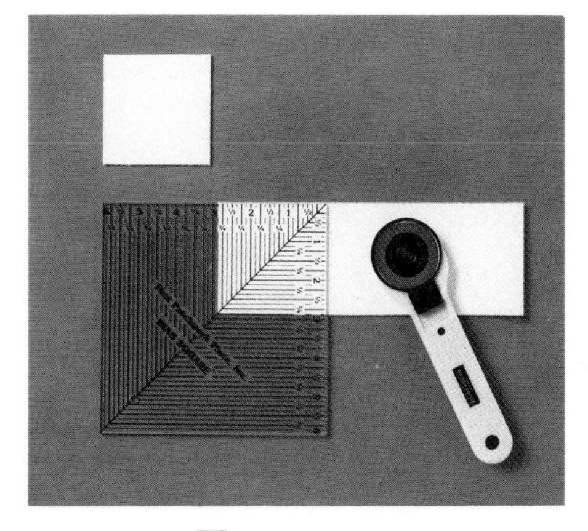

Triangles

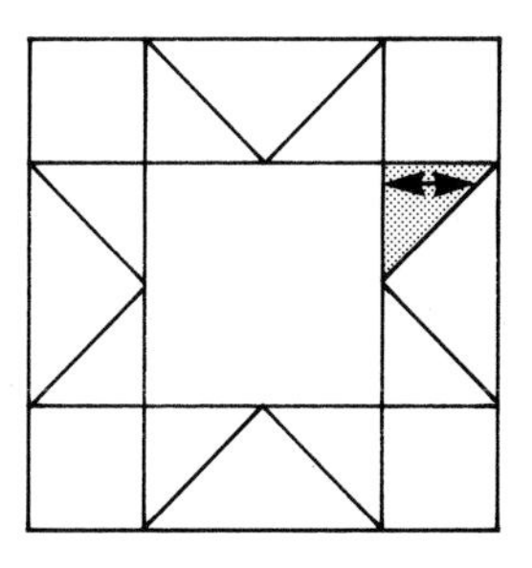

Half-Square Triangles. These triangles are half of a square cut diagonally, with the short sides on the straight grain of fabric and the long side on the bias. To cut these triangles, cut a square and then cut in half diagonally. Cut the square 7/8" larger than the finished short side of the triangle to allow for all seam allowances. Rotary cutting dimensions are given with each template in the Template section and in the directions for each quilt.

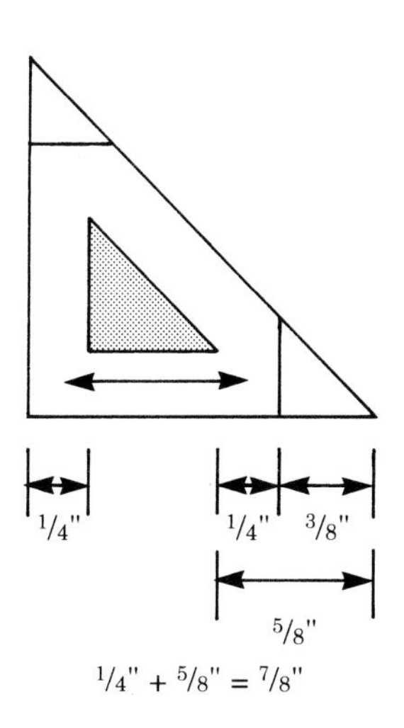

1. Cut a strip using the finished measurement of the short side of the triangle plus 7/8".
2. Cut into squares, using the same measurement.
3. Take a stack of squares and cut diagonally corner to corner. Check the first triangles you cut against the proper pattern pieces in the Template section to make sure they are the right size.
4. Use a Bias Square™ to trim points for easy matching (see page 18).

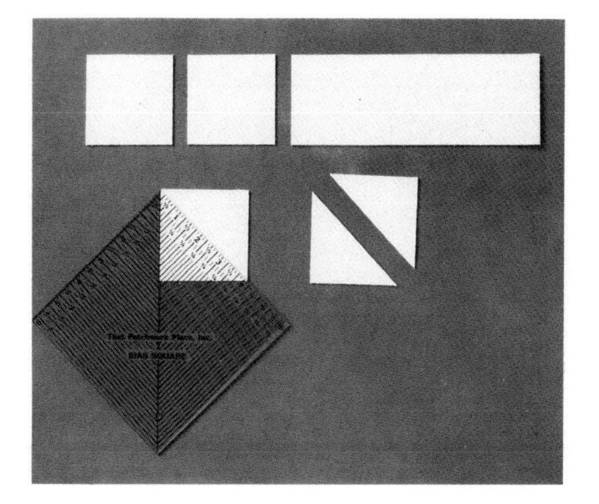

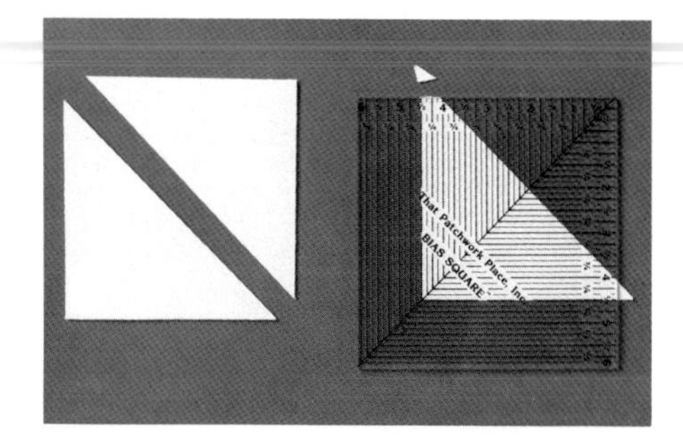

Trimming Points on Half-Square Triangles for Easy Matching

The Bias Square™ can be used to trim seam allowance points on half-square triangles. The measurement to use is the finished short side of the triangle plus 1/2" (1/4" seam allowance on each side). The example shown here is a half-square triangle with a finished dimension of 4".

1. To quick cut this triangle, including seam allowances, cut a 4 7/8" square of fabric and cut in half once on the diagonal.
2. To trim the points for easy matching, set the Bias Square™ at the 4 1/2" mark on the fabric triangle, as shown. The points of the triangle will stick out 3/8". Trim them off with the rotary cutter.

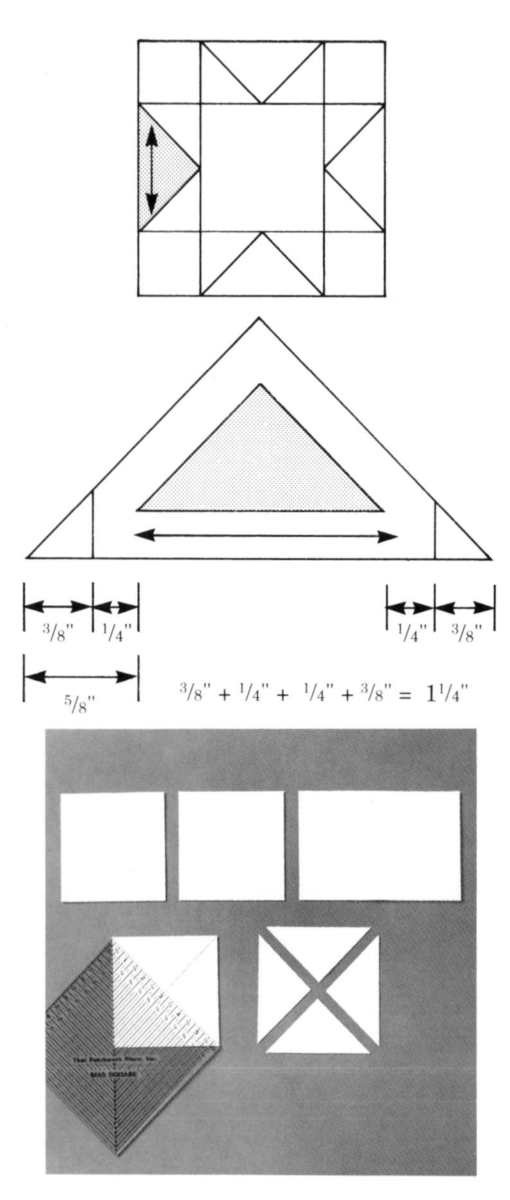

Quarter-Square Triangles. These triangles have their short sides on the bias and the long side on the straight grain. Placing the straight grain of the triangle on the outside edges of your block or quilt keeps it from stretching. These triangles are cut from squares. The square is cut 1 1/4" larger than the finished long side of the triangle.

1. Cut a strip the desired finished measurement plus 1 1/4".
2. Cut strip into squares, using the same measurement.
3. Taking a stack of these squares, line up the ruler from corner to opposite corner and cut diagonally. Without moving the squares, cut in the other direction. Each square will yield four triangles with the long sides on straight grain.
4. Use a template or ruler to trim 3/8" points off these triangles for easy matching (see page 12).

Asymmetrical Shapes and Reversals

An asymmetrical shape has unequal sides, and when it is flipped over, becomes the mirror image or reversal of its face-up self. Some examples are the parallelograms in the Scrap Basket block, the long skinny triangles in Darting Minnows, and the background pieces in the Pinwheel Daisy and Pinwheel blocks. When a design requires an asymmetrical shape in mirror images, as in Scrap Basket, there will be an "R" or reverse in the cutting instruction. From the right side of a single layer of fabric, cut the first number of pieces with the template face up and then flip it over, face down, to cut the remainder. A quicker way is to fold the fabric wrong side to wrong side to make two or four layers and cut with the template face up; the alternate layers will yield mirror image pieces.

Sometimes, an asymmetrical shape is used only one way in a design, such as the small background piece in the Pinwheel block. Then you have to be careful *not* to cut mirror images. In those cases, cut all pieces with the template face up on the right side of the fabric.

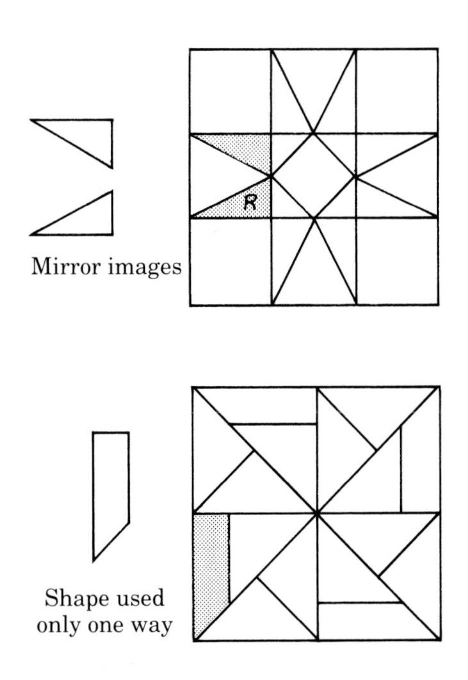

Mirror images

Shape used only one way

Skinny Triangles. The skinny triangles that form the points of Darting Minnows can be rotary cut from rectangles. Note that the block design requires skinny triangles cut as reversals or mirror images.

1. Cut straight strips as wide as the short side of the triangle, including seam allowances. The easiest way to arrive at this dimension is to draw the shape on graph paper and add 1/4" seam allowances.
2. Cut rectangles from strips, using the dimension of the long straight side of the triangle, including seam allowances.
3. Cut rectangles from corner to opposite corner to yield two identical skinny triangles. To get reversed skinny triangles, cut the next rectangle diagonally in the opposite direction.
4. Use a template to trim points for easy matching (see page 18).

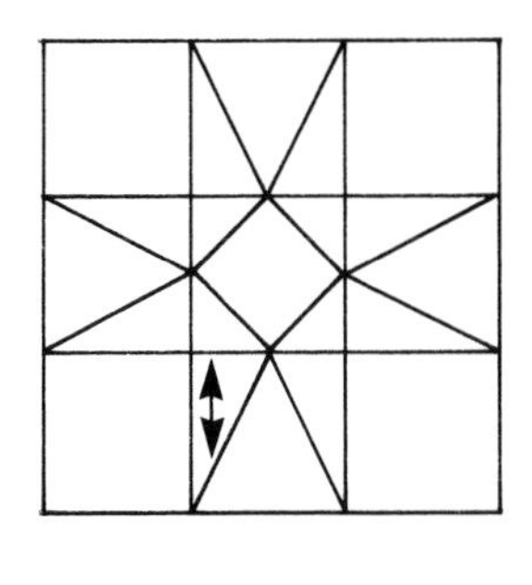

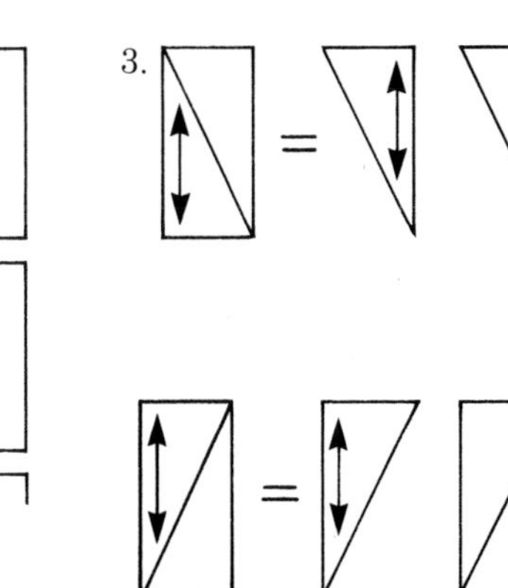

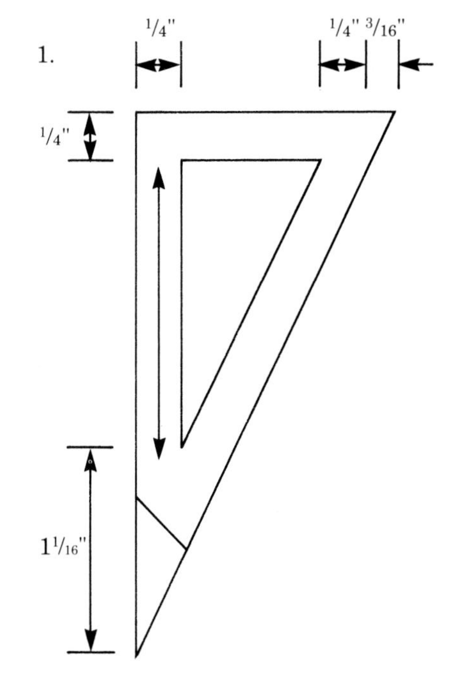

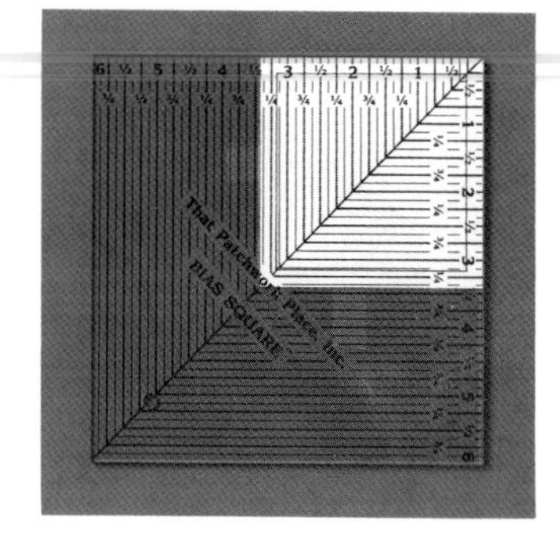

Combining Rotary Cutting with Paper Templates

If you are dedicated to using the rotary cutter, and many quilters are, you will figure out ways to cut out most any shape without touching scissors.

Often shapes and cut dimensions of pattern pieces do not correspond to markings on standard cutting guides. But, just because a square measures 4⁵⁄₁₆" does not mean it cannot be cut with a rotary cutter. For odd-size squares and rectangles, make an accurate paper template and tape it to the bottom of your cutting ruler with removable tape. You will then have the proper guide for cutting your shape.

Some shapes are more easily cut without taping the paper template to the ruler, by leaving it free. Carefully position the template on the fabric and place the cutting guide on top of it, lining up the edge of the ruler with the edge of the template. Be careful not to slice off bits of the template as you work.

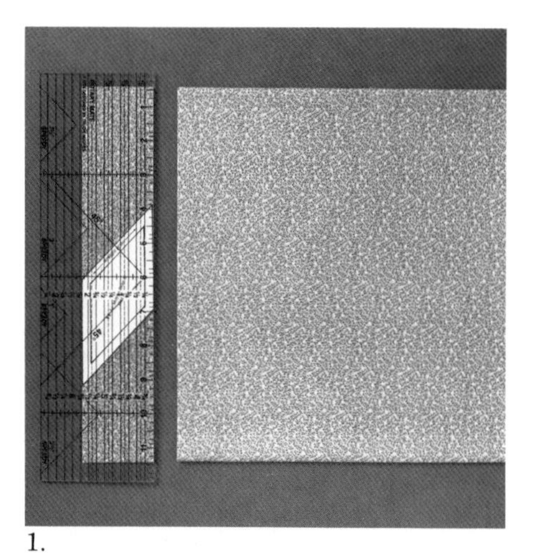

1.

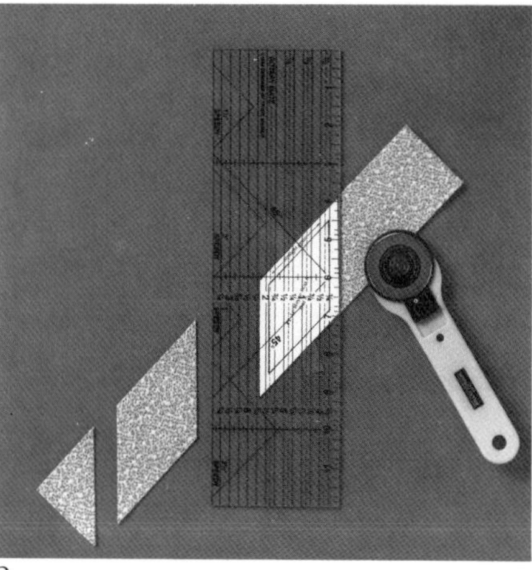

2.

Diamonds and Parallelograms. Diamonds can be cut using templates, by rotary cutting with rulers, or by combining the two techniques. Because the dimensions involved don't always easily match the markings on my ruler, I often find it easiest to use both a template and the rotary cutter.

1. Cut fabric strips the width of the finished diamond, plus seam allowances. Determine this width by measuring a drawn diamond template or simply taping the template to the bottom of the cutting guide.
2. Using the 45°-angle line on the ruler, make a first cut on the fabric strip. Then using either the measurement of the side of the diamond template or the template itself, make successive diagonal cuts to form diamonds. Check cut diamonds against templates for accuracy.
3. Use a template to trim points for easy matching or simply leave the points on; it will depend on the pattern. I leave points on when piecing simple Le Moyne Stars, but trim diamond points for more complex designs.

Machine Piecing

Sewing Machines

Your sewing machine is a tool. Don't be intimidated by it. Admittedly, some sewing machines are better suited to machine piecing than others, but I pieced for years on a less-than-wonderful machine and turned out very respectable patchwork. A lot of it is attitude. Get to know your machine and how it works. If it needs service, get it done or read the manual and do as much as you can yourself. Sometimes, all you need to do is sit down and sew pieces together for however long it takes to learn to use your particular machine.

Every machine is different and I haven't space to evaluate the performance of different brands, but the following are items I consider to be important in a machine that will be used primarily for patchwork.

1. Does the machine have an evenly locking straight stitch? Some machines that have the ability to do a lot of fancy stitches fall down on this basic stitch. For piecing, a machine that only does a straight stitch, but does it well, is all you need.
2. Does the machine have a backstitch that can be controlled manually? "Two stitches forward and two stitches back" is what is needed to backtack at the seam line; control is very important.
3. Will the machine start stitching at the edge of the fabric without chewing it up? A throat plate with a single hole for straight stitching (as opposed to an oblong hole for a zigzag stitch) can help solve the problem of the edge of the fabric being fed into the hole by the action of the needle and the feed dog. Another trick is to always use a starter scrap at the beginning of chain piecing.
4. Is there an appropriate presser foot? My favorite presser foot is 1/8" wide on the right or inner side. It allows the edges of the pieces to be seen (and sometimes held with the point of your seam ripper) as they are being stitched. With a wider presser foot, you lose sight of the fabric edges at this vital moment.
5. Does it have a light that works? Some new, inexpensive machines actually come without a light. It's something you don't think about until you don't have it.

Beyond these basics, there are a few adjustments and things you can do to set up your machine for piecing.

1. Experiment with different threads to find the one most suited to your machine. Since you most likely will be working with 100% cotton fabric and the thread should be compatible, the

choice is between 100% cotton thread and a cotton-wrapped polyester thread. Which kind produces the best stitch on your machine?

2. Set the stitch length at 10–12 stitches to the inch. The stitch length needs to be short (a short stitch is stronger than a long stitch), but not so short that you cannot easily use a seam ripper. The **General Rule** is that the length of the stitch should be no shorter than the width of the blade on your seam ripper.
3. Replace the needle frequently with a fresh one. A medium-weight, sharp needle for broadcloth is the best choice. Sewing machine needles are easily bent or burred as you sew, especially when going over pins or multiple thicknesses of fabric. A damaged needle can adversely affect the quality of the machine stitch and make little pulls in the fabric along the seam lines. So, change the needle often.
4. Adjust the tension. You need an evenly locking straight stitch that makes a strong flat seam with no puckers. Consult your sewing machine manual for the "how to" of adjusting the tension.
5. Establish a 1/4" seam-allowance guide that matches the seam allowance on your templates. To do this, place a template under the presser foot and gently lower the needle onto the seam line. The distance from the needle to the edge of the template is 1/4". Lay a piece of masking tape at the edge of the template to act as the 1/4" guide. If the edge of the template falls at a place where you cannot lay tape or another marking is not available, there are other things you can do. On some machines the width of the presser foot is 1/4" and can be used as a guide. Some machines have a left-to-right adjustment on the needle and the needle can be moved to the right for correct spacing.

   If you cannot find a satisfactory 1/4" marking on your sewing machine, then change the seam allowances on your templates to match the machine. It will not matter in the final product if your seam allowances are not exactly 1/4". They can be slightly narrower or wider, as long as they are consistent. Some quilters find that they sew consistently with seams a little wide or a little narrow, so they adjust their templates to the way that they actually sew. The beauty of drafting and making your own templates makes this custom fitting quite simple.

General Rules for Sewing

Stitching

1. Use white or neutral thread as light as the lightest fabric in the project. Use dark neutral thread for piecing dark solids. I

choose one color of thread and use it to piece the whole quilt regardless of color changes in the fabric. Lighter threads, if they don't get clipped completely, will not show through light fabrics in the finished quilt.

2. Sew exact 1/4" seams. See #5 on page 22.
3. Clip threads as you go. Make it a habit. Threads left hanging from the ends of seam lines can get in the way and be a real nuisance.
4. For most piecing, sew from cut edge to cut edge. Backtack if you wish, but when a seam line will be crossed and held by another, it is not necessary.
5 When sewing set-in seams, sew only to the 1/4" seam line, and backtack (see page 25).
6. Use chain piecing whenever possible to save time and thread. To chain piece, sew one seam, but do not lift the presser foot. Do not take the piece out of the sewing machine and do not cut the thread. Instead, set up the next seam to be sewn and stitch as you did the first. There will be a little twist of thread between the two pieces. Sew all the seams you can at one time in this way, then remove the "chain." Clip the threads.
7. To piece a unit block, sew the smallest pieces together first to form units. Join smaller units to form larger ones until the block is complete. (See Block Construction on pages 24–27).

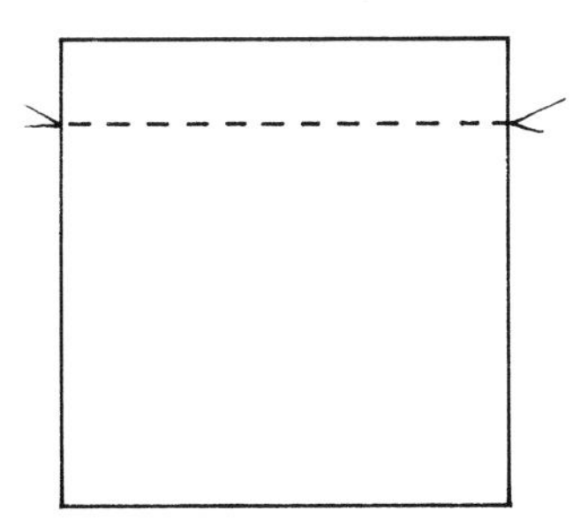

Stitching edge to edge

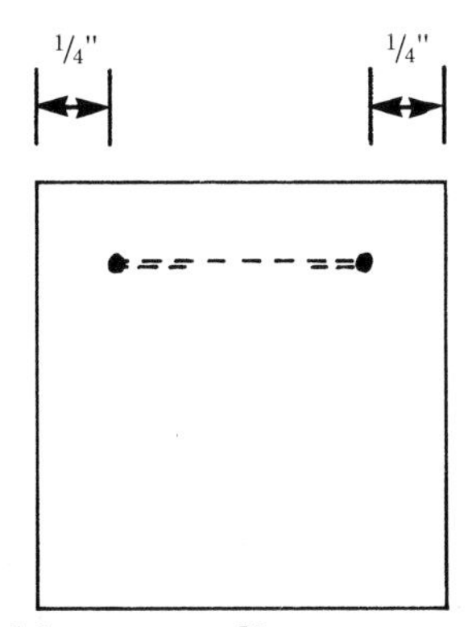

Stitching seam line to seam line with backtacking at 1/4"

Chain piecing

Pinning

The **General Rule** for pinning is that if you don't have to, don't do it. But if matching is involved, if your seams are longer than 4", or if you are unsure, then pin. Pin points of matching (where seam lines or points meet) first. Once these important points are firmly in place, pin the rest of the seam, easing if necessary (see Easing on page 25). Keep pins away from seam lines, as sewing over them tends to damage the needle and makes it hard to be accurate in tight places.

Pressing

To press or not to press? Some machine piecers press every seam immediately after it is sewn; others only finger press during sewing and save ironing for later, after the piecing of the block or even the whole quilt is complete.

I press with an iron at some places and finger press at others. It just depends on the situation, and experience will teach you what works best.

The **General Rule** for pressing is to press seams to one side, toward the darker fabric whenever possible. It is easier to press to one side, it puts the seam-line stress on fabric instead of stitches, and pressing toward the dark prevents a shadow line of the darker fabric from showing through the lighter.

The two main exceptions to the general rule of pressing to the dark are when seams are pressed open to distribute bulk, as in the feather rows of Feathered Stars, and when, for matching purposes, seams are pressed in opposite directions, regardless of which is the darker fabric.

For patchwork, I press with a dry iron that has a shot of steam when needed. Take care not to overpress. Overenthusiastic pressing can stretch and distort fabric pieces, as well as make the fabric shiny where there are bumps. In some situations, press from the top, in others only from the bottom. Press first from the top when pressing to the side, taking care to press the whole seam—don't leave little pleats at the ends. If you have a particularly bulky spot in your piecing, like the middle of a pinwheel where eight points come together, consider pressing the final seam open to distribute the bulk. Press only from the back to avoid making a shiny spot where the fabric layers come together.

Block Construction

Planning

To determine how best to approach constructing a design, first look for the longest seams in the block. Many blocks have long seams that run edge to edge on the vertical or horizontal. On others, the long edge-to-edge seams run diagonally.

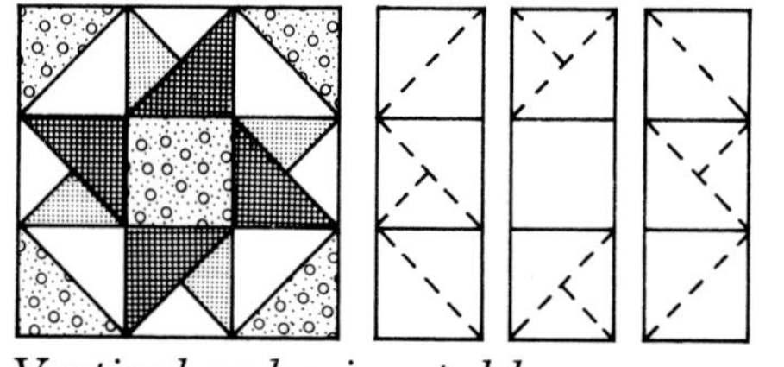

Vertical or horizontal long seams

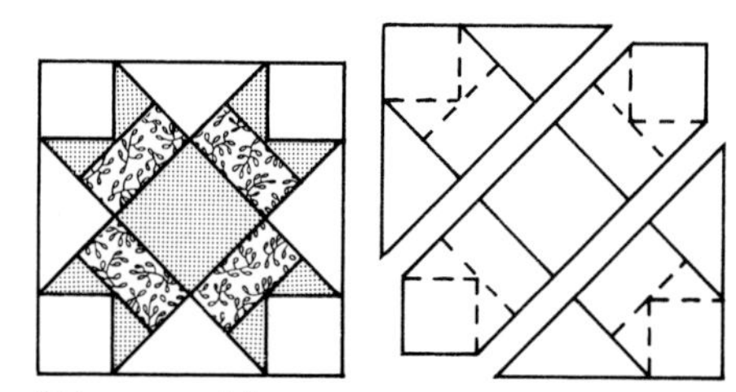

Diagonal long seams

Sometimes the longest seams don't run edge to edge but begin at an edge and end somewhere inside the block. In these cases, you either have asymmetrical construction, set-in seams, or halfway seams.

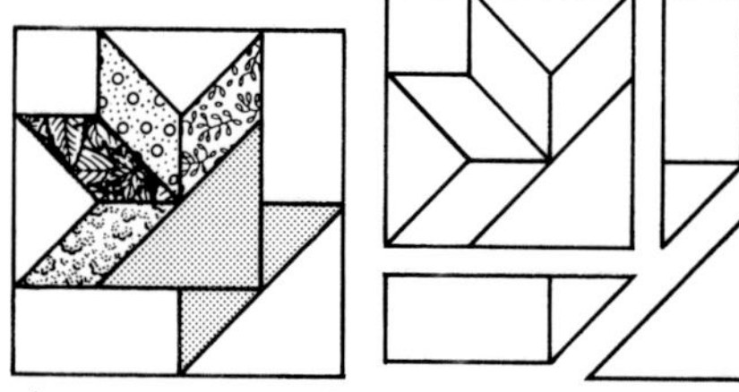

Asymmetrical construction

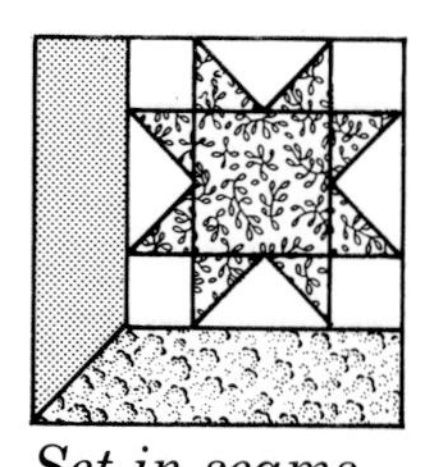

Set-in seams

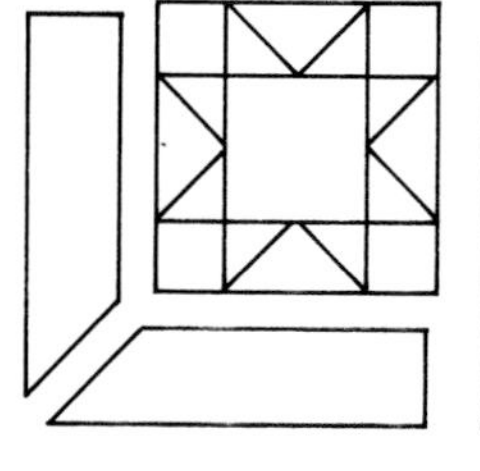

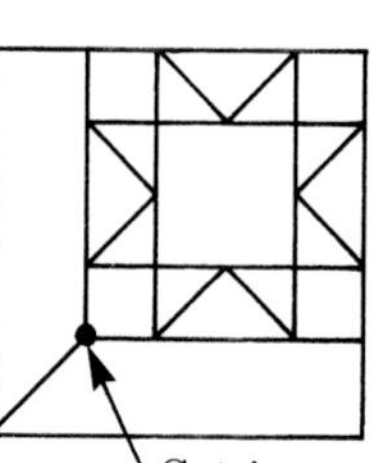

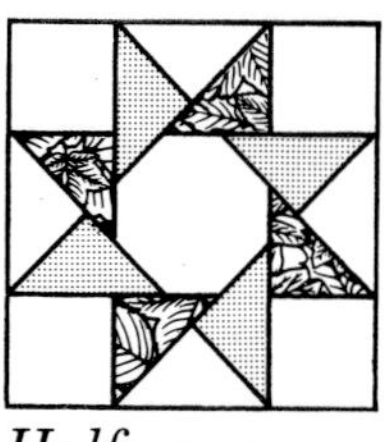

Halfway seams

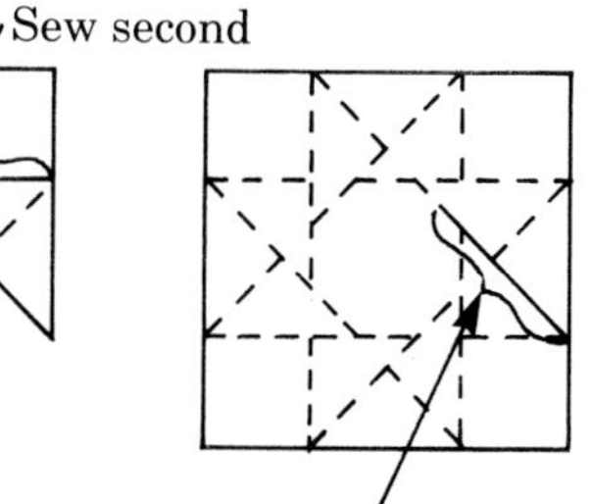

Matching

The following matching techniques can be helpful in many different piecing situations:

1. Opposing Seams. When stitching one seamed unit to another, press seam allowances in opposite directions on seams that need to match. The two "opposing" seams will hold each other in place and evenly distribute the bulk. Often, the opposing seams are diagonal seams. Plan pressing to take advantage of opposing seams.

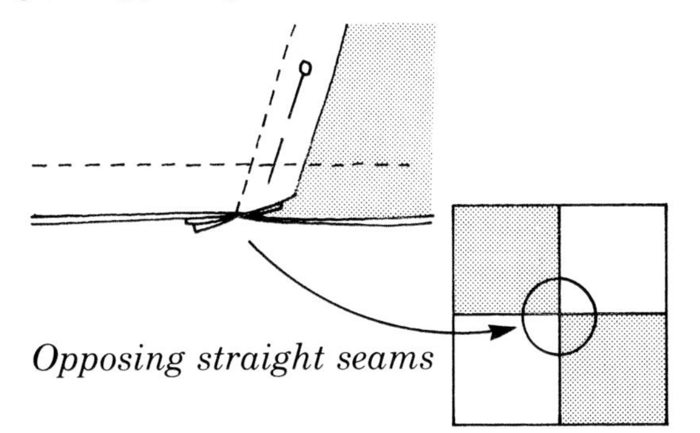

Opposing straight seams

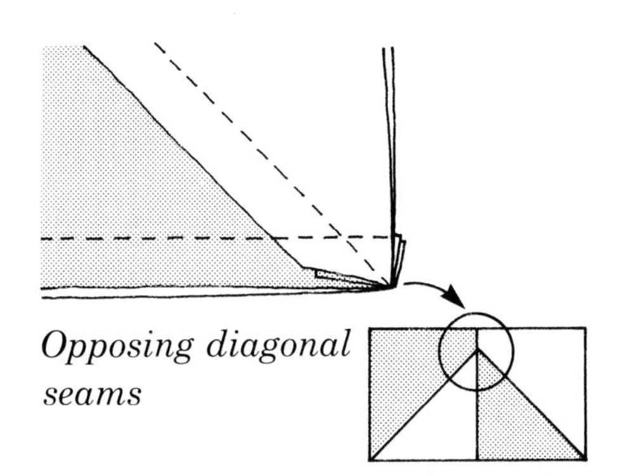

Opposing diagonal seams

2. Positioning Pin. A pin, carefully pushed straight through two points that need to match and pulled tight, will establish the proper point of matching. Pin the seam normally and remove the positioning pin before stitching.

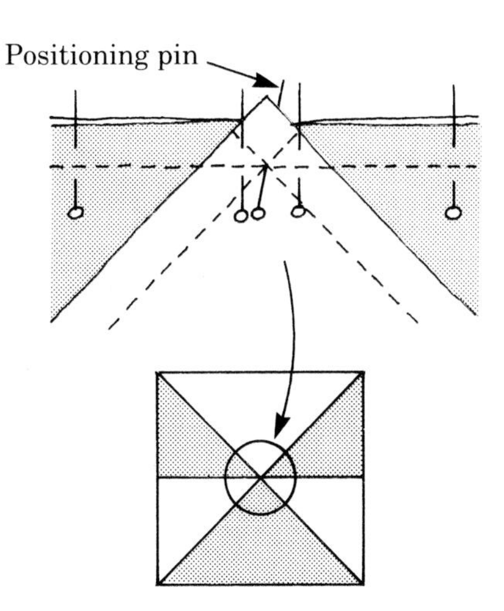

3. The X. When triangles are pieced, stitches will form an X at the next seam line. Stitch through the center of the X to make sure the points on the sewn triangles will not be chopped off. When seams are pressed open, the X will look like it does below. Sew right through the point indicated for crisply pieced points. Sew with these seams on top so the X can be seen clearly.

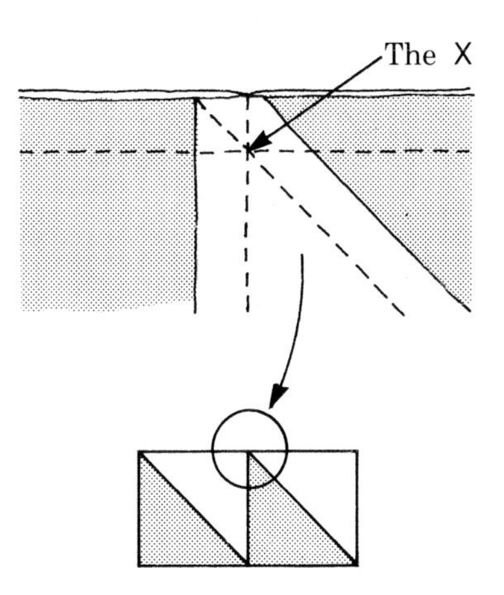

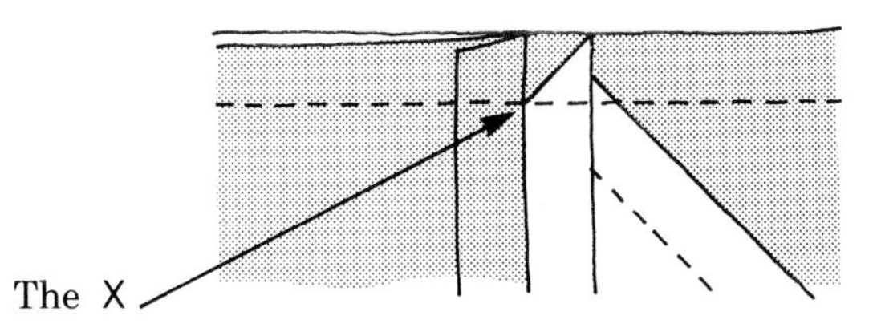

4. Easing. When two pieces to be sewn together are supposed to match but instead are slightly different lengths, pin the points of matching and stitch with the shorter piece on top. The feed dog eases the fullness of the bottom piece.

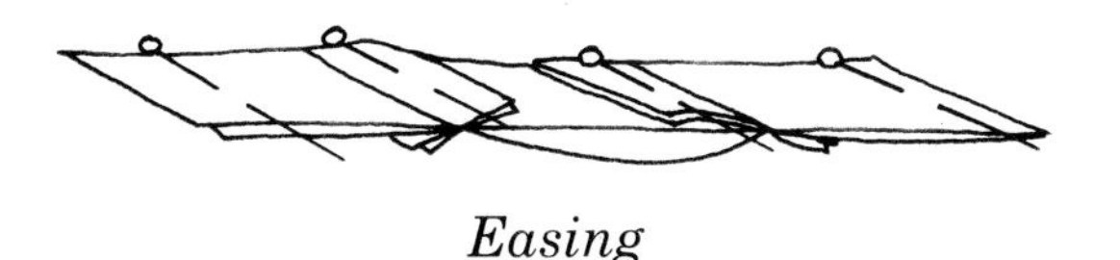

Easing

5. Set-in Seams. Where three seam lines come together at an angle, stop all stitching at the 1/4" seam line and backtack. I sometimes mark these points with a light pencil mark on the

wrong side of the fabric. Don't let even one stitch extend into the seam allowance. As each seam is finished, take the work out of the machine, position the next seam, and start stitching in the new direction. Backtacking is necessary because these seam lines will not be crossed and held by any other stitches.

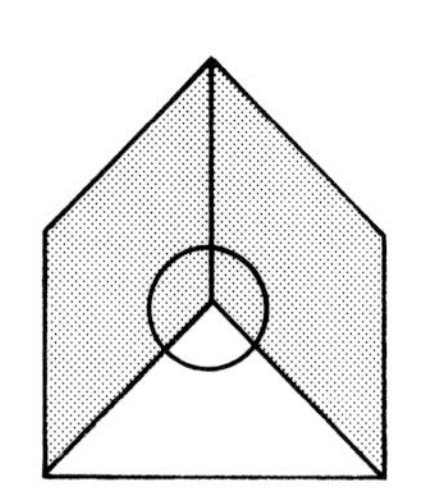

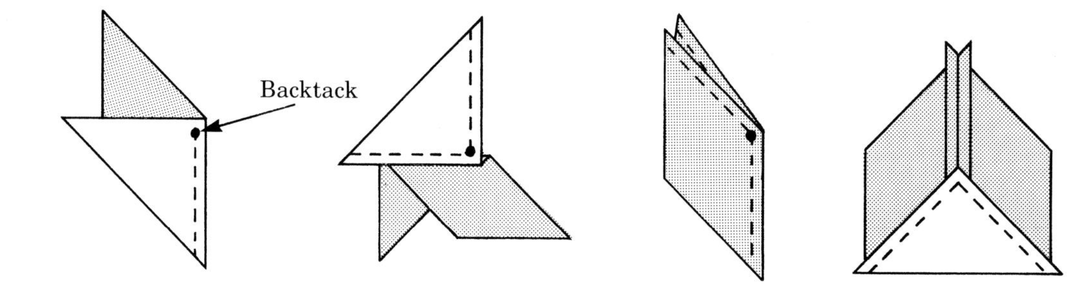

6. Halfway Seams. In some blocks, halfway seams are used to avoid set-in seams. Certain seams are sewn halfway, early in block construction, and then completed in the last stages of sewing. Begin and end these stitching lines with backtacking.

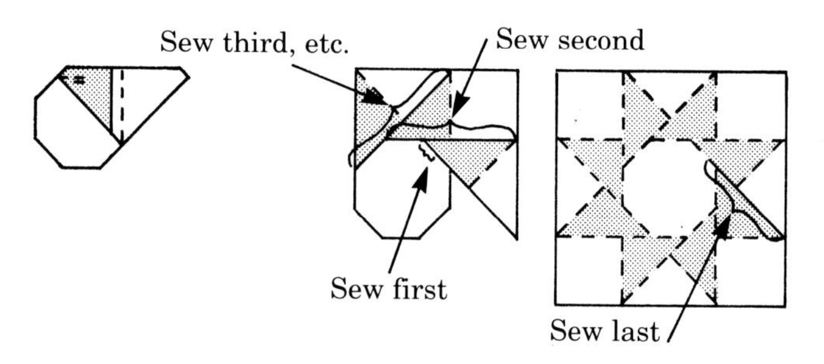

7. Curved Seams. In preparation for sewing, carefully score each concave curve. With the tips of your scissors, make 1/16" clips, 1/16" apart, along the inside curved edge. Some long gentle curves do not need scoring, so, on a new pattern, I usually try one seam without scoring to determine whether the curve has enough stretch. If scoring is unnecessary, don't bother with it.

Find the center of each piece by folding it in half and finger pressing. Match the centers of the pieces and pin. With the scored piece (concave curve) on top, match the edges at the beginning and end of the seam and pin. Pin in between, as needed.

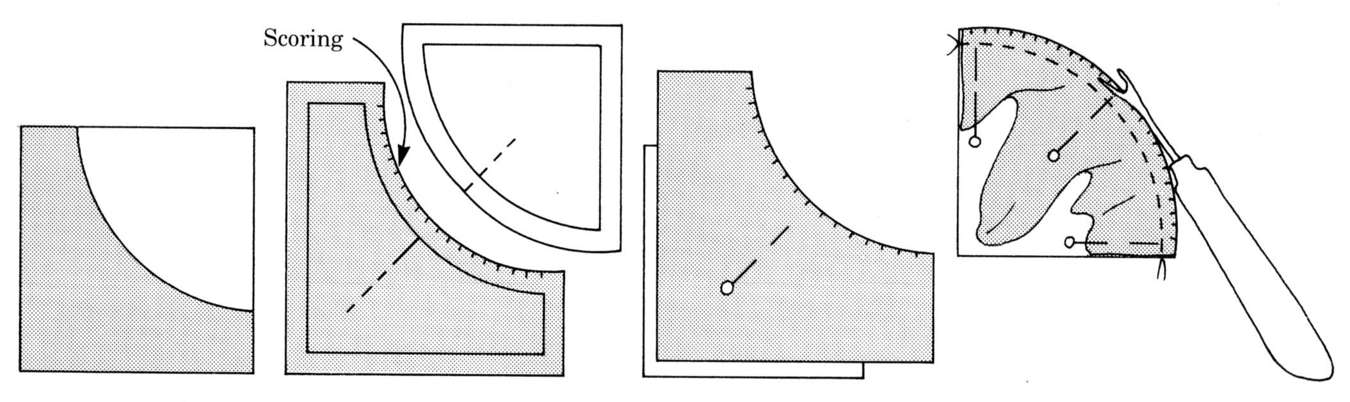

Begin stitching the $\frac{1}{4}$" seam slowly, only four or five stitches at a time, matching fabric edges along the curve as you go. The tip of a seam ripper can be used as a stylus to help match the fabric edges where your fingers won't fit. Stop often to make adjustments, keeping the fullness of the top piece from pleating into the seam. The scored edge is mostly bias and will stretch easily to accommodate the convex shape underneath. Continue stitching past the center pin to the end. Remember to go slowly. A few practice seams and you'll have it.

Press seams toward the dark fabric; they will lie flat in either direction.

Using a Seam Ripper

Seam ripper is really a bad name for this handy little tool, because we don't really "rip" seams; we just take stitches out that are in the wrong place. To "unsew" a seam, simply slip the blade of the seam ripper into the stitches on the top or bottom of a seam and break about every third stitch along the length of the seam. The two pieces of cloth then can be easily pulled apart without undo stress on you or the fabric.

Strip Piecing

In patchwork, every edge must be cut, every seam must be sewn. Sometimes the order in which these two operations take place can be changed to save time or to achieve more accurate results. In strip piecing, fabric strips are cut on the straight grain of the fabric and sewn together in units called strata. The strata are then cut into shorter portions. Finally, these small units are recombined to form simple designs. Many quiltmakers feel that strip piecing is a preferred way to work and deliberately choose designs where the technique can be used.

Straight Strip Piecing

Straight strip piecing is a great time-saver for checkerboard-type designs, like Four Patches, Ninepatches, and Irish Chains, and for piecing parts of designs that have regular repetitions of squares and rectangles.

To determine the width to cut strips, add a $\frac{1}{4}$" seam allowance to each side of the finished dimension of the desired shape. For example, if the finished dimension of a square will be 2", cut $2\frac{1}{2}$" strips. Both finished and cutting dimensions are provided for squares and rectangles in the Template section, beginning on page 82.

Cut strips from the length of the fabric, when possible, because it's easier to keep them on grain. When it is necessary to use the cross grain to get the required length, be sure to straighten the fabric so strips will be cut as close to true grain as possible (see pages 11–12). Fold the fabric so two or four layers can be cut at one time. Mark strip widths and cut with sharp scissors or use rotary cutter and ruler. Take care and be accurate. Time saved with quick methods is wasted if the work is done poorly.

Sew long strips together with 1/4" seam allowances. Press seam allowances toward the darker fabric, pressing from the top of the work so the fabric won't pleat along the seam lines. Usually, pressing toward the dark will result in opposing seams at points of matching. If the coloring of the strips doesn't work out that way, press for opposing seams instead of always to the dark.

Measure and mark crosswise cuts, using templates or rotary cutter and ruler. Join strip-pieced units as shown in the illustrations to make Four Patch, Ninepatch, and other desired units.

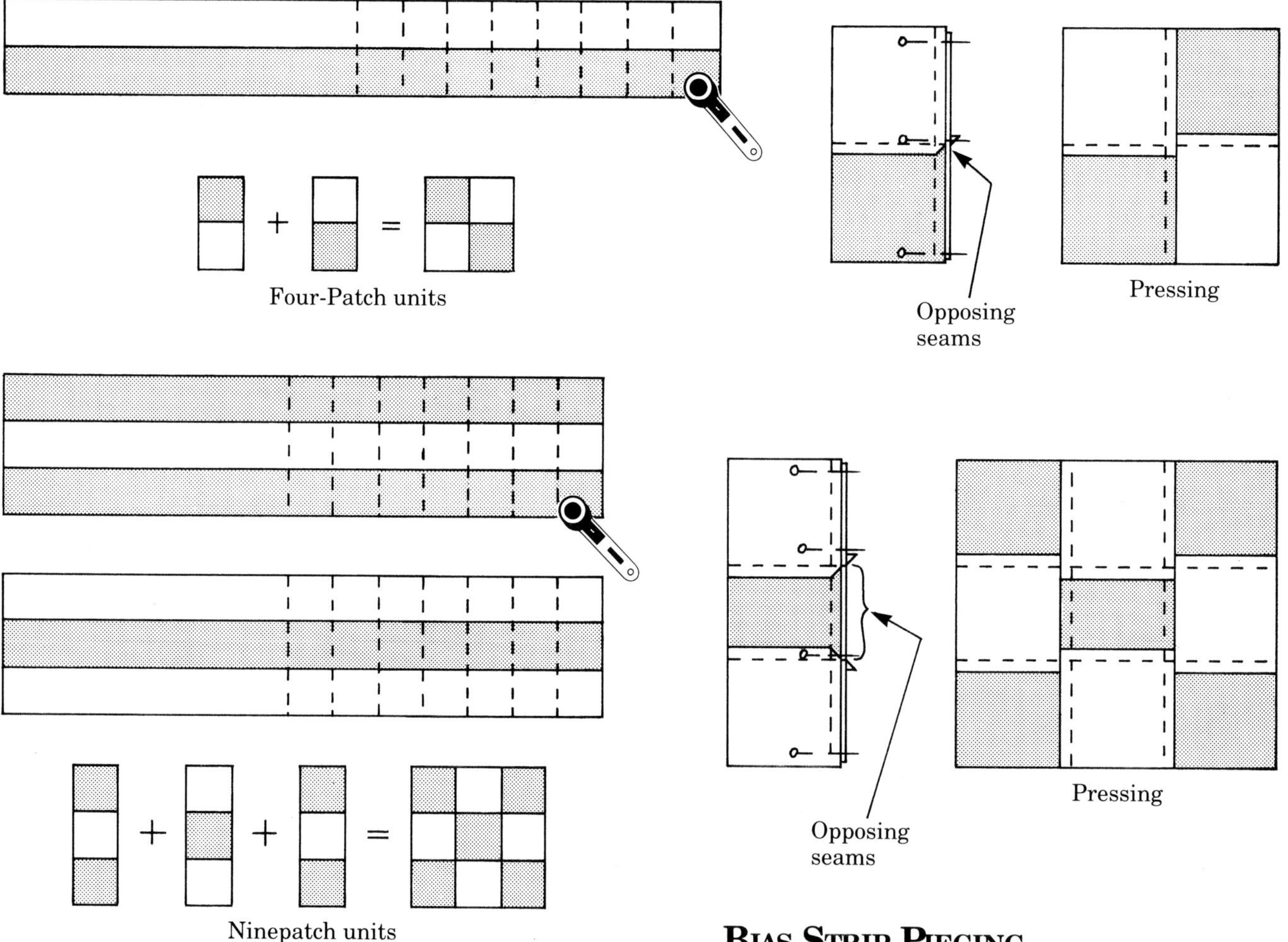

Bias Strip Piecing

I learned the basic principle of bias strip piecing many years ago and have since used it extensively, improving it and adding many new twists. In this strip-piecing method, strips are cut on the bias rather than on the straight grain, and the cut shapes are triangles rather than squares and rectangles. Because the seams are sewn on bias edges, the resulting two-triangle pieced squares have the straight grain along the outer edge. It is an accurate and fast method for piecing squares made of half-square triangles or any other shapes consisting of two equal triangles. It is great for any design that includes many of these triangle units, like Ocean Waves, Feathered Stars, or the Star Puzzle quilt on page 40 with its Sawtooth border.

Bias strip piecing can be either a template or rotary technique, as long as the strips of fabric are cut on the bias. To avoid struggling with a lot of yardage, cut the fabric that will be cut into bias strips into manageable chunks. I prefer squares or rectangles of 14"–18" that fit nicely on my cutting mat.

1. Cut two squares of contrasting fabric and place right sides together. (Both layers will be cut at the same time.)
2. Align the 45° marking of the Bias Square™ along the edge of the fabric square and use a long ruler to make the first diagonal cut.
3. Measure the desired width of the strip from the first cut and cut again. Continue until the whole square has been cut into bias strips.

   The width of the bias strips will depend on the desired size of the two-triangle squares that you are cutting. The table to the right shows strip widths for different-sized squares.

Cut size of Bias Square	Strip Width
1" to 1¼"	1½"
1½" to 1¾"	2"
2"	2"
2¼"	2¼"
2½"	2½"
2¾"	2¾"
3"	2¾"
3 ¼"	3"
3¾"	3½"
4"	3¾"

Making bias strips

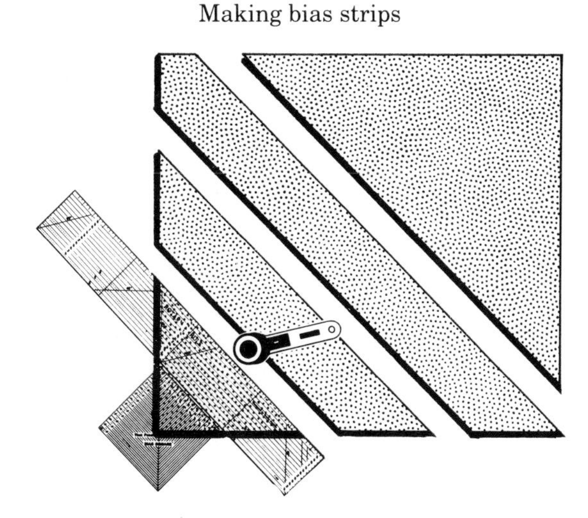

4. Pick up matching strips and sew the strips together on the long bias edge, using ¼" seam allowance. Press seams open for squares cut 1¾" or smaller. Press seams toward the darker fabric for larger squares.

Template Method. If you choose a template and scissors technique, place a stiffened square template on the right side of the bias-strip unit, lining up opposite corners with the seam line. Trace around the template. Start at one end and make a string of squares the length of the seam line. Carefully cut out the fabric squares, cutting just inside the drawn lines. This will yield several squares made up of two triangles, with outside edges on

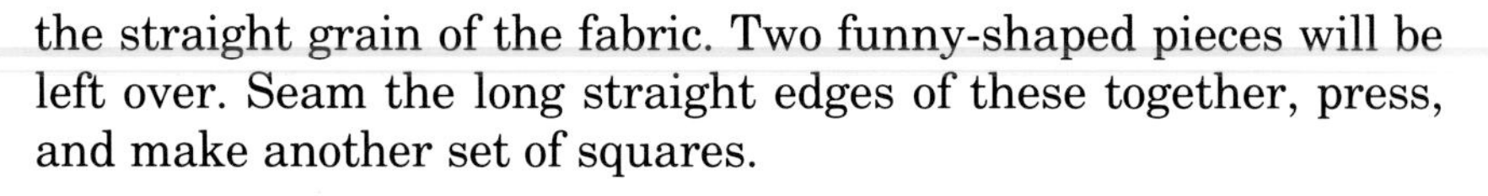
the straight grain of the fabric. Two funny-shaped pieces will be left over. Seam the long straight edges of these together, press, and make another set of squares.

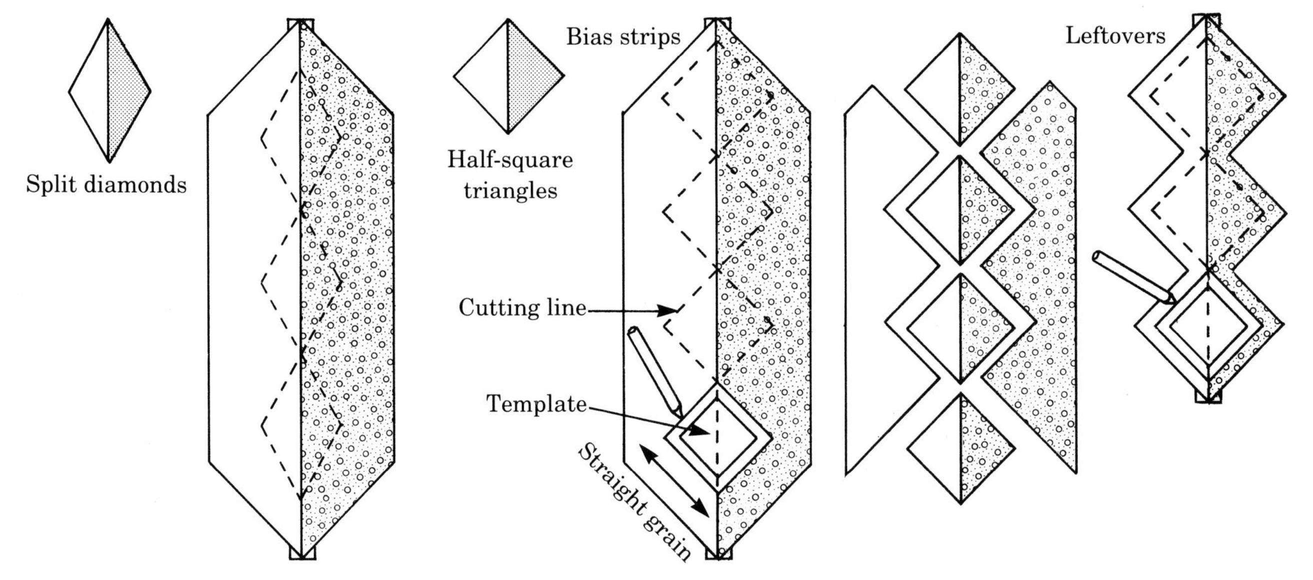

Bias strip piecing may be used to cut shapes made of two equal triangles.

Template Method for Bias Strip Piecing

Rotary Method. For the rotary method of cutting bias squares, cut strips and sew them together just as you would for the template method. The next step is to then sew two or three bias-strip pairs together. Use 1/4" seams and press.

Using a Bias Square™ and rotary cutter, begin at lower end and cut bias squares from the lowest points, as shown. If you have joined three or more strips, cut bias squares from alternate rows, working up the strip. Waste triangles of the background color and a print will result. Continue cutting bias squares, alternating rows until you have used all of the fabric.

Rotary Method for Bias Strip Piecing

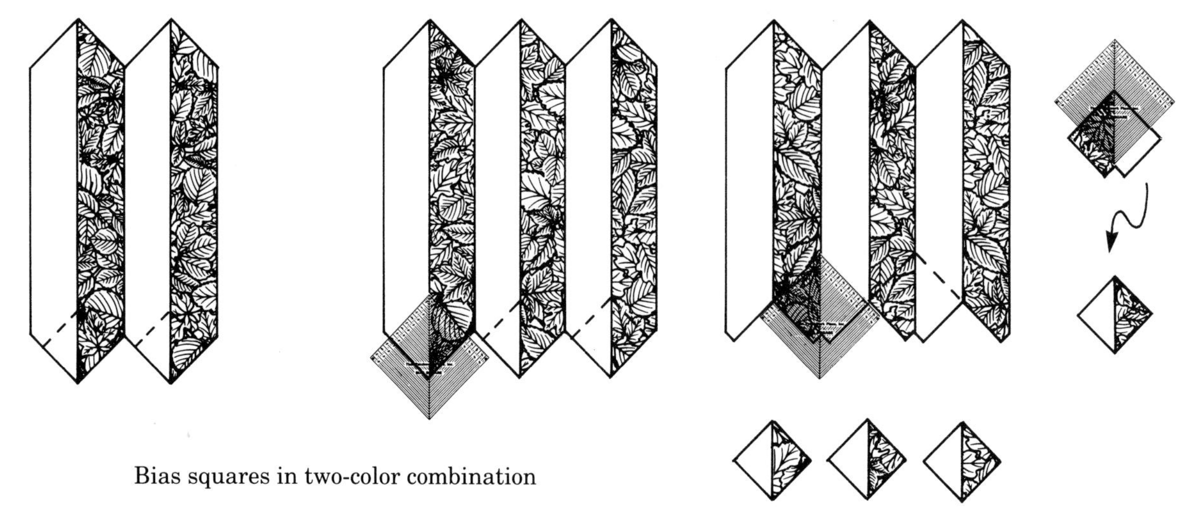

Bias squares in two-color combination

A variety of bias square fabric combinations can be obtained by sewing strips of different colors together. For instance, if you only want bias squares in a two-color combination, alternate light and dark strips. If you want a scrappy look with many different fabric combinations in your bias square units, cut strips of many different fabrics and sew them together, as shown below. Each seam will yield a different fabric combination. This cutting format is suggested for the Star Puzzle quilt on page 40.

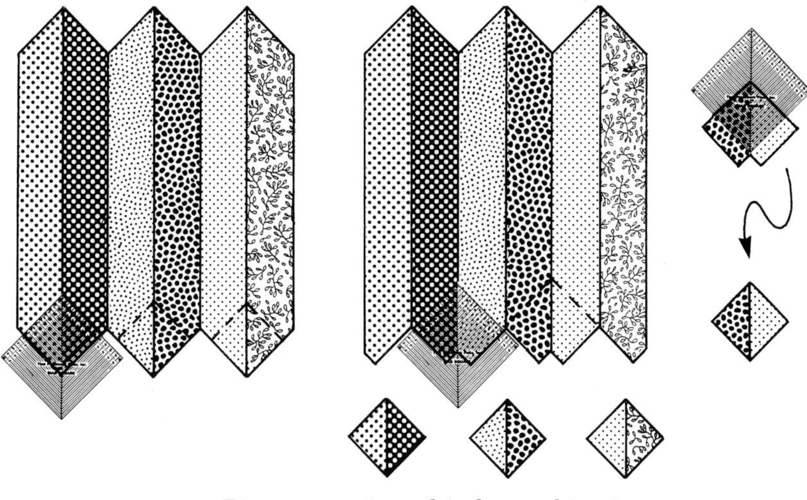

Bias squares in multicolor combinations

Waste Triangles

When bias strip piecing is combined with rotary techniques as described above, there will be triangular scraps or "waste triangles" left over from the outside edge strips. These pieces need not be wasted as they are a perfect size for single half-square triangles, which are used in many designs (like Ocean Waves) that involve bias squares.

To resize your waste triangles, find the proper triangle for your pattern in the Template section and use it to cut the desired piece. When the pattern I am working on does not require single triangles in the waste triangle size, I simply save them in a shoe box until I come to a pattern that does need them. They are great for adding variety to scrap quilts.

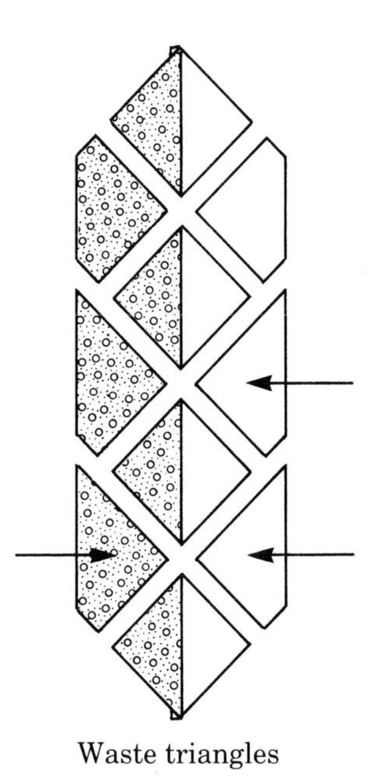

Waste triangles

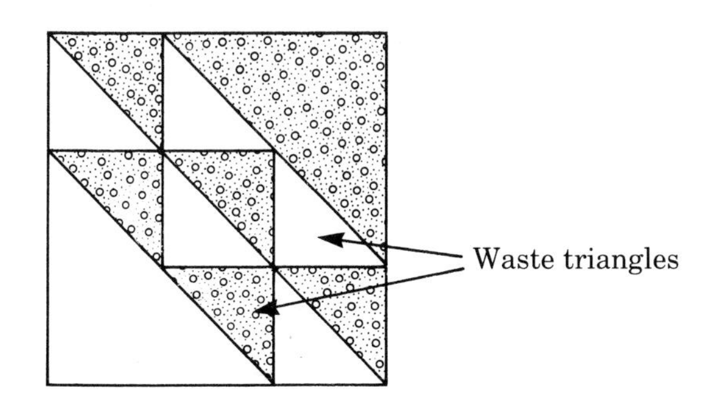

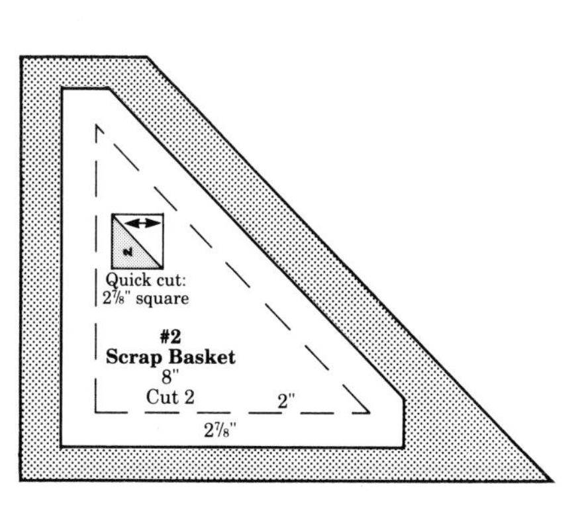

The Lessons and Quilt Patterns

There is no better way to learn a skill or technique than to do it. So, in this book the lessons in machine piecing are in the form of ten quilt patterns. Each quilt is fairly simple and was chosen for a set of specific drafting, piecing, or construction situations. The skills covered in each lesson are typical of a whole group of patchwork designs and therefore will be applicable to much of your machine piecing.

Each lesson/quilt pattern includes directions for drafting sample templates, fabric requirements, complete cutting instructions, and detailed sewing instructions for piecing the blocks and completing the quilt top. A color photo of each quilt can be found in the Gallery on the next page. For each quilt that has pieced borders, a simplified border easily could be added instead. Turn to page 93 for specific instructions on adding simple borders.

General drafting, along with cutting and sewing instructions for piecing blocks, are given in the front of the book. Quilt construction (setting and borders) and quilt finishing are given in the Glossary of Techniques, beginning on page 91. These will be referred to as needed, so a quick read-through of these sections before you begin a quilt lesson would be a good idea.

Almost all the quilts in this section are scrap or multifabric quilts. When a Materials list calls for 1½ yards total assorted fabrics, it means that several different prints in the same color range should be chosen, and the actual combined amount needed will be 1½ yards. However, you may need to purchase more fabric to get the desired variety. Approximate fabric amounts needed for bias bindings are given in the Glossary of Techniques on page 95 under Binding.

Plate 1. *Quail's Nest by Marsha McCloskey, 1988, Seattle, Washington, 48" x 56½". A design that has been known by many names, Quail's Nest is a great block for beginning piecers. The patchwork design blocks in this quilt were all made as classroom demonstrations over a period of two years. Quilted by Freda Smith.*

***Plate 2.** Star Puzzle by Marsha McCloskey, 1988, Seattle, Washington, 64" x 78". Star Puzzle is also known as Barbara Fritchie's Star. Each of these blocks and the Pinwheel set squares were made over several years as classroom demonstrations of "how to make eight points come together crisply." The two-triangle square units in the blocks and the Sawtooth border can be made with bias strip piecing. Quilted by Virginia Lauth.*

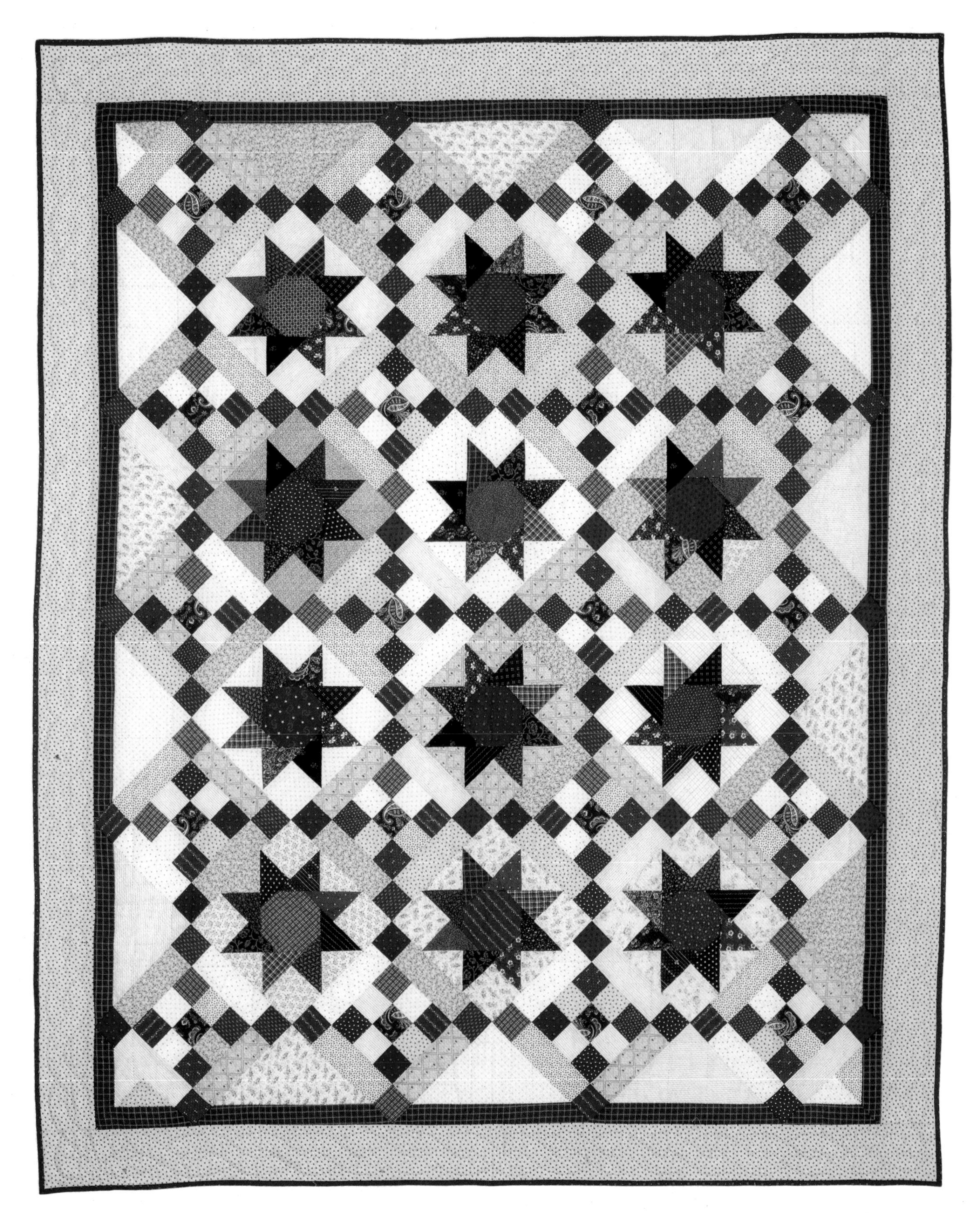

Plate 3. *Star Highway by Marsha McCloskey, 1989, Seattle, Washington, 66" x 80". Star Highway is a two-block design. The first block, Twisting Star, is based on the Le Moyne drafting and involves "halfway" or partial seams. The King's Highway blocks were quickly constructed, using rotary-cutting and strip-piecing techniques. Quilted by Virginia Lauth.*

Plate 4. *LeMoyne Star by Marsha McCloskey, 1989, Seattle, Washington, 44" x 54". The Le Moyne Star is an old pattern that involves special drafting and sewing techniques. The blocks in this quilt were made as class demonstrations. The back was also pieced to use up extra blocks.*

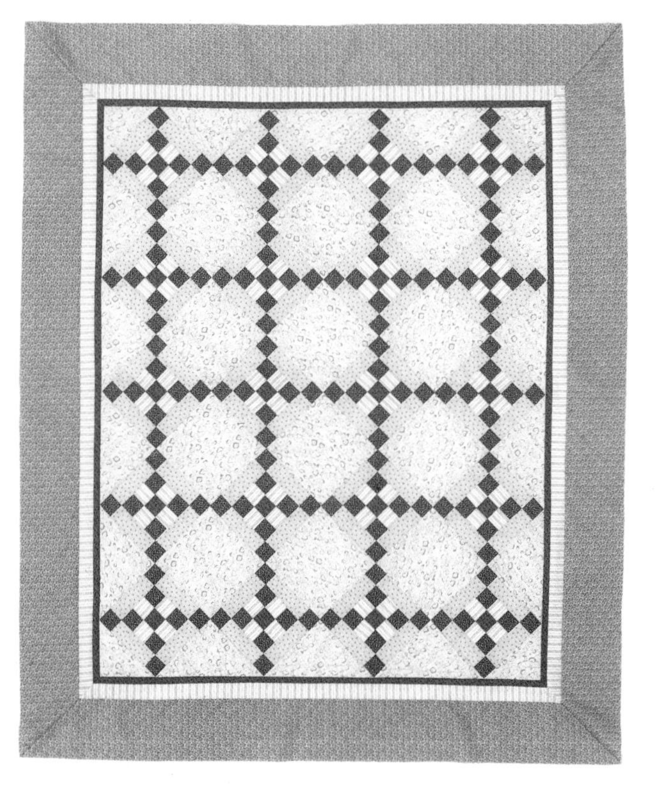

Plate 5. *King's Highway (top) by Marsha McCloskey, 1989, Seattle, Washington, 38" x 45". With rotary cutting and strip piecing, this baby quilt top took only a few hours to make.*

Plate 6. *Scrap Basket by Marsha McCloskey, 1988, Seattle, Washington, 39½" x 53¾". The colors in this Scrap Basket quilt were inspired by antique quilts seen on a teaching trip to Iowa. The blocks are from class demonstrations and involve set-in seams and asymmetrical construction (sounds hard, but they're really easy). Quilted by Freda Smith.*

Plate 7. *Pinwheel by Marsha McCloskey, 1987, Seattle, Washington, 49½" x 60". Sewn in Fourth of July red-white-and-blue scraps, this quilt has crisply matched triangles and a pieced border. Quilted by Freda Smith.*

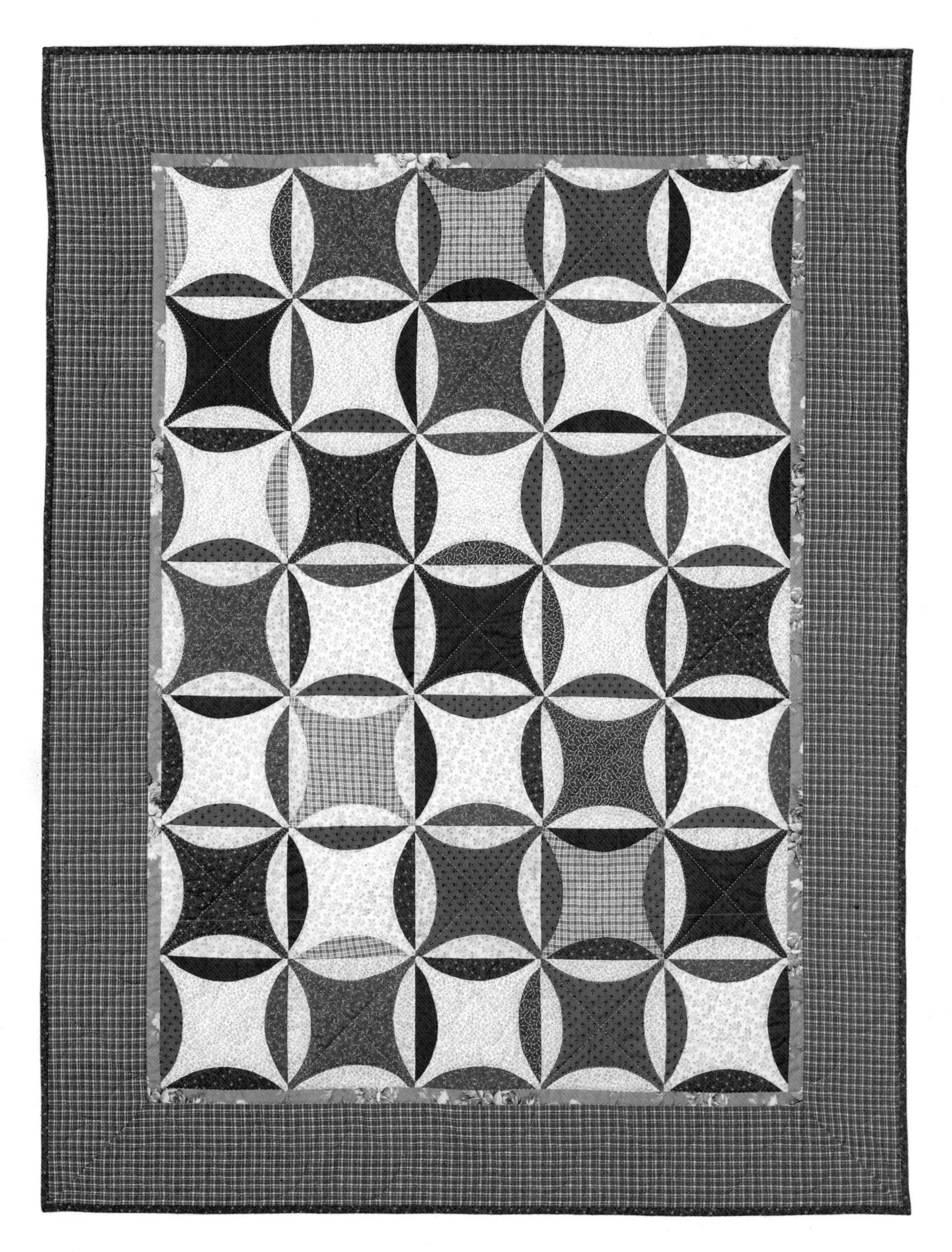

Plate 8. *Dolly Madison's Workbox by Marsha McCloskey, 1988, Seattle, Washington, 40" x 52". Cool and crisp in blues, this traditional curved seam design is surprisingly easy to piece and delightful to live with. Quilted by Freda Smith.*

Plate 9. *Darting Minnows by Marsha McCloskey, 1989, Seattle, Washington, 41" x 49". The boundaries of the Darting Minnows blocks were erased to eliminate seams, resulting in bar quilt construction. The quilt was also an exercise in contrast of different intensities of yellow with a white or ecru background. Quilted by Freda Smith.*

Plate 11. *Drunkard's Path block samples by Marsha McCloskey. The curved seam Drunkard's Path in a dark/light design is very versatile. Many different designs can be formed by simply changing the positions of light and dark fabrics.*

Plate 10. *Pinwheel Daisy by Marsha McCloskey, 1989, Seattle, Washington, 44" x 55". This quilt was begun as a test of a 1930s pattern for Sara Nephew's book,* My Mother's Quilts: Designs from the Thirties. *The curved seam piecing and the 1930s scraps were so appealing, it was eventually finished as a sample for this book. A variation of this quilt pattern is found on page 80. Quilted by Freda Smith.*

Quilt Lesson #1:

Quail's Nest

This is an old pattern that, over time and in different parts of the country, has been known by many names. You might recognize it as Sherman's March, Monkey Wrench, or Churn Dash. It is the first block I teach in my Machine Piecing workshop. It is easy to draft, has only three templates, and the sewing is straightforward.

Drafting category: nine-square grid

Preferred cutting: no templates, rotary cutter

Sewing: straight seam, cut edge to cut edge

Matching concerns: opposing seams at four corner intersections, crisp triangle points

Drafting

The nine-square grid is the basis for many traditional pieced blocks. Quail's nest is based on such a grid.

The size of the grid squares is determined by dividing the measurement of the side of the square (6") by the number of equal divisions along that side (3). So, 6" ÷ 3 = 2".

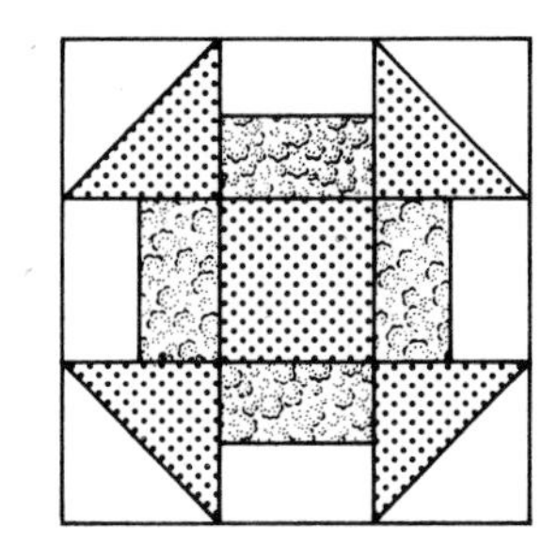

1. Draw a 6" square on 1/4" graph paper.
2. Draw a grid of nine 2" squares in the 6" square.
3. Divide each corner square in half on the diagonal, as shown.
4. Divide each middle side square in half to make two equal rectangles.
5. Identify a square, triangle, and rectangle as shapes needed for templates and color them in.
6. Add a consistent 1/4" seam allowance around each template shape. Refer to page 13 for making different types of templates.

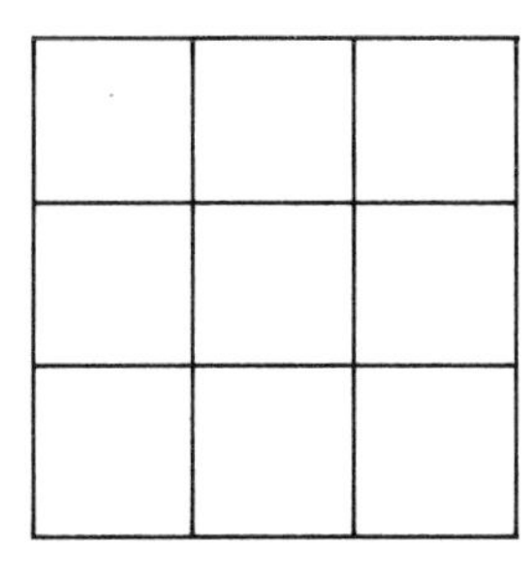

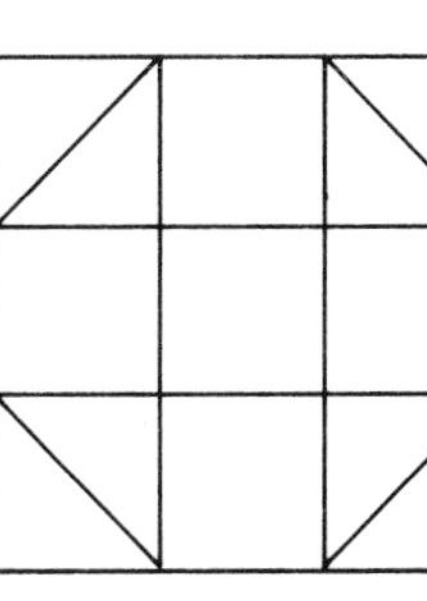

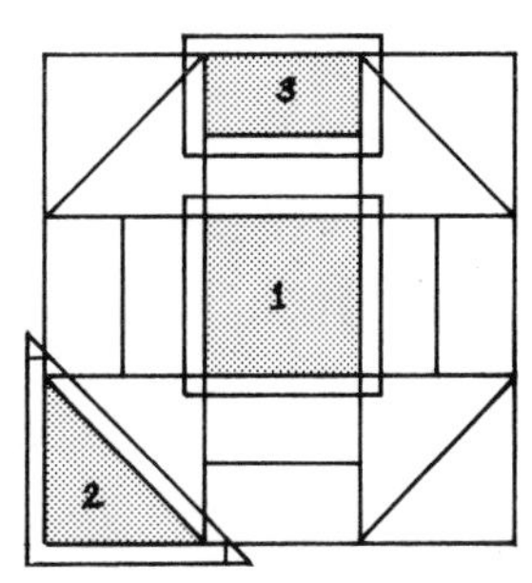

Cutting

Quail's Nest has three fabrics: a light, a dark, and an accent color. It has simple shapes that are easy to measure, so it is a good place to use a no-template, rotary-cutting technique. Use the templates on page 83 for cutting dimensions and to compare your cut pieces for accuracy.

For one Quail's Nest block:

Template #1: Cut one square, 2 1/2" x 2 1/2", of dark fabric.

Template #2: Cut two squares, 2 7/8" x 2 7/8", of dark fabric and two of light fabric. Cut squares diagonally to yield four dark, plus four light, half-square triangles. Trim points for easy matching with a Bias Square™, as shown on page 18.

Template #3: Cut four rectangles, 2 1/2" x 1 1/2", of accent fabric and four of light.

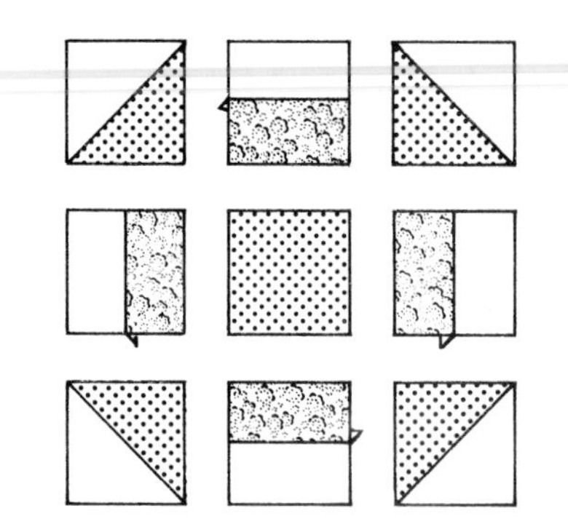

Piecing

1. Lay the cut pieces together on the table, following the design, to determine which to sew first and whether you need to change the colors you have chosen. Beginning with the corner triangles, chain piece four square units, as shown. Then sew the rectangles together to make four chain-pieced squares. Cut the chains and press seams toward the darker fabric.

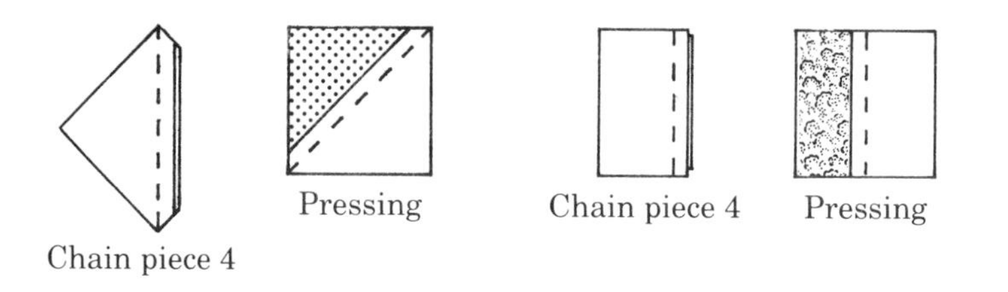

2. Use chain piecing to sew the square units together in three rows.

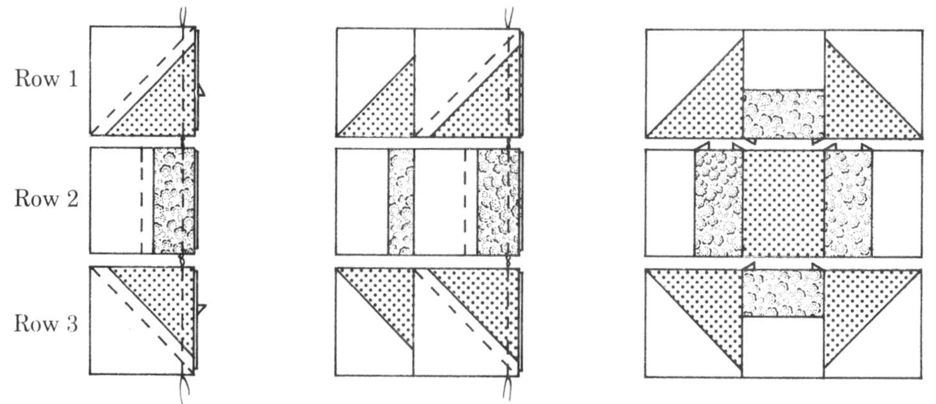

3. Pressing to take advantage of opposing seams, pin Row 1 and Row 2, as shown, and stitch the long seam. Join Row 3 to Row 2 in the same manner. Press, as shown.

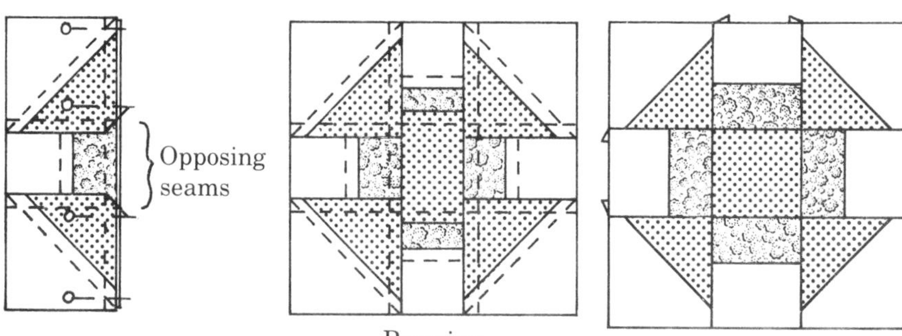

Quail's Nest Quilt

Plate 1
Templates are on page 83.

Dimensions: 48" x 56 1/2"

Materials: (45" wide fabric)
Dark: 1 1/2 yds. total assorted dark green prints for piecing and set pieces
Light: 1 yd. total assorted light green prints for piecing and middle border
Accent: 1/2 yd. total assorted pink prints for piecing and inner border
Outer border: 1 3/4 yds. dark (green)
Backing: 2 7/8 yds.
Batting, binding, and thread to finish

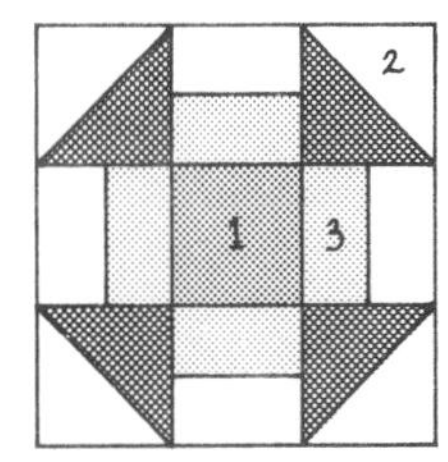

Quail's Nest, 6"
Make 20

Set piece I
Cut 12

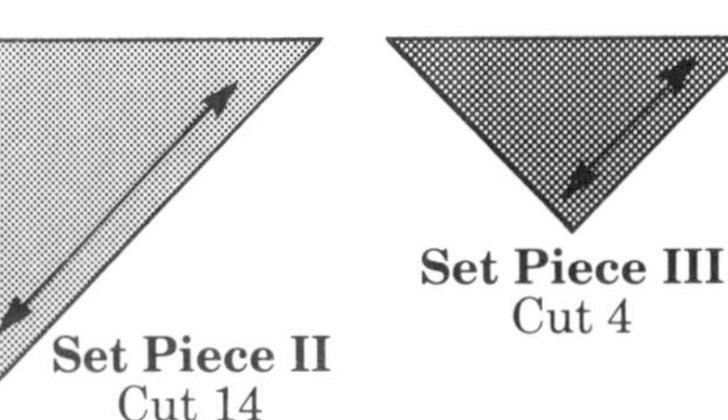

Set Piece II
Cut 14

Set Piece III
Cut 4

Set Piece II
Quick cut:
9 3/4" square

Set Piece III
Quick cut:
5 1/8" square

CUTTING

Borders

Cut the following border strips and set aside. Strips are longer than needed and will be trimmed to fit later.

Hint: The width of the inner and middle borders can be adjusted to accommodate the actual sewn dimensions of the pieced border and the pieced center of the quilt. You may want to wait to cut and sew these "spacer" borders until the other piecing is completed. See Pieced Borders on page 94 for help in making pieced borders fit.

1. Inner border: From crosswise grain of accent fabric, cut enough 1" wide strips (5) so that with seaming, there will be 2 strips, 48" x 1", and 2 strips, 39" x 1".
2. Middle border: From crosswise grain of light fabric, cut enough 1 1/2" wide strips (5) so that with seams, there will be 2 strips, 48" x 1 1/2", and 2 strips, 39" x 1 1/2".
3. Outer border: From the length of outer border fabric, cut 4 strips, 4 1/2" wide (extra length will be trimmed later).

Pieced Borders

1. Cut 16 squares, 4 1/16" x 4 1/16", of assorted dark fabrics. Cut twice diagonally to yield 62 quarter-square triangles (Template #2).
2. Cut 16 squares, 4 1/16" x 4 1/16", of assorted light fabrics. Cut twice diagonally to yield 62 quarter-square triangles (Template #2).

Quail's Nest Blocks

1. Cut 20 squares, 2 1/2" x 2 1/2", of assorted dark fabrics (Template #1).
2. Cut 80 rectangles, 1 1/2" x 2 1/2", of assorted accent fabrics (Template #3).
3. Cut 80 rectangles, 1 1/2" x 2 1/2", of assorted light fabrics (Template #3).
4. Cut 40 squares, 2 7/8" x 2 7/8", of assorted dark fabrics. Cut diagonally to yield 80 half-square triangles (Template #2).
5. Cut 40 squares, 2 7/8" x 2 7/8", of assorted light fabrics. Cut diagonally to yield 80 half-square triangles (Template #2).

Set Pieces

1. Cut 12 squares, 6 1/2" x 6 1/2", of assorted dark fabrics for Set Piece I.
2. Cut 4 squares, 9 3/4" x 9 3/4", of assorted dark fabrics. Cut twice diagonally to yield 14 quarter-square triangles for Set Piece II.
3. Cut 2 squares, 5 1/8" x 5 1/8", of dark fabrics. Cut diagonally to yield 4 half-square triangles for Set Piece III.

Directions

1. Piece 20 Quail's Nest blocks.
2. Stitch pieced blocks and set pieces together in diagonal rows, as shown. Sew rows together to complete pieced center section of the quilt. Refer to pages 91–92 for tips on setting blocks together.
3. For inner and middle borders, stitch the 1" wide accent color strips together with the 1½" wide light strips to form 4 border units. Stitch to center pieced section and miter the corners (see Mitering Corners on pages 93–94).
4. Sew pieced border sections for top and bottom of quilt and one for each side, as pictured. Sew to quilt center, adding corner pieces last.
5. Add 4½" wide outer borders, using mitered or blunt-sewn corners.
6. Add backing and batting; quilt.
7. Finish edges with bias binding.

Quilt Lesson #2:
Star Puzzle

This design is an exercise in piecing triangles and getting points to come out crisply. It is an excellent place to use bias strip piecing to make wonderfully accurate half-square triangle units.

Drafting category: sixteen-square grid
Preferred cutting: no templates, bias strip piecing, rotary cutter
Sewing: straight seam, cut edge to cut edge
Matching concerns: making eight points come together in center of pinwheel unit, making the flying geese unit, using positioning pins, making crisp triangle points

Drafting

The finished size of this block is 9". The design is based on a sixteen-square grid. To get the size of the grid squares, divide the side of the square (9") by the number of divisions counted along that side (4). So, 9" ÷ 4 = $2\frac{1}{4}$".

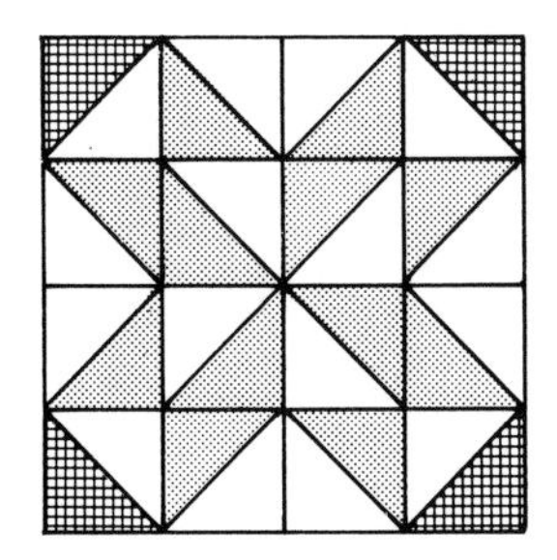

1. Draw a 9" square on $\frac{1}{4}$" graph paper.
2. Draw a grid of sixteen $2\frac{1}{4}$" squares in the 9" square.
3. Divide each grid square in half on the diagonal to create half-square triangles. The direction of each line is shown in the accompanying drawing.
4. Two templates are needed for this design: the smaller half-square triangle and a larger quarter-square triangle along the outside edge. Identify these two shapes as templates and color them in. If you plan to use bias strip piecing, also identify one $2\frac{1}{4}$" square as a template shape.
5. Add a consistent $\frac{1}{4}$" seam allowance around each template shape. Refer to page 13 for making different types of templates from a drafting.

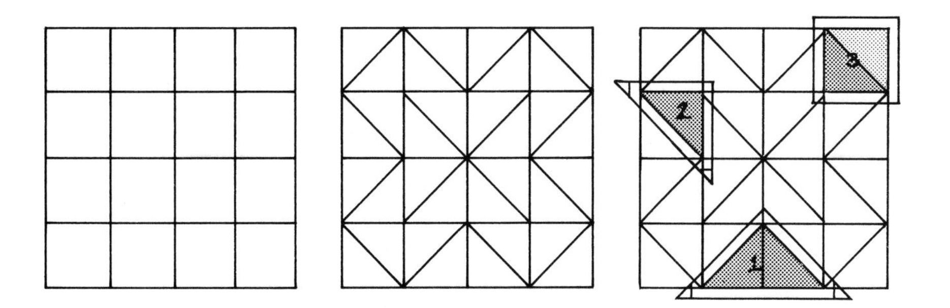

Cutting

This version of Star Puzzle has three colors: a light, a dark, and an accent color. It has simple shapes that are easy to measure, so it is a good candidate for rotary cutting techniques that don't require templates. Use the templates provided on page 83 for cutting dimensions and to compare your cut pieces for accuracy. It is also a great design for bias strip piecing.

For one Star Puzzle block:

Template #1: Cut one square, 5¾" x 5¾", of light fabric. Cut twice diagonally to yield four quarter-square triangles. Use the template to trim points for easy matching.

Template #2: Cut four squares, 3⅛" x 3⅛", of dark fabric. Cut diagonally to yield eight half-square triangles. Trim points for easy matching with the Bias Square™ at the 2¾" mark, as shown on page 18.

Template #3: Cut four bias square units, 2¾" x 2¾", of the light/dark fabric combination and four of the light/accent fabric combination. Cut bias strips 2¾" wide and follow the bias strip piecing instructions on pages 28–30. Press seams toward the darker fabric.

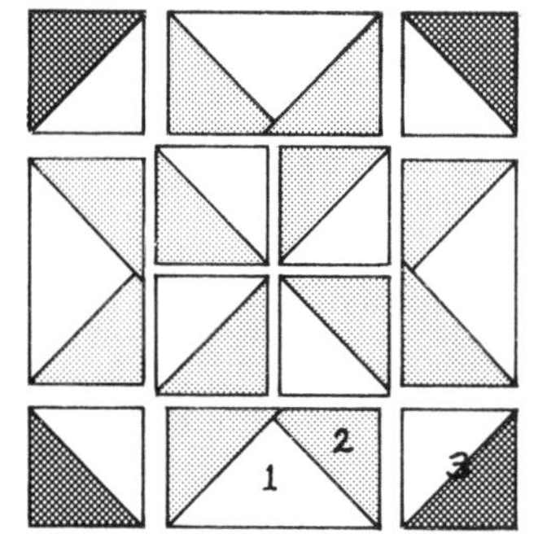

Piecing

1. Lay the cut pieces and the bias squares on the table to determine which pieces to sew together first and to evaluate your fabric choices. Beginning with the four light/dark squares, piece the pinwheel unit in the center, as shown.

   a. Matching diagonal opposing seams, chain piece two halves of the pinwheel unit. Make sure the triangles meet exactly at the ¼" seam allowance.

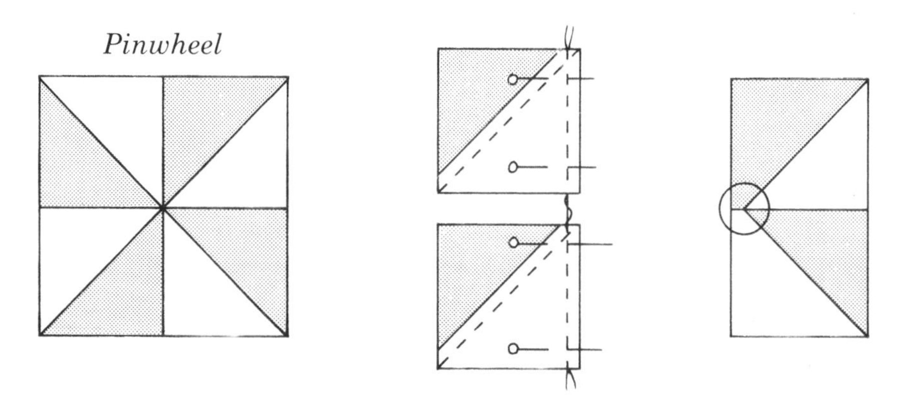

   b. Press seams toward the lighter fabric; this procedure will result in "circular" pressing. With a positioning pin, match the centers. Opposing vertical and diagonal seams will "nest." Pin, as shown. Stitch center seam through the X. Press center seam open to distribute bulk.

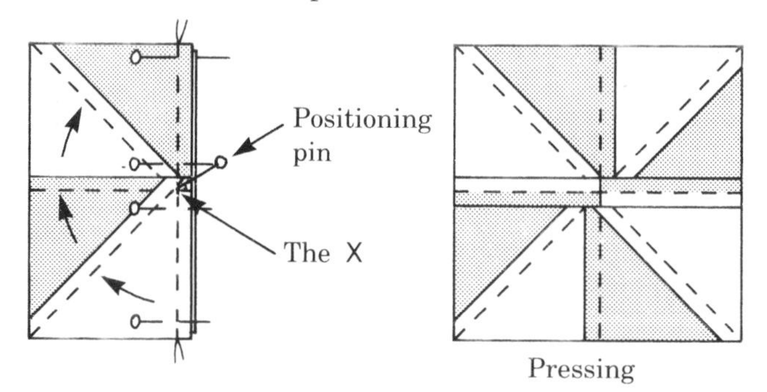

2. Using chain piecing, make four flying geese units, as shown. Press seams away from the large triangle.
   a. Sew the #2 triangle to the #1 triangle. Press.

Flying geese unit

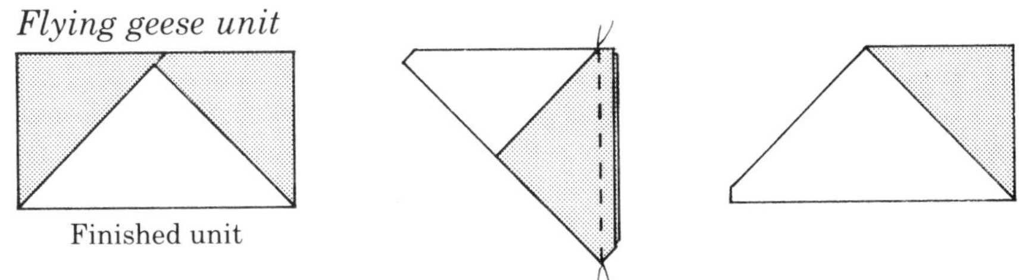

   b. Sew the second #2 triangle to the #1/#2 triangle unit. Press.

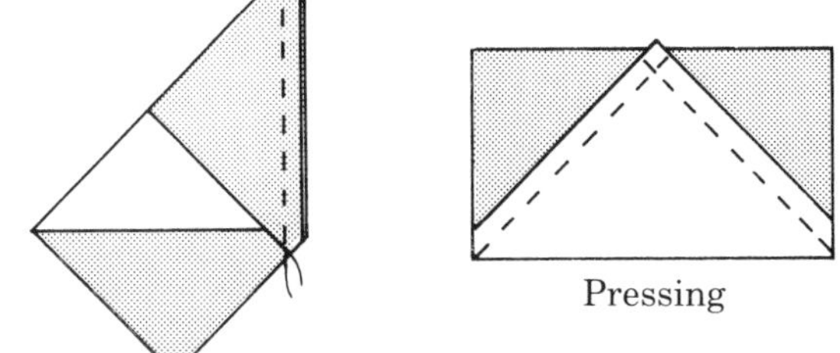

3. Use chain piecing to sew the flying geese units, together with the corner bias squares and the center pinwheel unit, in three rows.

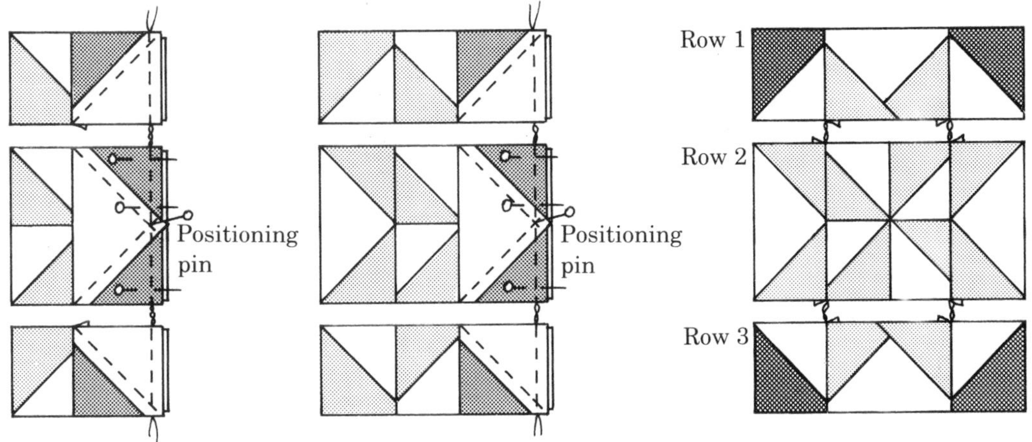

4. Pressing to take advantage of opposing seams, pin Row 1 and Row 2, as shown. Stitch long seam. Join Row 3 to Row 2 in the same manner. Press, as shown.

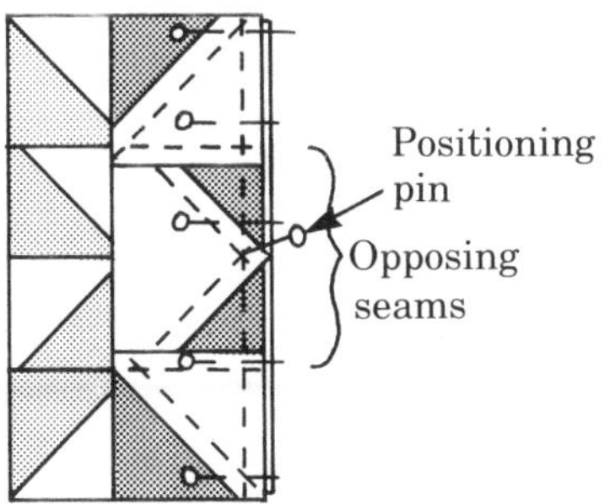

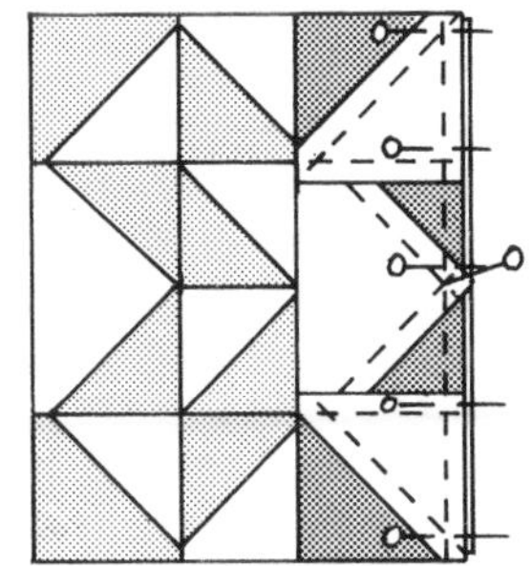

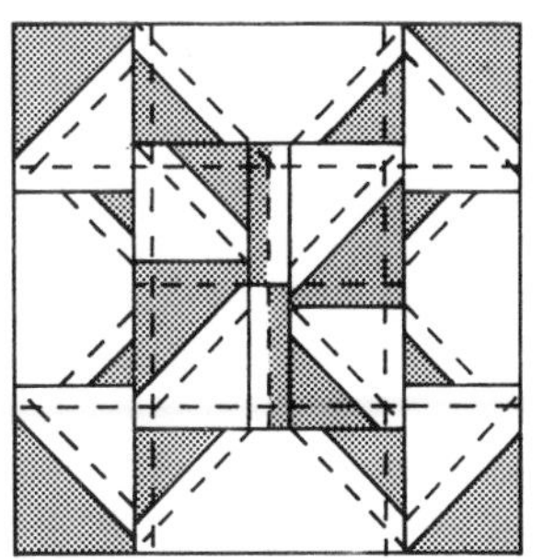

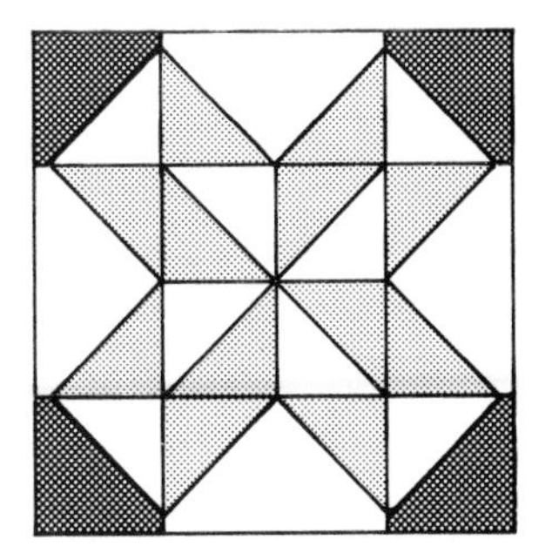

Star Puzzle Quilt

Plate 2
Templates are on page 83.

Dimensions: 64" x 78"

Materials: (45" wide fabric)
Dark: 1½ yds. total assorted green prints for piecing
Medium: 1¼ yds. gray print for lattices
Light: 1¼ yds. total assorted gray prints for piecing
Accent: ½ yd. total assorted blue prints for piecing
Inner border: ⅝ yd. light (gray print)
Middle border: ⅜ yd. dark (green print)
Outer border: ¾ yd. accent color (blue print)
Backing: 3¾ yds.
Batting, binding, and thread to finish

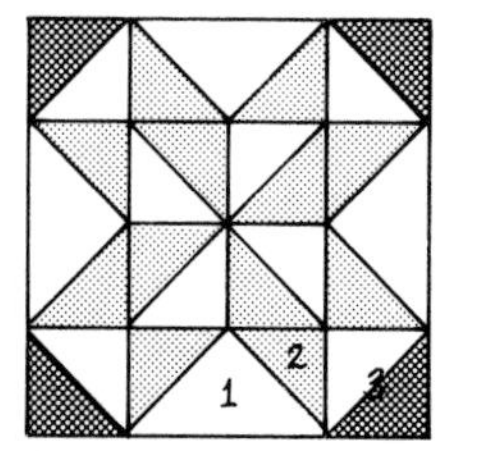

Star Puzzle, 9"
Make 20

Lattice
Cut 31

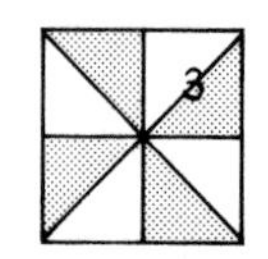

Set Square
Make 12

Border Unit
Make 112

Cutting

Borders

Cut the following border strips and set aside. Strips are longer than needed and will be trimmed to fit later.

Hint: The width of the inner and middle borders can be adjusted to accommodate the actual sewn dimensions of the pieced border and the pieced center of the quilt. You may want to wait to cut and sew these "spacer" borders until the other piecing is completed. See Pieced Borders on page 94 for help in making pieced borders fit.

1. Inner border: From the crosswise grain of the light gray print, cut enough 2¼" strips so that with seaming there will be 2 strips, 2¼" x 56", and 2 strips, 2¼" x 70".
2. Middle border: From the crosswise grain of the green print, cut enough 1" wide strips (8) so that with seaming there will be 2 strips, 1" x 56", and 2 strips, 1" x 70".
3. Outer border: From the crosswise grain of the blue print, cut enough 3" wide strips (8) so that with seaming there will be 2 strips, 1" x 56", and 2 strips, 1" x 70".

Star Puzzle Blocks

1. Cut 80 bias squares, 2¾" x 2¾", of assorted light and accent combinations (Template #3). See Bias Strip Piecing on pages 28–30. Use cutting format for bias squares in multifabric light/dark combinations.
2. Cut 80 bias squares, 2¾" x 2¾", of assorted light and dark combinations (Template #3).
3. Cut 20 squares, 5¾" x 5¾", of assorted light prints. Cut twice diagonally to yield 80 quarter-square triangles (Template #1).
4. Cut 80 squares, 3⅛" x 3⅛", of assorted dark prints. Cut diagonally to yield 160 half-square triangles (Template #2).

Set Pieces

1. For pieced pinwheel cornerstone units, cut 48 bias squares, 2¾" x 2¾", of assorted light and dark combinations (Template #3).
2. For lattice pieces, cut 31 rectangles, 5" x 9½", of medium print.

Sawtooth Border

Cut 112 (total) bias squares, 2¾" x 2¾", of both light/accent and light/dark combinations (Template #3).

Directions

1. Piece 20 Star Puzzle blocks.
2. Piece 12 pinwheel units for cornerstones.
3. Sew Star Puzzle blocks, pinwheel units, and lattice pieces together in rows, as shown in quilt diagram; then sew rows together.

4. Prepare inner and middle borders by stitching the light $2\frac{1}{4}$" strips to the 1" dark strips to form 4 border units. Stitch to center section and miter the corners (see Mitering Corners on pages 93–94).

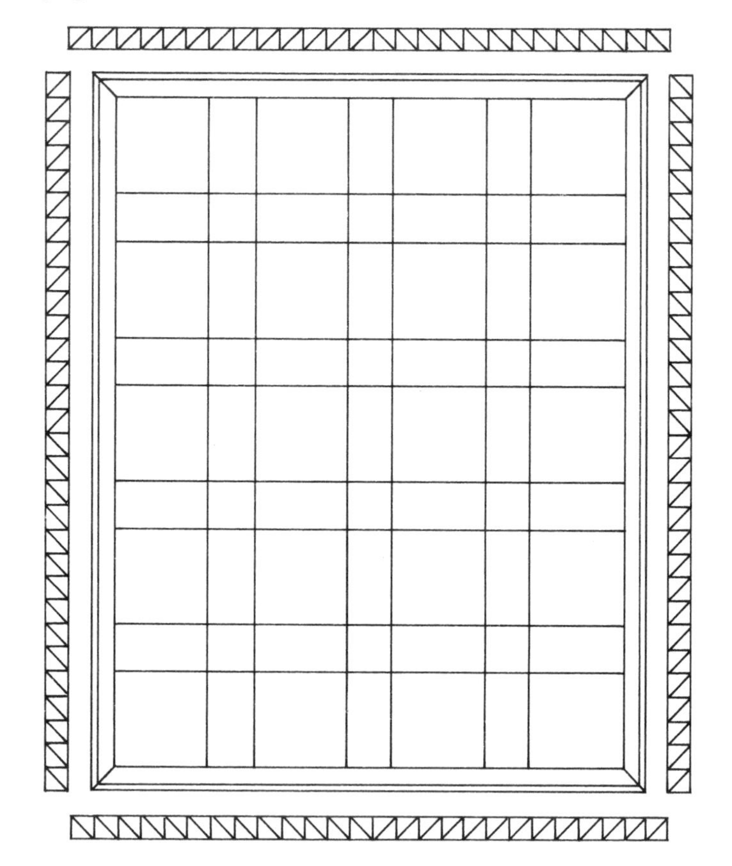

5. Piece Sawtooth border sections, as pictured. The top and bottom borders each contain 24 bias squares; the side borders have 30 bias squares each. First, sew borders to quilt sides, then to top and bottom.
6. Add the 3" wide outer border strips, using mitered or blunt-sewn corners.
7. Add backing and batting; quilt.
8. Finish edges with bias binding.

Quilt Lesson #3:

Le Moyne Star

The Le Moyne Star is one of the most basic patterns in patchwork. It has set-in seams and takes a little more time to sew than the designs in the previous lessons, but mastering the stitching is worth the effort.

Drafting category: Le Moyne Star
Preferred cutting: paper templates and rotary cutter or templates and scissors
Sewing: straight seam with some set-in seams
Matching concerns: perfecting the set-in seam, making eight points come together in center, making crisp star points

Drafting

Refer to the basic drafting instructions for the Le Moyne Star on pages 8–9 to draft this 8" design.

1. Draw an 8" square and follow the instructions to draft the Le Moyne Star.
2. Identify the three template shapes (diamond, triangle, and square) and add a consistent 1/4" seam allowance around each one. Refer to pages 10–13 for making templates. Use Method II and make a set of paper or stiffened templates. Compare your templates and cut pieces to those given on page 84 for accuracy.

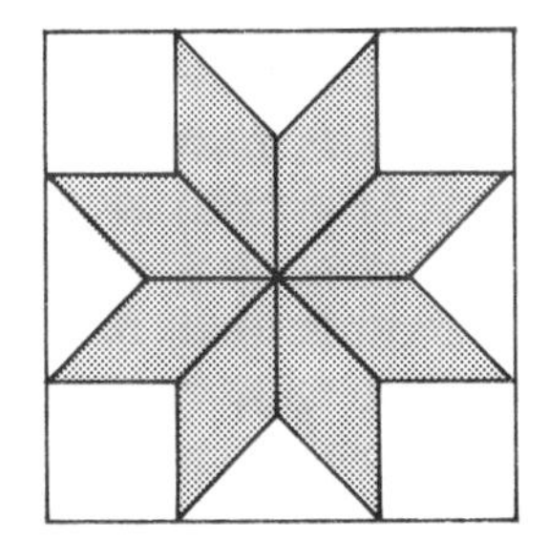

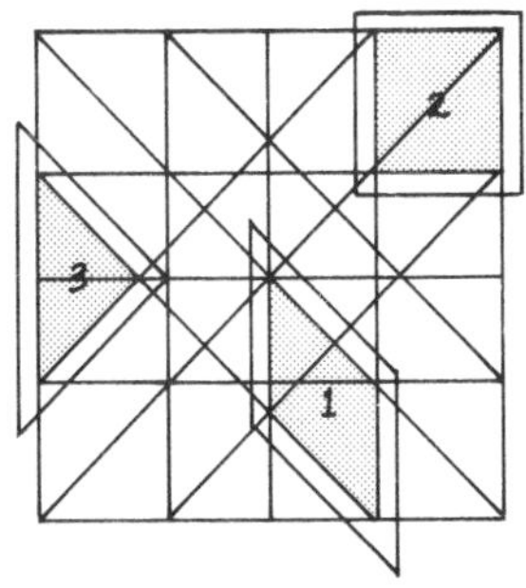

Cutting

This version of the Le Moyne Star has only two fabrics: a dark for the star and a light for the background. Because of the nature of the drafting, the measurements of the templates do not necessarily correspond with markings on standard cutting guides. So, this is a good pattern for cutting methods that include templates (see page 20 for special help on cutting diamonds).

For one Le Moyne Star block:
Template #1: Cut eight of dark fabric.
Template #2: Cut four of light fabric.
Template #3: Cut four of light fabric.

Piecing

1. Lay the cut pieces on the table to determine which to sew together first. Begin with Unit A, the diamond-diamond-triangle unit. Make four.

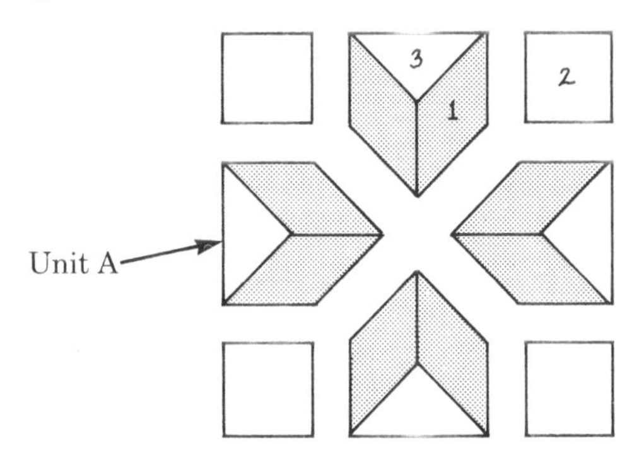

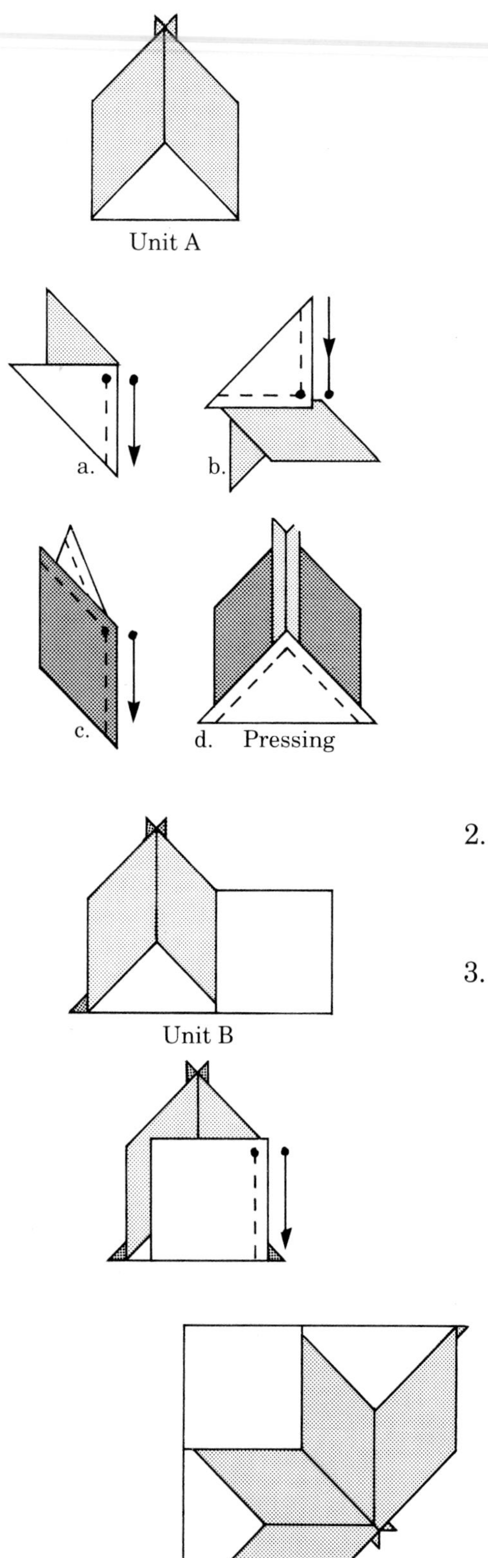

a. Sew a diamond to a triangle. With triangle on top, begin to sew at the 1/4" seam line. Backtack by sewing two stitches forward and two stitches back, taking care not to stitch into the seam allowance. (Backtacking is necessary here to hold the stitches, as they will not be crossed and held by another line of stitching.) Sew the remainder of the seam, ending at the cut edge of the fabric. (No backtacking is necessary here, as this seam will be crossed and held by another.)

b. Sew the second diamond to the same triangle. With the triangle on top, sew from the outside edge of the fabric, ending with a backtack at the 1/4" seam line.

c. Folding the triangle out of the way, match the points of the diamonds to position them for the third seam. Stitch the diamonds together, beginning with a backtack at the inner 1/4" seam line and ending at the raw edge of the fabric.

d. With an iron, lightly press the center seam open. Press the other two seams toward the diamonds. (Sometimes, especially when working with fabric that has a low thread count, it is better to finger press while piecing to avoid stretching bias edges. Use the iron only to press the finished block.)

2. Make four Unit B. Sew a corner square to the right edge of each completed A unit. With the square on top, begin stitching with a backtack at the inner 1/4" seam line and sew to the outside raw edge.
3. Make two Unit C.
   a. Join two B units to form Unit C by first matching the corner square of one B unit to the diamond of the next. With the square on top, stitch from the outside edge, ending with a backtack at the inner 1/4" seam line.
   b. To sew the diamonds together, match the points, folding the rest of the block out of the way. Use a positioning pin to match the center seams. Pin normally; remove the positioning pin. Beginning with a backtack, stitch from inner 1/4" seam line through the center seams to the raw edge of the fabric. Press center seams open and corner-square seams toward the center.

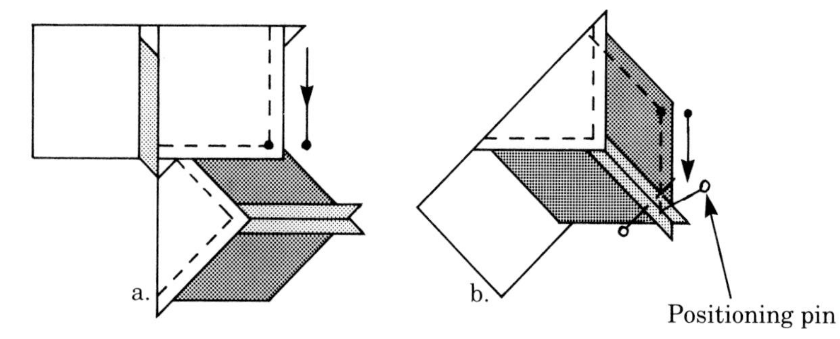

4. Join the C units.
   a & b. Joining the two C units and completing the Le Moyne Star will take three more seams. Follow the same procedure as in step 3a to join the first two seams at the corner squares.
   c. The final seam is the center seam. Use a positioning pin to carefully match the center at the center point. Pin the seam securely and remove the positioning pin before stitching. Backtacking at the 1/4" seam line, stitch precisely through the center, ending with another backtack at the 1/4" seam.

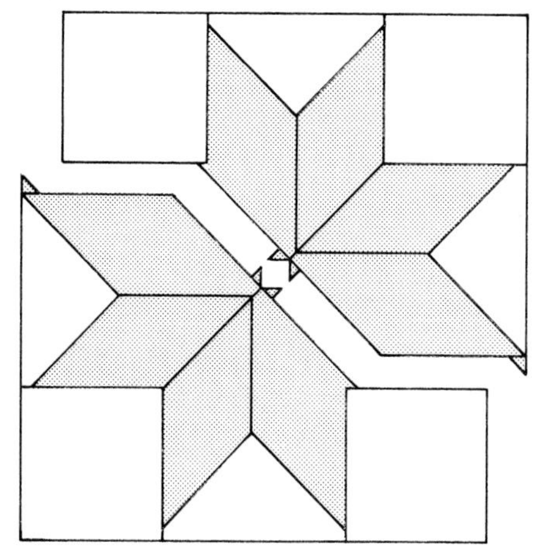
Two C units

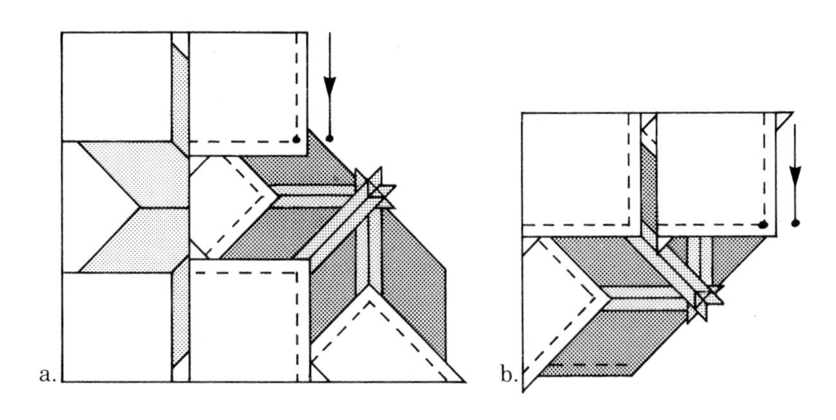

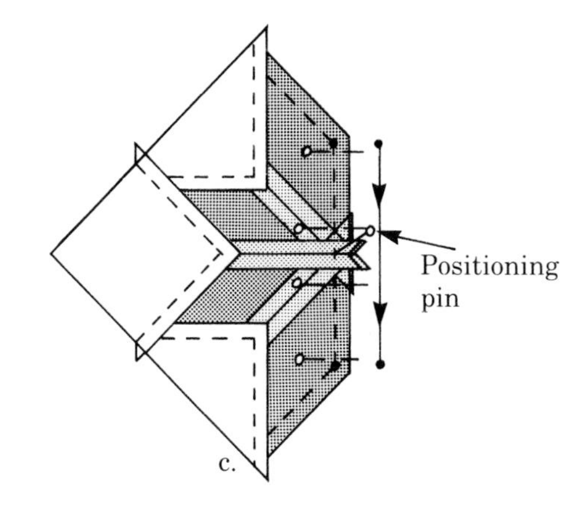

   d. Press the center seam open and the remaining seams toward the center.

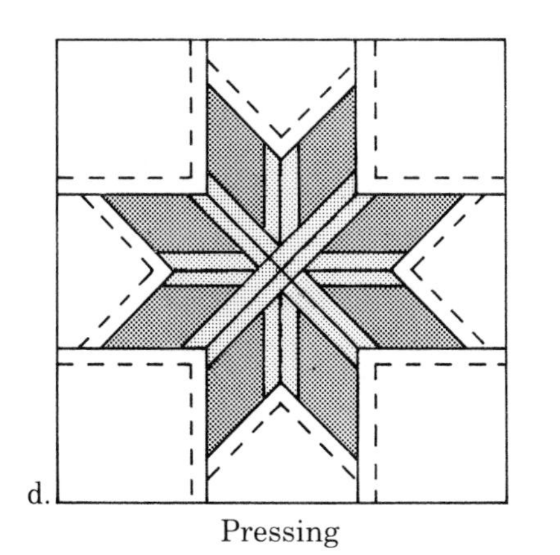

Pressing

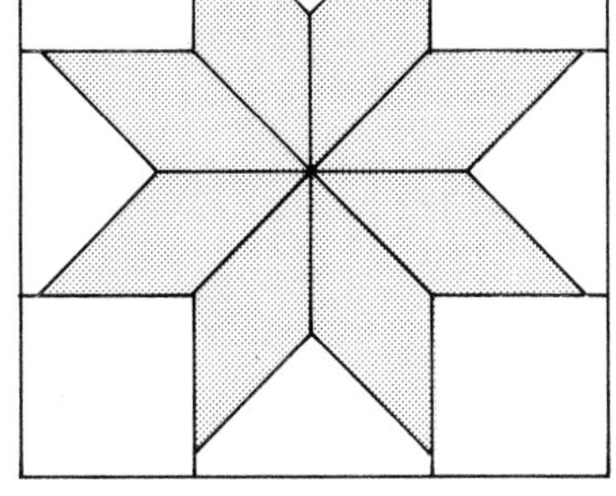

Le Moyne Star Quilt

Plate 4
Templates are on page 84.

Dimensions: 44" x 54"

Materials: (45" wide fabric)
Dark: 1½ yds. total assorted brown/cinnamon/red and pink prints for stars, cornerstones, and pieced border
Medium: ⅜ yd. brown/rust plaid for lattices
Light: ¾ yd. unbleached muslin for star backgrounds
Inner border: 1⅝ yds. medium pink/red print for lengthwise cuts; ⅝ yd. for crosswise cuts
Outer border: 1⅝ yds. cinnamon plaid for lengthwise cuts; ⅜ yd. for crosswise cuts (seam for length)
Backing: 1⅝ yds.
Batting, binding, and thread to finish

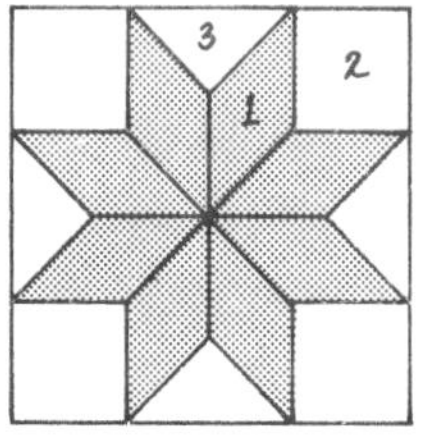

LeMoyne Star, 8"
Make 12

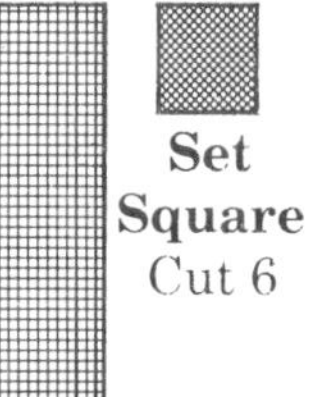

Set Square
Cut 6

Lattice
Cut 17

Cutting

Borders

Cut the following border strips and set aside. Strips are longer than needed and will be trimmed later to fit.

1. Inner border: From inner border fabric, cut 2 strips, 4½" x 46", and 2 strips, 4½" x 56".
2. Outer border: From outer border fabric, cut 2 strips, 2½" x 46", and 2 strips, 2½" x 56".

Le Moyne Star Blocks

1. Cut 96 diamonds of assorted brown, cinnamon, and pink prints for stars (Template #1).
2. Cut 48 squares (Template #2) and 48 quarter-square triangles (Template #3) from unbleached muslin for star backgrounds.

Set Pieces

1. Cut 6 squares, 2½" x 2½", of reddish print for cornerstones.
2. Cut 17 rectangles, 2½" x 8½", of brown/rust plaid fabric for lattices.

Pieced Border

1. Cut 66 parallelograms (Template #4) and 4 triangles (Template #5) of assorted brown, cinnamon, and pink prints for pieced border. (Pattern differs slightly from quilt pictured in Plate 4.)

Directions

1. Piece 12 Le Moyne Star blocks.
2. Sew completed blocks together in rows with lattices and cornerstones, as shown. Sew rows together to complete center pieced section.
3. Using #4 parallelograms and #5 triangles, piece 2 border sections that contain 14 parallelograms and 1 triangle each, for the top and bottom. For each side, make a section that contains 19 parallelograms and 1 triangle. Colors are placed randomly.
4. Sew the pieced border sections to the quilt center, using set-in seams at the corners (see pages 25–26).
5. Add inner and outer border strips, using either mitered or blunt-sewn corners.
6. Add batting and backing; quilt.
7. Finish edges with bias binding.

Quilt Lesson #4:

King's Highway

King's Highway in the 10" size is used as an alternate block with Twisting Star in the Star Highway quilt on page 55. A 5" block is used for the baby quilt on page 51. It is a simple block and a good lesson in rotary cutting and strip piecing.

Drafting: twenty-five-square grid
Preferred cutting: no templates, rotary cutter
Sewing: strip piecing
Matching concerns: opposing seams

Drafting

King's Highway is based on a twenty-five-square grid. To keep the measurements of the pieces compatible with the markings on standard rulers, a 10" block is used. To get the size of the grid squares, divide the side of the square (10") by the number of divisions counted along that side (5). So, 10" ÷ 5 = 2".

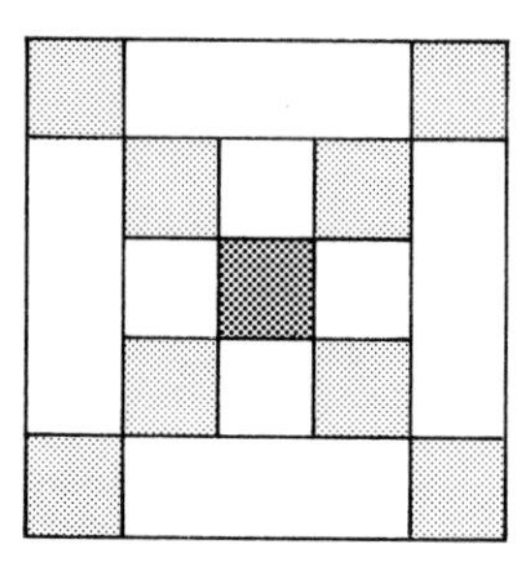

1. On 1/4" graph paper, draw a 10" square.
2. Draw a grid of twenty-five 2" squares in the 10" square.
3. Using the grid lines for a guide, identify the rectangle and square that will be templates. Add a 1/4" seam allowance around each piece.
4. See pages 10–13 for making templates. Use Method III to determine measurements of pieces without actually making templates. Compare your measurements and cut pieces with templates found on page 87.

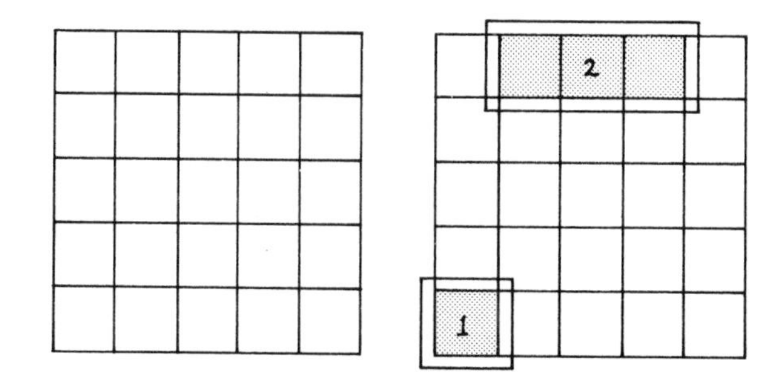

Cutting

Rotary cutting and strip piecing are used for this block, so a lot of blocks can be made quickly. Rather than give cutting and piecing for just one block, these instructions will yield twenty 10" King's Highway blocks, enough for the Star Highway quilt pattern on page 55. For these blocks, you will need three fabrics: a dark, a medium, and a light. Cut fewer strips for fewer blocks.

For twenty 10" King's Highway blocks:
Dark fabric: Cut twelve strips cross-grain 2½" wide.
Medium fabric: Cut two strips cross-grain 2½" wide.
Light fabric: Cut six strips cross-grain 6½" wide and seven strips 2½" wide.

Piecing

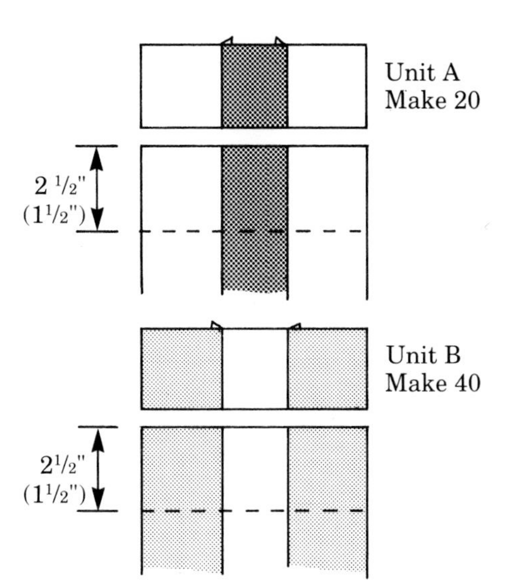

1. Sew three 2½" (1½")* wide strips together in a light/medium/light color order to form two (one) sets of strips, like the one pictured. Press seams toward darker fabric. Make cross cuts 2½" (1½") apart to make twenty Unit A.

2. Sew three 2½" (1½") wide strips together in a dark/light/dark color order to form three (two) sets of strips, like the one pictured. Press seams toward the darker fabric. Make cross cuts 2½" (1½") apart to make forty Unit B.

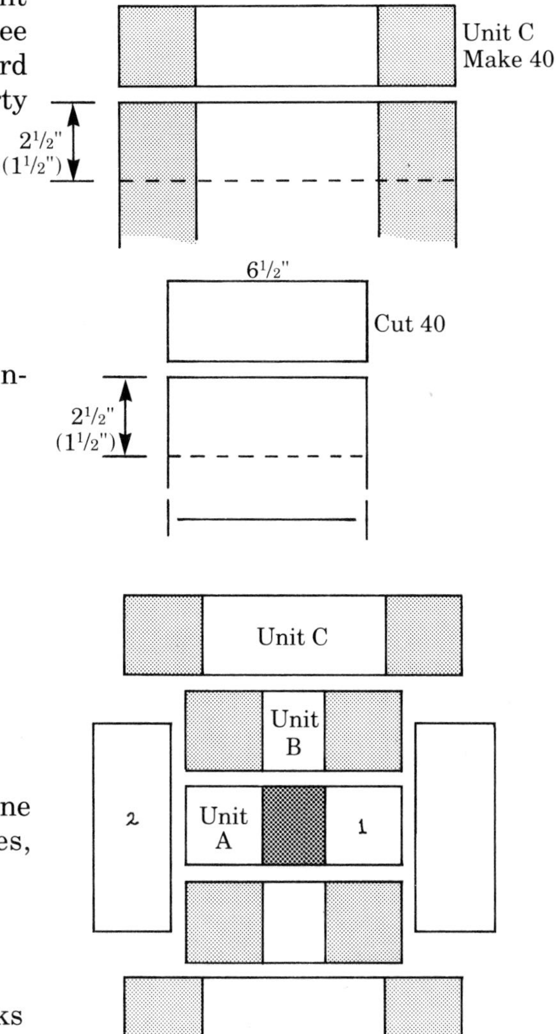

3. Sew 2½" (1½") wide dark strips and 6½" (3½") wide light strips together in a dark/light/dark color order to make three (two) sets of strips, like the one pictured. Press seams toward lighter fabric. Make cross cuts 2½" (1½") apart to make forty Unit C.

4. Make cross cuts 2½" (1½") apart on the three (two) remaining 6½" (3½") wide light strips to make forty rectangles.

5. Piece twenty King's Highway blocks. Each block contains one Unit A, two Unit B, two Unit C, and two rectangles, 2½" x 6½" (1½" x 3½").

*Numbers in parentheses are for the 5" King's Highways blocks used in the baby quilt pattern on page 51.

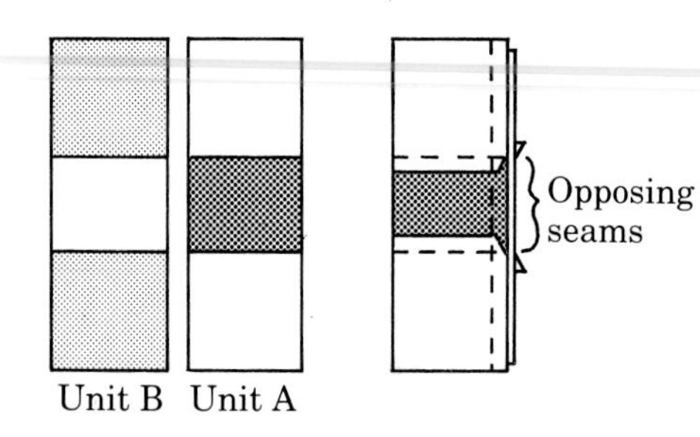

a. Chain piece twenty A units to twenty B units, utilizing opposing seams for matching.

b. Chain piece twenty B units to the preceding units to make Ninepatches. Press seams away from center.

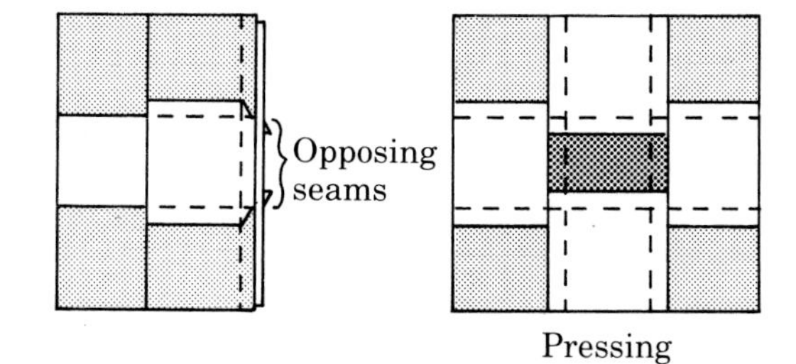

Unit B Unit A Unit B

c. Chain piece the 2½" x 6½" (1½" x 3½") rectangles to the Ninepatches. Press seams away from center.

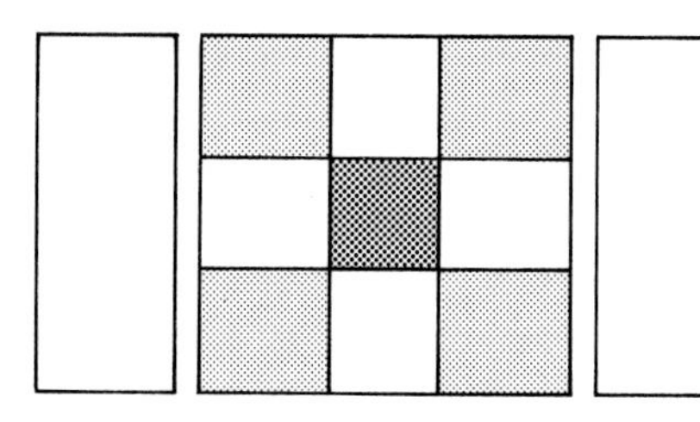

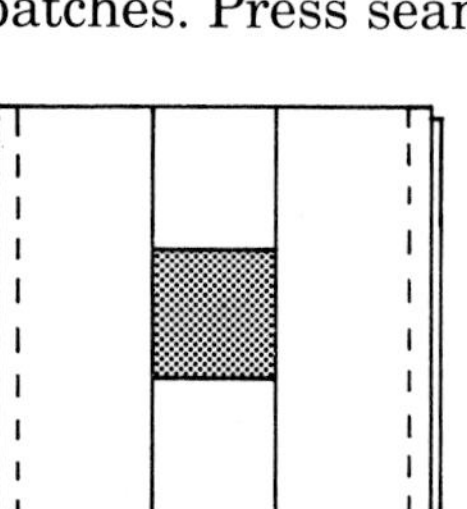

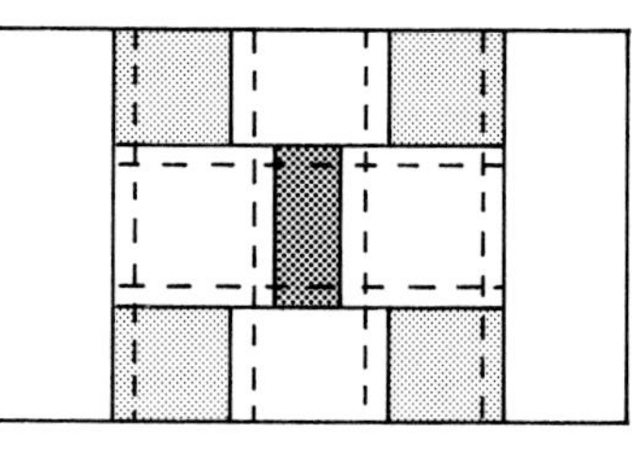

d. Add C units with chain piecing. Utilize opposing seams for matching. Press seams away from center.

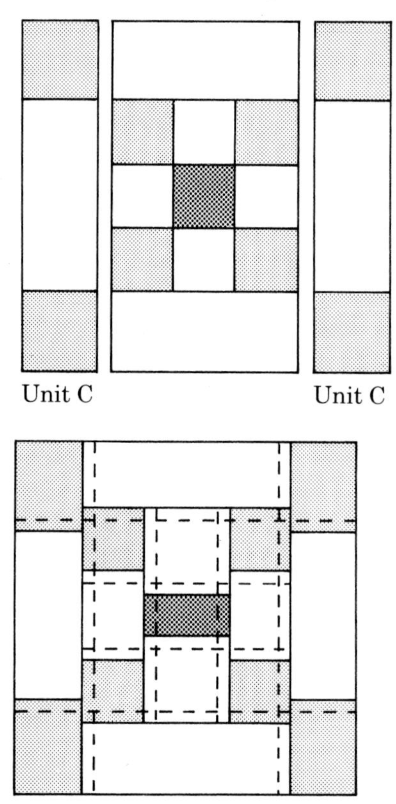

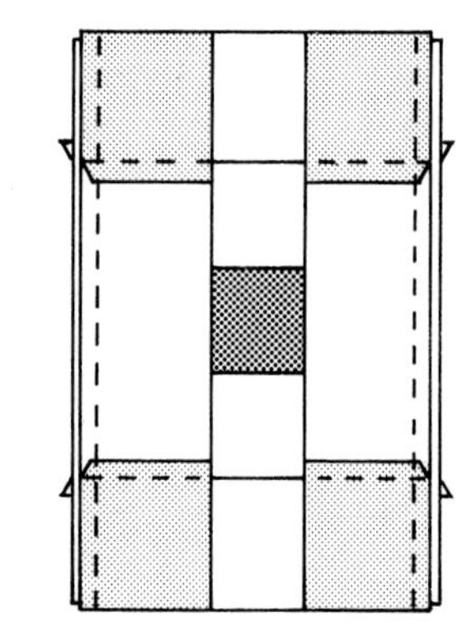

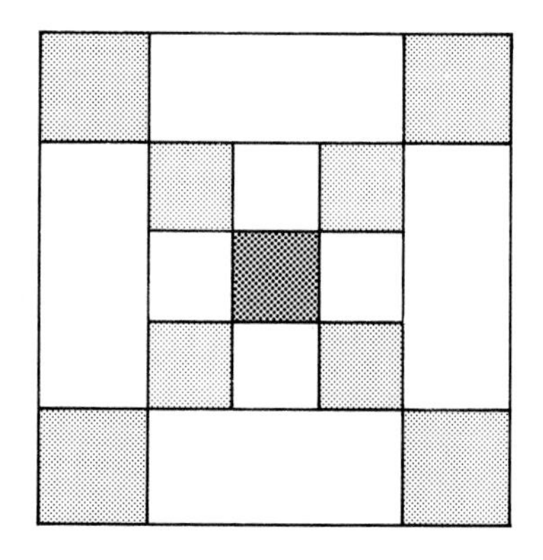

King's Highway Baby Quilt

Plate 5

Dimensions: 38" x 45"

Materials: (45" wide fabric)
Dark: $1\frac{3}{8}$ yd. brown print for outer border and block piecing
Medium: $\frac{1}{4}$ yd. rose print for inner border and block piecing
First light: $\frac{3}{8}$ yd. light blue print for block piecing
Second light: $\frac{1}{4}$ yd. light blue stripe for block piecing and middle border
Third light: $\frac{3}{4}$ yd. light blue print for set pieces
Backing: $1\frac{3}{8}$ yds.
Batting, binding, and thread to finish

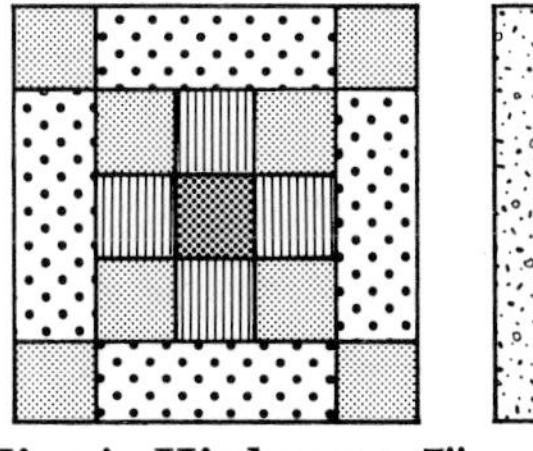

King's Highway, 5"
Make 20

Set Piece I
Cut 12

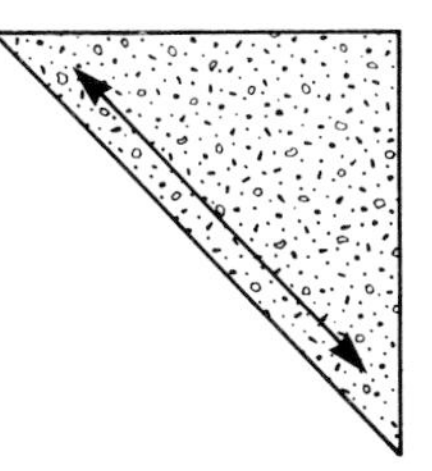

Set Piece II
Cut 14

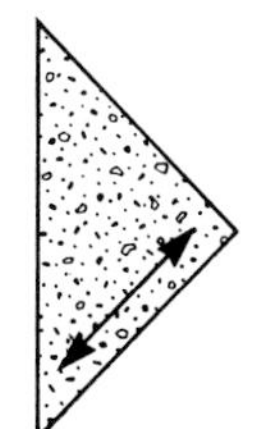

Set Piece III
Cut 4

Cutting

Borders

1. Inner border: Cut 4 strips, 1" wide from the crosswise grain of the medium fabric.
2. Middle border: Cut 4 strips, $1\frac{1}{2}$" wide, from the crosswise grain of the second light.
3. Outer border: Cut 4 strips, 4" wide, from the lengthwise grain of the dark fabric.

King's Highway Blocks

1. From dark fabric, cut 6 strips, $1\frac{1}{2}$" wide, on the lengthwise grain.
2. From medium fabric, cut 1 strip, $1\frac{1}{2}$" wide, on the crosswise grain.
3. From first light, cut 3 strips, $3\frac{1}{2}$" wide, on the crosswise grain.
4. From second light, cut 4 strips, $1\frac{1}{2}$" wide, on the crosswise grain.

Set Pieces

1. From third light, cut 12 squares, $5\frac{1}{2}$" x $5\frac{1}{2}$", for Set Piece I.
2. From third light, cut 4 squares, $8\frac{1}{4}$" x $8\frac{1}{4}$". Cut twice diagonally to yield 14 quarter-square triangles for Set Piece II.
3. From third light, cut 2 squares, $4\frac{3}{8}$" x $4\frac{3}{8}$". Cut diagonally to yield 4 half-square triangles for the corner pieces, Set Piece III.

Set Piece II

Quick cut:
$8\frac{1}{4}$" square

Set Piece III

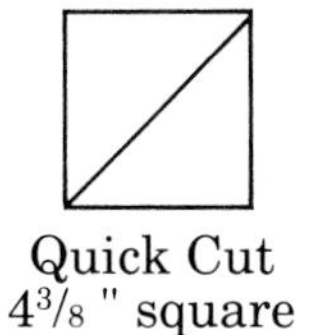

Quick Cut
$4\frac{3}{8}$ " square

Directions

1. Following the instructions on page 49, piece twenty 5" King's Highway blocks. (The dimensions for the 5" blocks are in parentheses. The piecing order is the same.)
2. Arrange the pieced blocks, alternate blocks, and set triangles in diagonal rows, as shown in the quilt diagram, and stitch.
3. Sew the rows together to complete the pieced section of the quilt.
4. Sew the border strips together in color order in preparation for mitering. Sew to quilt and miter the corners (see Mitering Corners on pages 93–94).
5. Add batting and backing; quilt.
6. Finish edges with bias binding.

Quilt Lesson #5:

Twisting Star

The Twisting Star is based on the Le Moyne Star drafting. The piecing, however, does not include set-in seams. This design has halfway seams that are partially sewn early in block construction and finished later. The procedure can be applied to many designs that may appear to have set-in piecing, most notably Feathered Star designs.

Drafting category: Le Moyne Star
Preferred cutting: paper templates and rotary cutter, or templates and scissors
Sewing: straight seam, cut edge to cut edge, with some halfway seams
Matching concerns: making accurate triangle points that end 1/4" from raw edge of fabric

Drafting

Refer to the basic drafting instructions for the Le Moyne Star on pages 8–9 to draft this 10" block.

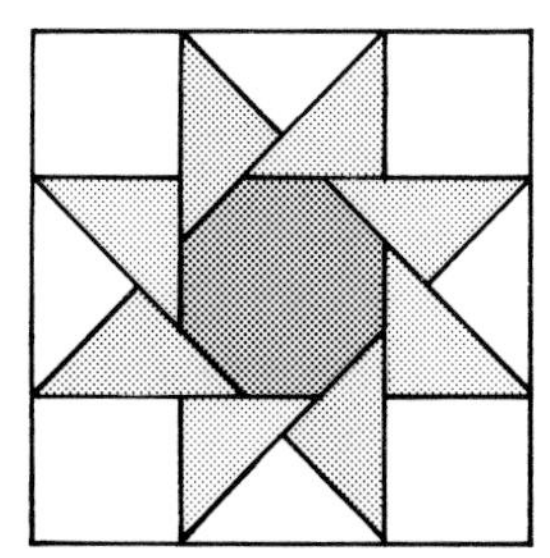

1. Draw a 10" square and follow the drafting instructions for the Le Moyne Star.
2. Identify the three template shapes (an octagon, triangle, and square). Color them in and add a consistent 1/4" seam allowance around each one. Refer to pages 10–13 for making templates. Use Method II and make a set of paper or stiffened templates. Compare your templates and cut pieces to the templates found on page 85 for accuracy.

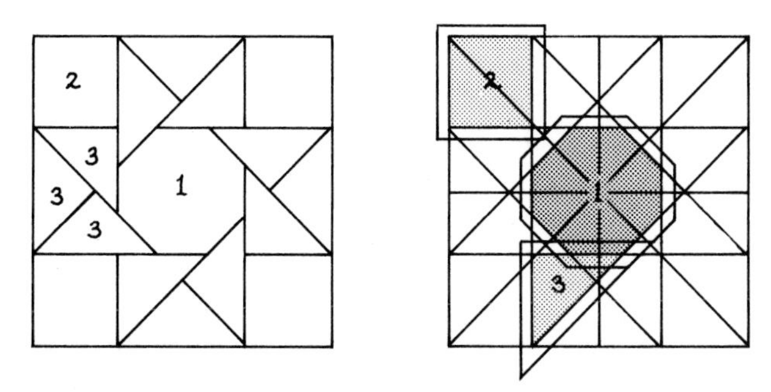

Cutting

This version of the Twisting Star has three colors: a medium color for the center octagon, a dark fabric for the star points, and a light fabric for the background. Because of the nature of the drafting, the measurements of the templates do not necessarily correspond with markings on standard cutting guides. So, this is a good pattern for cutting methods that include templates.

For one Twisting Star block:
Template #1: Cut one octagon of the medium fabric.
Template #2: Cut four triangles of the background fabric and eight triangles of the dark fabric.
Template #3: Cut four corner squares of background fabric.

PIECING

1. Lay the cut pieces out to determine which to sew together first and to evaluate your fabric choices. To begin, chain piece four Unit A (triangle to square) and four Unit B (triangle to triangle).

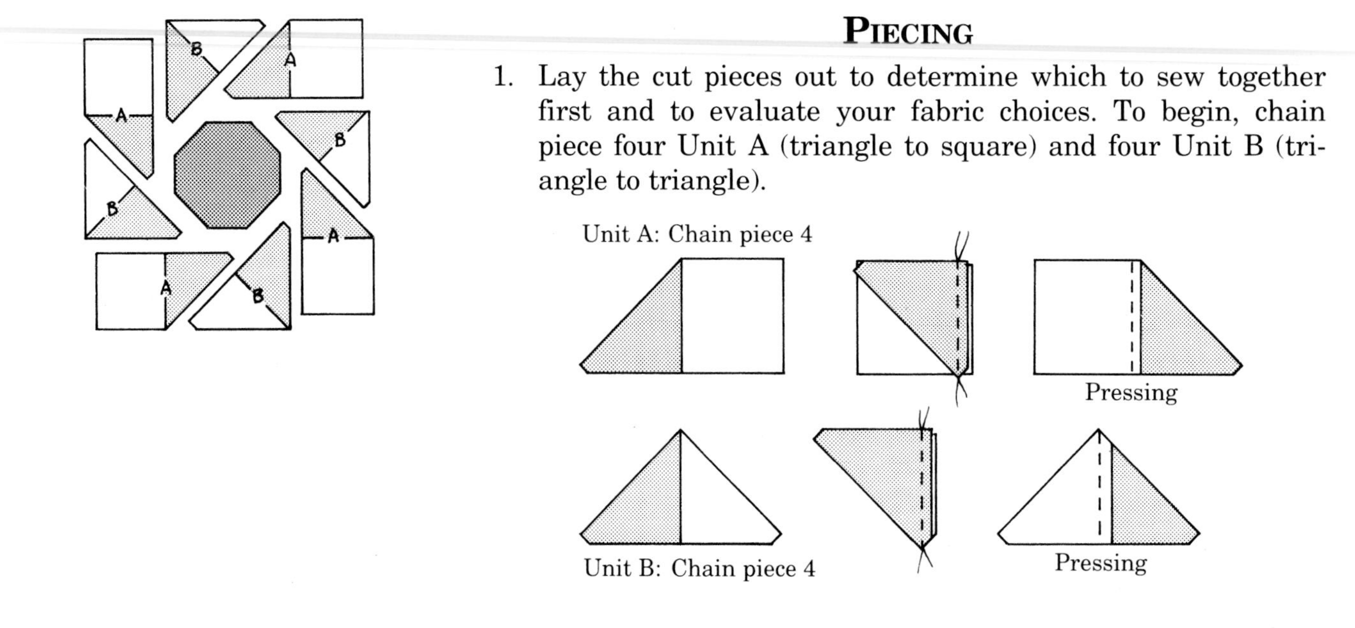

2. Sew the first Unit B to the center octagon with a halfway seam, as shown. Begin stitching at the edge of the fabric and end with a backtack midway on the side of the octagon. Press seam away from the center.

3. Sew the first Unit A to the previous section, as shown, with a straight seam, sewing cut edge to cut edge. Continue adding remaining B and A units alternately. Press seams away from center.

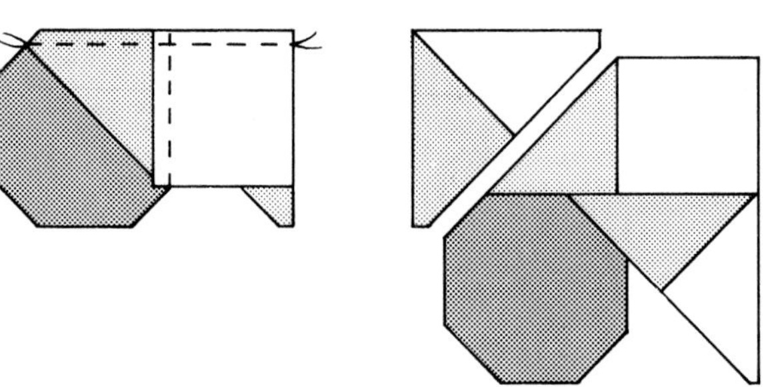

4. The last step is to complete the halfway seam. Stitch, as shown, beginning with a backtack where the first portion of the halfway seam ended. Sew to outside edge of block. Press.

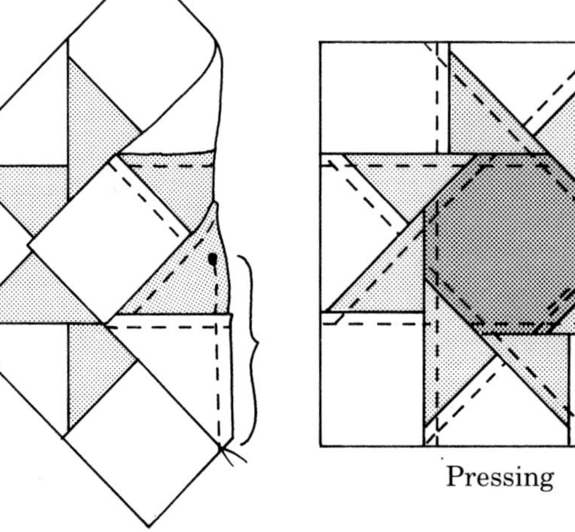

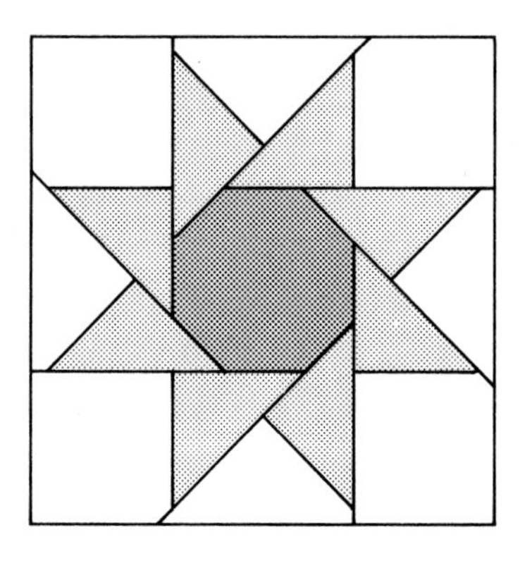

Cutting

Borders

Cut 4 strips 5 1/2" wide from the length of the border fabric and set aside. Extra length will be trimmed later.

Twisting Star Blocks

1. Cut 12 octagons of assorted medium prints (Template #1).
2. Cut 48 squares of assorted light prints (Template #2).
3. Cut 96 triangles of assorted dark prints and 48 triangles of light prints (Template #3).

King's Highway Blocks

Follow the cutting instructions on page 48 for 10" blocks.

Set Pieces

1. Cut 7 squares, 8 7/8" x 8 7/8", of assorted light prints. Cut diagonally to yield 14 half-square triangles for Set Piece I.
2. Cut 14 trapezoids of a medium print (Set Piece II).
3. Cut 4 squares, 3 7/8" x 3 7/8", of assorted light prints. Cut diagonally to yield 8 half-square triangles for the corner pieces (Set Piece III).
4. Cut 8 trapezoids from a medium print (Set Piece IV).

Directions

1. Piece 12 Twisting Star 10" blocks.
2. Piece 20 King's Highway 10" blocks.
3. Piece 14 side set triangles, as pictured.

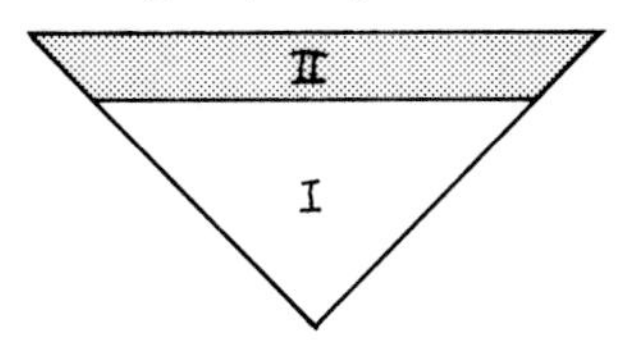

4. Piece 4 corner units, as pictured.

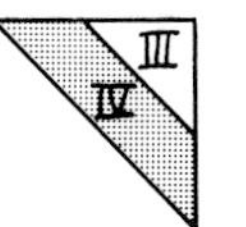

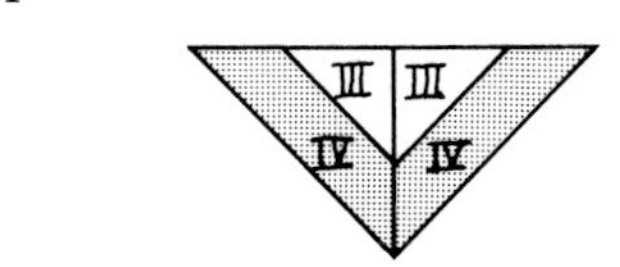

5. Stitch Twisting Star blocks, King's Highway blocks, and the side and corner triangular units together in diagonal rows, as shown. Sew rows together to complete pieced center section.
6. Add 5 1/2" wide border strips, using mitered or blunt-sewn corners.
7. Add batting and backing; quilt.
8. Finish edges with bias binding.

Star Highway Quilt

Plate 3
Templates are on pages 84–85, 87.

When making this quilt, check the first few blocks you make of each design to make sure they are of equal size. If they don't match, adjust your sewing to compensate. I found my King's Highway blocks were coming out smaller than the Twisting Star blocks, so I began using a scant 1/4" seam on the King's Highway blocks, and they were then the proper size.

Dimensions: 66" x 80"

Materials: (45" wide fabric)
Dark: 1 3/8 yds. total assorted red prints for piecing
Medium: 1 1/2 yds. total assorted green prints for piecing
Light: 4 1/4 yds. total assorted light prints for block backgrounds
Borders: 2 1/2 yds. light print
Backing: 5 yds.
Batting, binding, and thread to finish

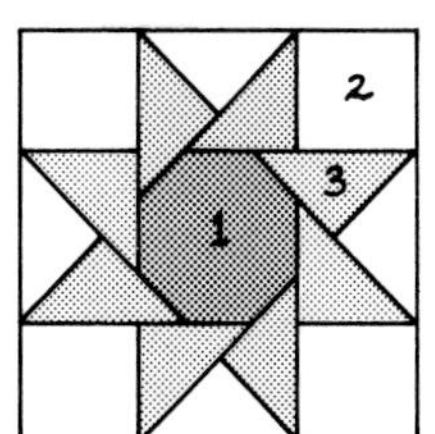

Twisting Star, 10"
Make 12

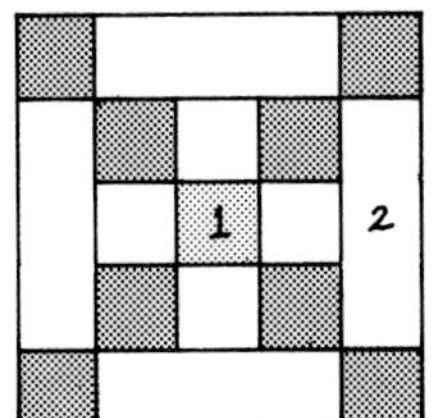

King's Highway, 10"
Make 20

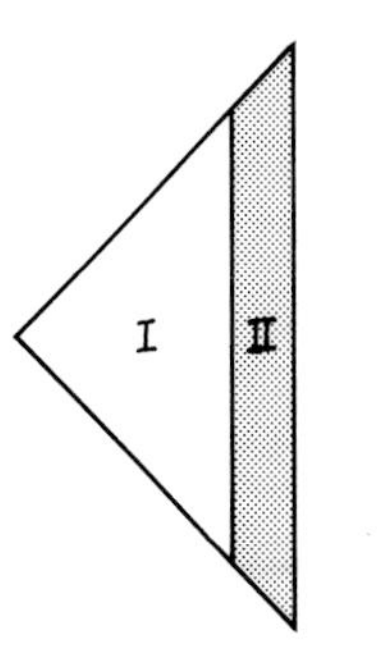

Side Set Triangle
Make 14

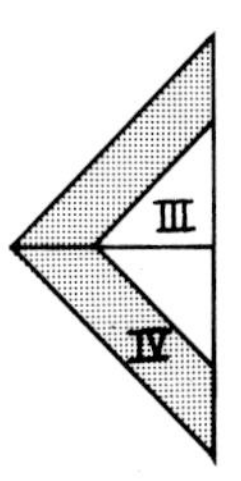

Corner Unit
Piece 4

Quilt Lesson #6:
Scrap Basket

The Scrap Basket design introduces the concept of asymmetrical piecing. The construction units on this and many other "picture" blocks are not all alike. It also involves asymmetrical shapes, reversals or mirror images, and set-in seams.

Drafting category: sixteen-square grid
Preferred cutting: rotary techniques combined with paper template for parallelogram
Sewing: set-in seams and straight seams, cut edge to cut edge
Matching concerns: asymmetrical construction, parallelograms are mirror images

Drafting

The Scrap Basket design is based on a sixteen-square grid. The finished block measures 8". To get the size of the grid squares, divide the side of the square (8") by the number of divisions counted along that side (4). So, 8" ÷ 4 = 2".

1. Draw an 8" square on 1/4" graph paper.
2. Draw a grid of sixteen 2" squares in the 8" square.
3. Study the drafting example and draw the appropriate diagonal lines to make the design.
4. Identify the six shapes that need to be templates (not every grid line is a seam line) and color them in. You will find a 2" square, a 2" x 4" rectangle, three triangles, and a parallelogram.
5. Add a consistent 1/4" seam allowance around each template. Refer to page 13 for making different types of templates. Templates for this design are found on page 86.

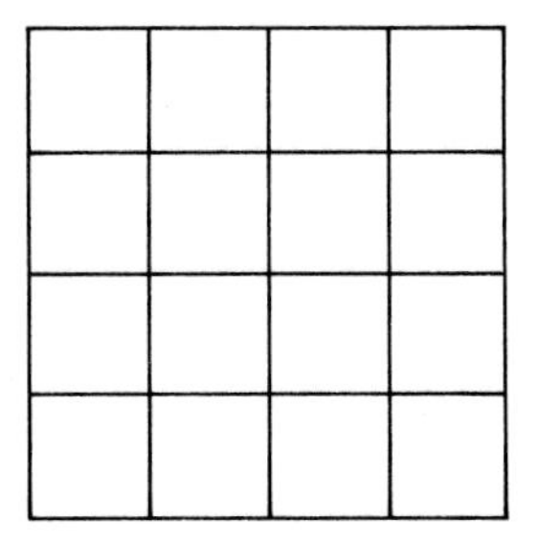

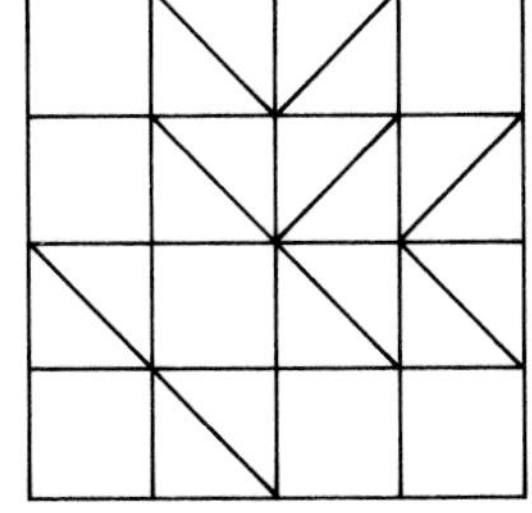

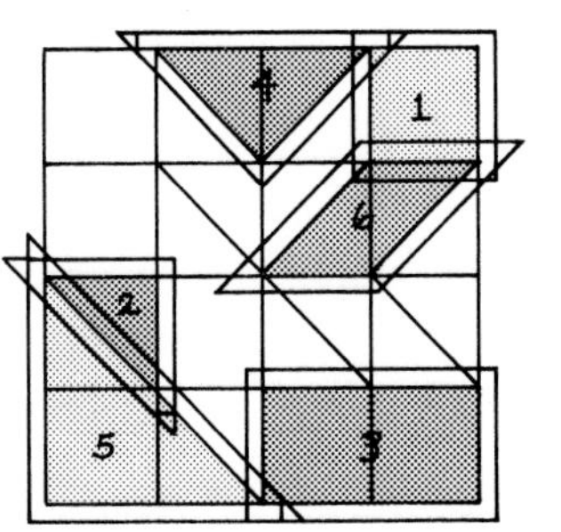

Cutting

This version of the Scrap Basket has three main colors: a light, a dark, and a medium. The quilt pattern on page 61 calls for assorted print fabrics for each color category. With the exception of the parallelogram (Template #6), Scrap Basket has simple, easy-to-measure shapes that are perfect for no-template rotary cutting.

For one Scrap Basket block:

Template #1: Cut one square, 2½" x 2½", of light fabric.

Template #2: Cut one square, 2⅞" x 2⅞", of dark fabric. Cut diagonally to yield two half-square triangles. Trim points for easy matching with the Bias Square™ at 2½" mark, as shown on page 18.

Template #3: Cut two rectangles, 2½" x 4½", of light fabric.

Template #4: Cut one square, 5¼" x 5¼", of light fabric. Cut twice diagonally to yield four quarter-square triangles (only two are needed for one block). Use a template to trim points for easy matching.

Template #5: Cut one square, 4⅞" x 4⅞", of dark fabric and one square of light fabric. Cut each diagonally to yield half-square triangles. One light and one dark of each color are needed to complete the block. Trim points for easy matching with the Bias Square™ at 4½" mark, as shown on page 18.

Template #6: Using a paper template and the instructions for cutting parallelograms on page 20, cut two, plus two reversed, of medium fabric. Refer to page 19 for cutting reversals.

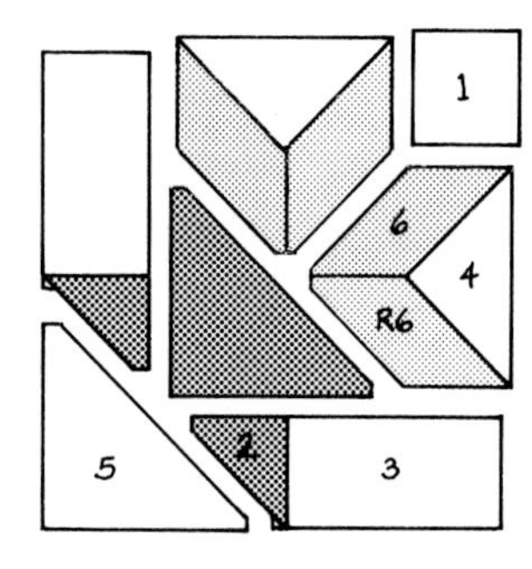

PIECING

1. Lay the cut pieces out to determine which to sew together first. Begin with Unit A, which consists of two parallelograms and a triangle.
   a. Keeping in mind that the #6 parallelograms have two long sides and two short sides and are mirror images, begin by sewing the long side of the left parallelogram to the short side of the #4 triangle. With the triangle on top, begin to sew at the ¼" seam line. Backtack and sew the remainder of the seam ending at the cut edge of the fabric.
   b. Sew the long side of the right-hand parallelogram to the same triangle. With the triangle on top, sew from the outside edge of the fabric, ending with a backtack at the ¼" seam line.
   c. Folding the triangle out of the way, match the points of the parallelograms to position them for the third seam. Stitch the parallelograms together, beginning with a backtack at the inner ¼" seam line and ending at the raw edge of the fabric.
   d. With an iron, lightly press the center seam open. Press the other two seams toward the parallelograms.

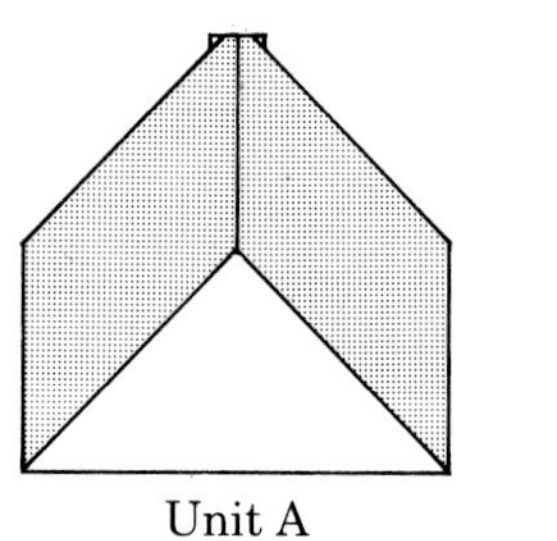

Unit A

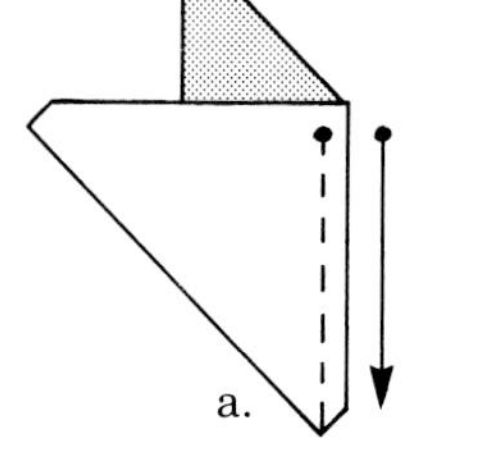

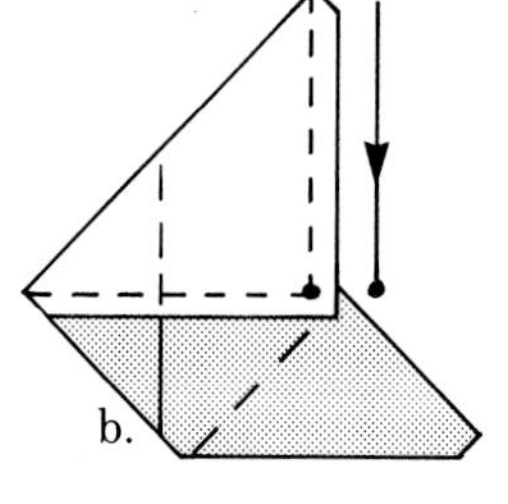

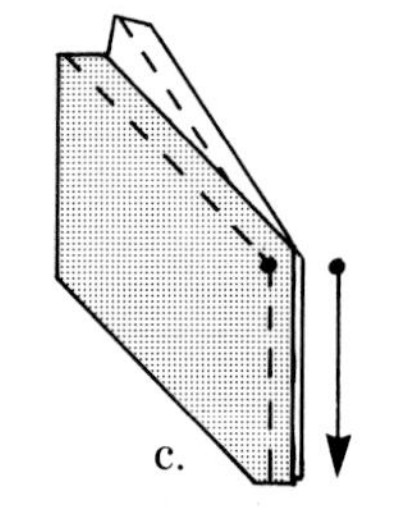

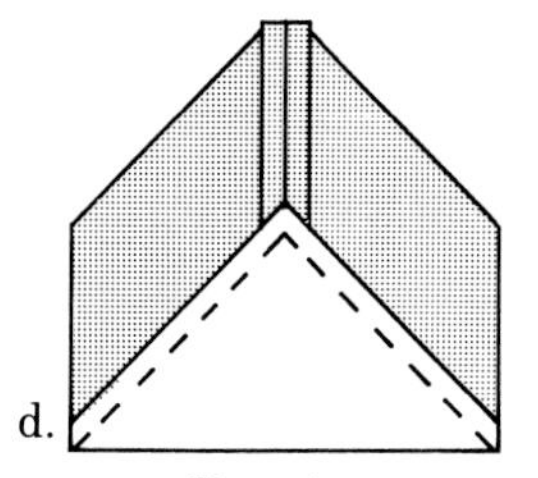

Pressing

2. Unit B combines the two Unit A's with the #1 corner square. Make one.
   a. With the #1 square on top, stitch the square to Unit A. Beginning with a backtack at the inner 1/4" seam line, sew to cut edge of the fabric.
   b. Join the above unit to the remaining Unit A by placing the corner square, as shown. With the square up, stitch from the outer cut edge to the inner 1/4" seam line and backtack.
   c. Folding the rest of Unit B out of the way, match the points of the parallelograms. Use a positioning pin to match the center seams. Pin normally; remove the positioning pin. Beginning with a backtack, stitch from the inner 1/4" seam line through the center seams to the cut edge of the fabric.
   d. Press center seam open and corner square seams toward the center.

Unit B

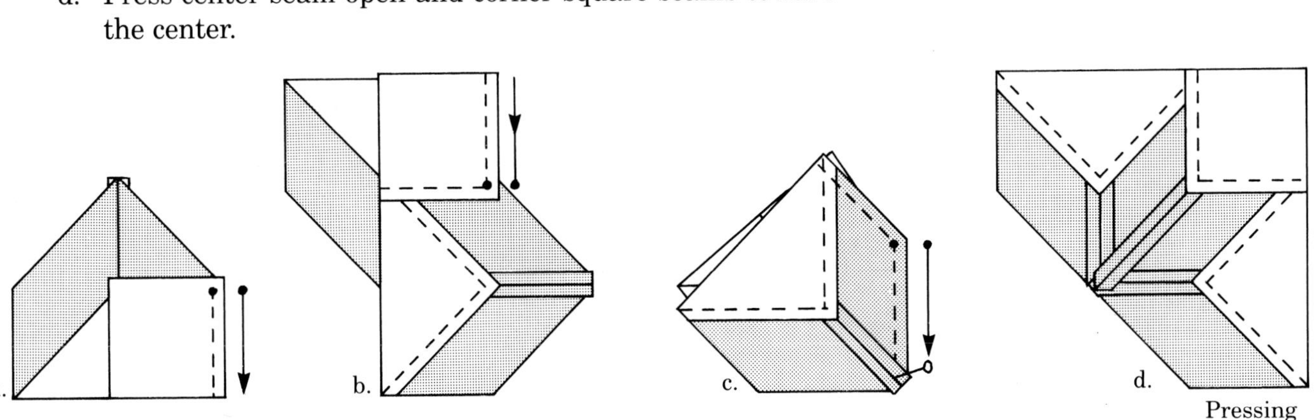

3. Sew the large dark triangle to Unit B to make Unit C.

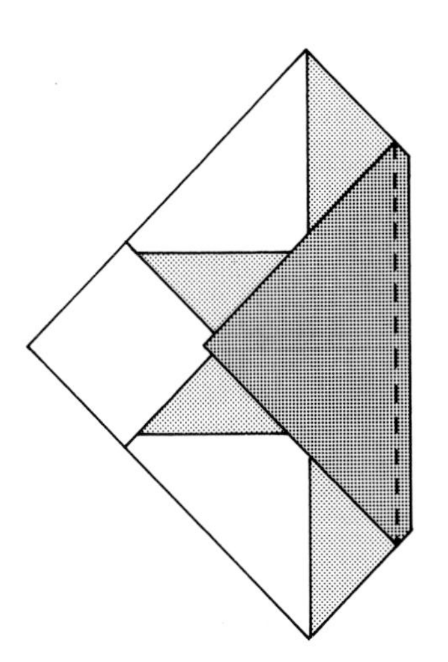

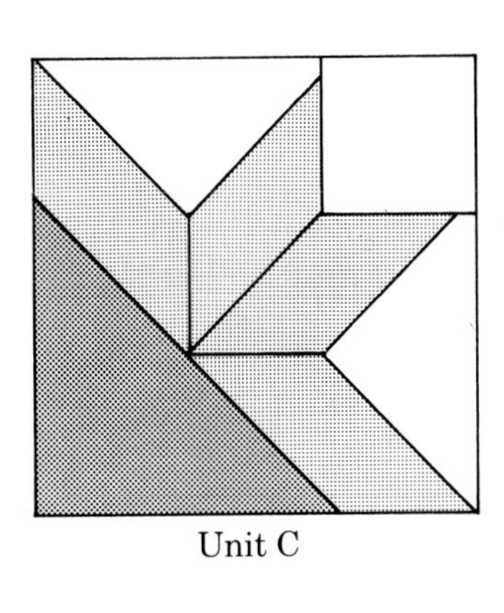

Unit C

4. The two side units, each made of a rectangle and a triangle, are mirror images. Stitch and press, as shown.

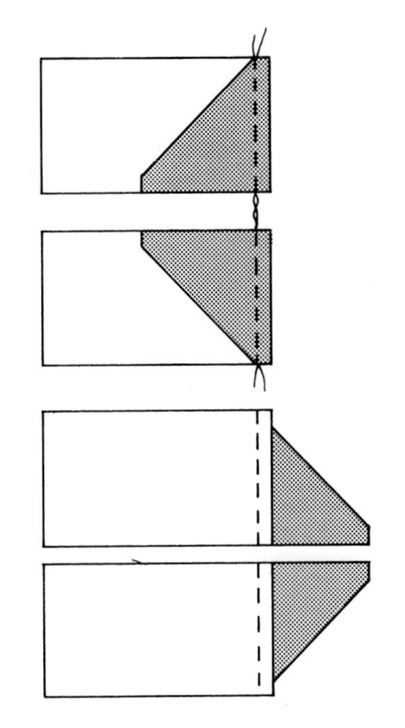

5. Sew the side units to Unit C, as shown, to create Unit D.

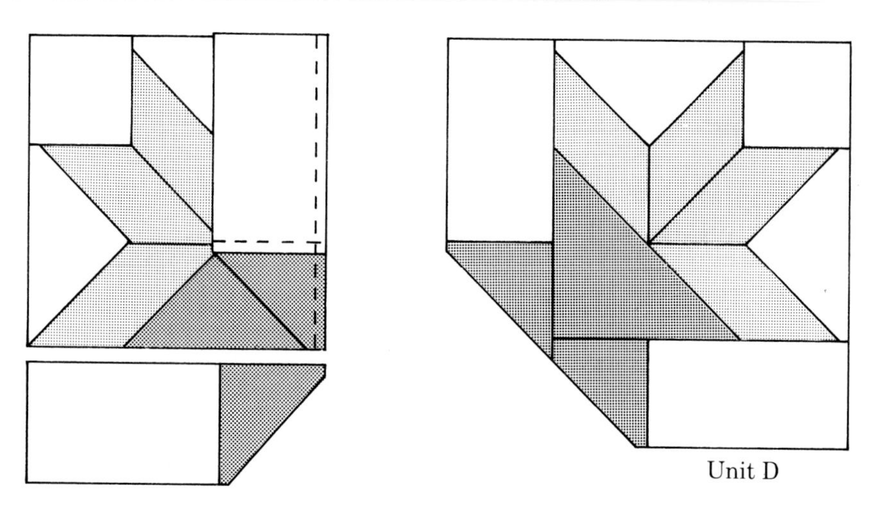

Unit D

6. Sew the large light triangle to Unit D. Press, as shown.

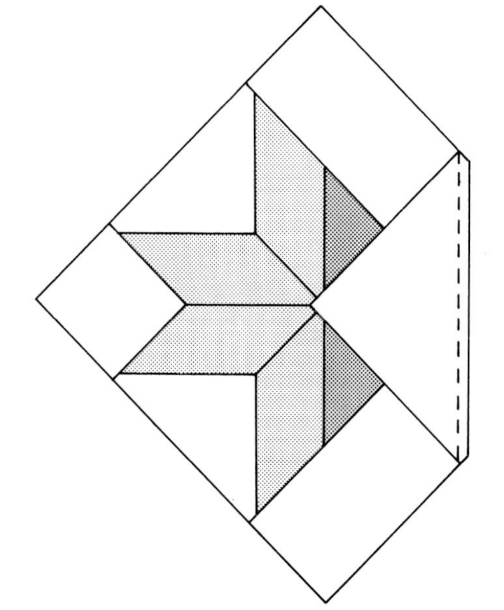

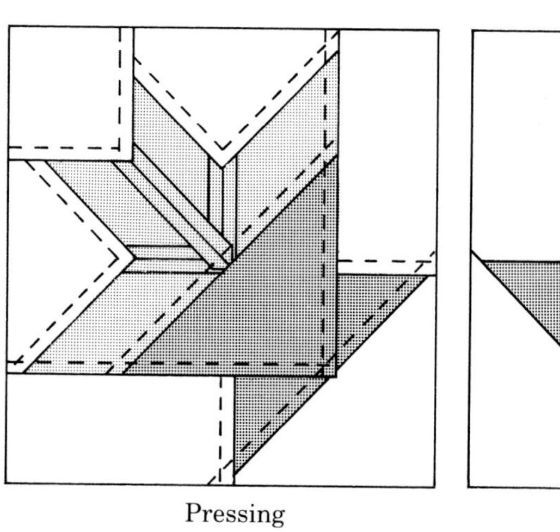

Pressing

Scrap Basket Quilt

Plate 6
Templates are on page 86.

Dimensions: 39½" x 53¾"

Materials: (45" wide fabric)

First dark: ½ yd. total assorted navy prints for baskets and pieced border

Second dark: ¾ yd. black print for alternate blocks and pieced border

Medium: ⅝ yd. total assorted maroon/cinnamon/brown or gold prints for baskets and pieced border

Light: ⅜ yd. total assorted white-with-small-dark-figure prints for block backgrounds

Inner border: ½ yd. gold print

Middle and outer borders: 1⅝ yds. maroon print (if cut from lengthwise grain or ½ yd. if cut from crosswise grain)

Backing: 1⅝ yds.

Batting, binding, and thread to finish

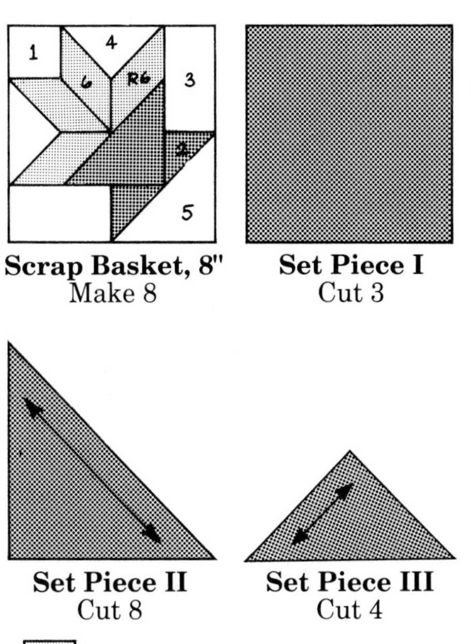

Scrap Basket, 8" Make 8

Set Piece I Cut 3

Set Piece II Cut 8

Set Piece III Cut 4

Border Pieces

Cutting

Borders

Cut the following border strips and set aside. Extra length will be trimmed later.

Hint: The width of the inner and middle borders can be adjusted to accommodate the actual sewn dimensions of the pieced border and the pieced center of the quilt. You may want to wait to cut and sew these "spacer" borders until the other piecing is completed. See Pieced Borders on page 94 for help in making pieced borders fit.

1. Inner border: From the crosswise grain of gold print, cut enough 2¾" strips (6) so that with seaming there will be 2 strips, 2¾" x 30", and 2 strips, 2¾" x 53".
2. Middle and outer borders: From the crosswise or lengthwise grain, cut enough strips so that you have 2 strips that measure 1⅛" x 30" and 2 strips, 1⅛" x 53". From the same fabric, cut 2 strips, 2" x 42", and 2 strips, 2" x 55", for outer border.

Pieced Border

1. Cut 60 squares, 2½" x 2½", of assorted medium prints (Template #1).
2. Cut 14 squares, 4¹⁄₁₆" x 4¹⁄₁₆", of assorted navy prints. Cut twice diagonally to yield 56 quarter-square triangles (Template #2).
3. Cut 15 squares, 4¹⁄₁₆" x 4¹⁄₁₆", of black fabric. Cut twice diagonally to yield 60 quarter-square triangles (Template #2).
4. Cut 2 squares, 2¼" x 2¼", of navy fabric. Cut diagonally to yield 4 half-square triangles (Border Template).
5. Cut 2 squares, 2¼" x 2¼", of black fabric. Cut diagonally to yield 4 half-square triangles (Border Template).

Scrap Basket Blocks

1. Cut 8 squares, 2½" x 2½", of light fabric (Template #1).
2. Cut 8 squares, 2⅞" x 2⅞", of navy fabric. Cut diagonally to yield 16 half-square triangles (Template #2).
3. Cut 16 rectangles, 2½" x 4½", of light fabric (Template #3).
4. Cut 4 squares, 5¼" x 5¼", of light fabric. Cut twice diagonally to yield 16 quarter-square triangles (Template #4).
5. Cut 4 squares, 4⅞" x 4⅞", of assorted navy prints. Cut diagonally to yield 8 half-square triangles (Template #5).
6. Cut 4 squares, 4⅞" x 4⅞", of light fabric. Cut diagonally to yield 8 half-square triangles (Template #5).
7. Cut 16 parallelograms, plus 16 reversed, of assorted medium fabrics (Template #6).

Set Pieces

1. Cut 3 squares, 8½" x 8½", of black fabric for Set Piece I.
2. Cut 2 squares, 12½" x 12½", of black fabric. Cut twice diagonally to yield 8 quarter-square triangles for Set Piece II.

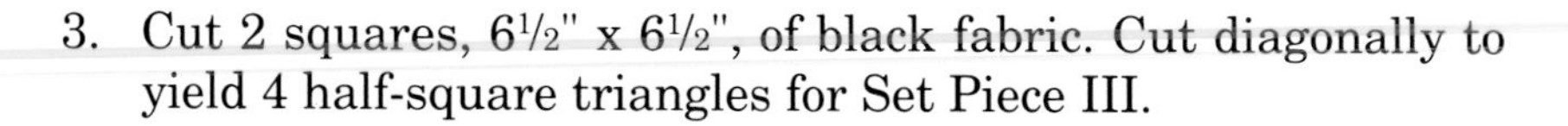

3. Cut 2 squares, 6½" x 6½", of black fabric. Cut diagonally to yield 4 half-square triangles for Set Piece III.

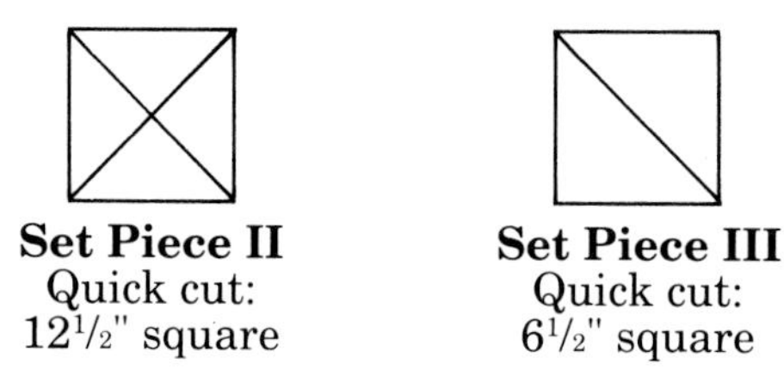

Set Piece II
Quick cut:
12½" square

Set Piece III
Quick cut:
6½" square

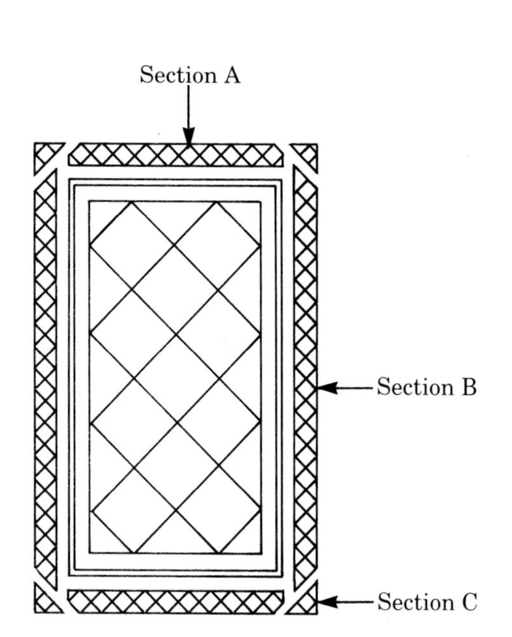

Directions

1. Piece 8 Scrap Basket blocks.
2. Sew blocks and set pieces together in diagonal rows, as shown. Sew rows together to complete center pieced section.
3. Add first and second inner border strips, using blunt-sewn or mitered corners.
4. Piece Chain of Squares border sections: Make two A sections for top and bottom of quilt, two B sections for sides, and four C sections for corners.
5. Sew a Section A to the top and to the bottom of the quilt, then sew a Section B to each side. Add C sections to corners last.
6. Add outer border with blunt-sewn or mitered corners.
7. Add backing and batting; quilt.
8. Finish edges with bias binding.

Quilt Lesson #7:
Pinwheel

This simple traditional pattern reinforces some items covered in other lessons: using a compass to take a measurement, cutting asymmetrical shapes, and making the eight points in the center come together crisply. The quilt pattern includes a lovely pieced border that uses as its main element the same large triangle used in the Pinwheel block.

Drafting category: four-square grid
Preferred cutting: paper templates and rotary cutter for asymmetrical shapes, no-template and rotary cutter for triangles
Sewing: straight seam, cut edge to cut edge
Matching: making eight triangle points come together in center

Drafting

The finished size of this block is 8". The design is based on a four-square grid. To arrive at the size of the grid squares, divide the side of the block (8") by the number of divisions on a side (2). 8" ÷ 2 = 4".

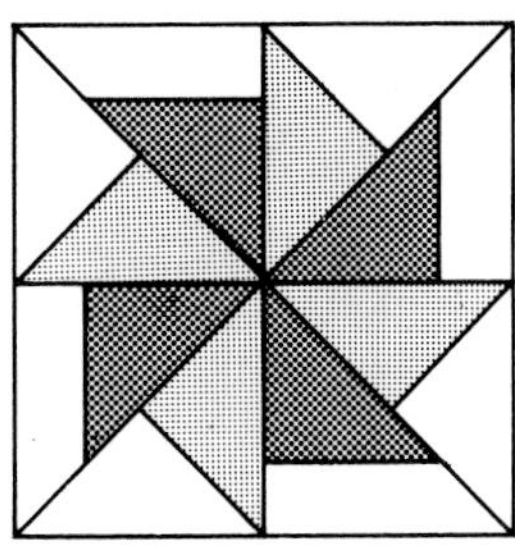

1. Draw an 8" square on 1/4" graph paper.
2. Draw a grid of four 4" squares.
3. Draw two opposing diagonal lines corner to corner across the 8" square to create eight large triangles.
4. Draw diagonal lines in every other large triangle to divide each into two smaller triangles, as shown.
5. To draw the smaller triangle in the remaining spaces, use a compass to take a measurement of the long side of the small triangle from the center of the square to the triangle point. Rotate the compass and mark the distance thus obtained on the four diagonal lines, as indicated.
6. Complete the four new triangles by using the compass marks as the ends and drawing appropriate lines parallel to the sides of the square.
7. Two templates are needed for this design: a triangle that makes the Pinwheel blades and part of the background, and a smaller asymmetrical quadrilateral that completes the background. Identify these two shapes as templates and color them in.
8. Add a consistent 1/4" seam allowance around each template shape. Refer to pages 10–13 for making different types of templates from a drafting. Compare your templates and cut pieces with the templates found on page 87.

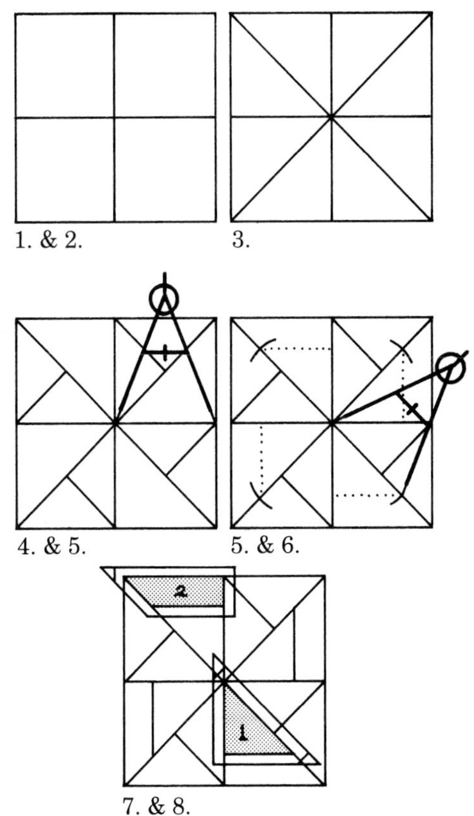

Cutting

This Pinwheel block has three colors: a light, an accent, and a dark. The triangles are easily cut with a no-template rotary technique. The asymmetrical background piece can be rotary cut, using the "paper template taped to cutting guide" technique described for diamonds and parallelograms on page 20.

For one Pinwheel block:

Template #1: Cut one square 5 1/4" x 5 1/4" from each fabric color, so you have a light, an accent, and a dark square. Cut each diagonally twice to yield four dark quarter-square triangles, four accent, and four light. Trim points for easy matching, using a template as a guide.

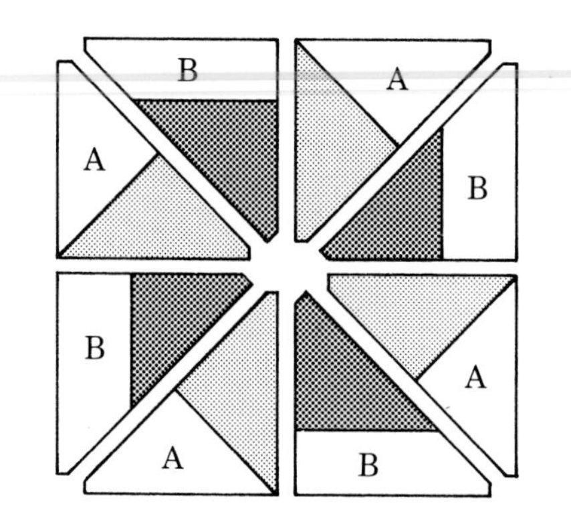

Template #2: Cut four of this shape, using a paper template taped to the bottom of a rotary cutting guide to cut strips. Change the orientation of the template on the ruler to cut diagonals. Be careful to cut these four shapes all the same. This shape is asymmetrical and should be cut with the right side of the fabric up. Inattention will yield mirror images.

Piecing

1. Lay the pieces out to determine which to sew together first. To begin, chain piece four Unit A and four Unit B. Press seams toward the darker fabric.

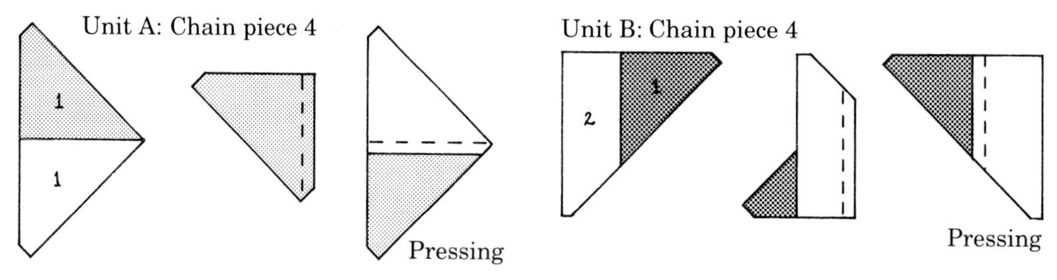

2. Sew the four A units to the four B units to form four square C units. Press seam toward Unit B.

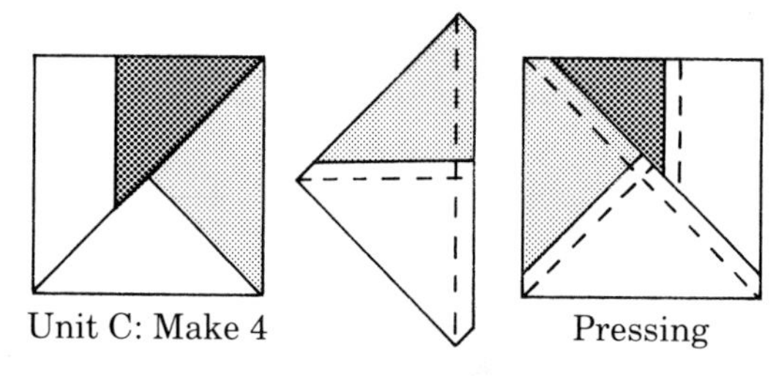

3. Matching diagonal opposing seams, chain piece the C units together to make two block halves. Make sure the triangle points at the center meet at the 1/4" seam line. Press center seams to one side, so they are opposing when matched.

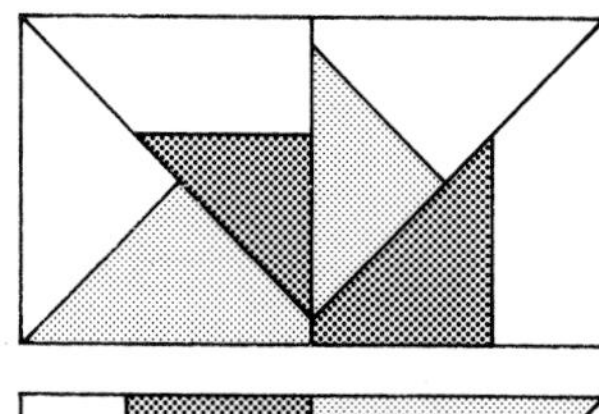

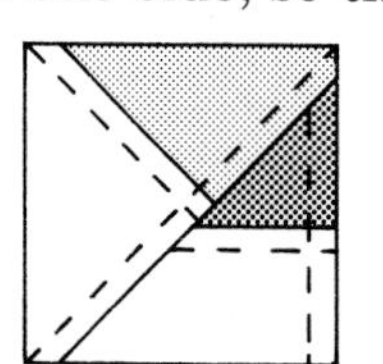

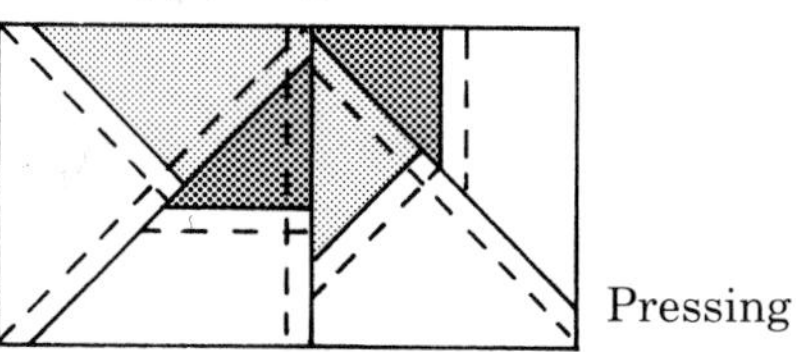

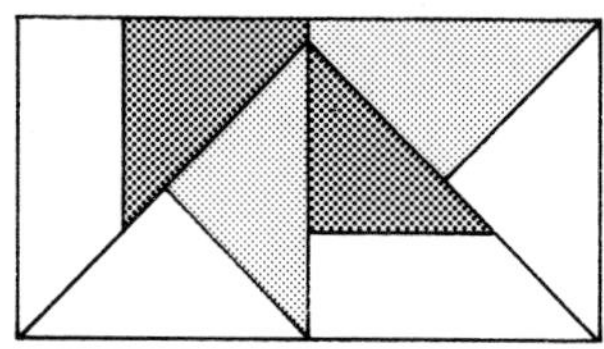

4. With a positioning pin, match the centers of the block halves. Opposing vertical and diagonal seams will "nest." Pin, as shown. Stitch center seam through the X. Press center seam open to distribute bulk.

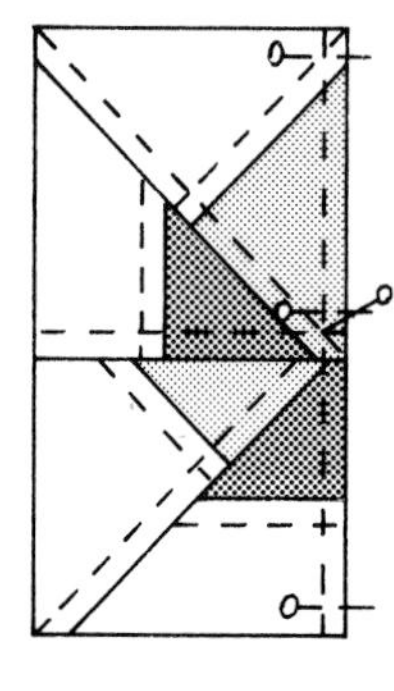

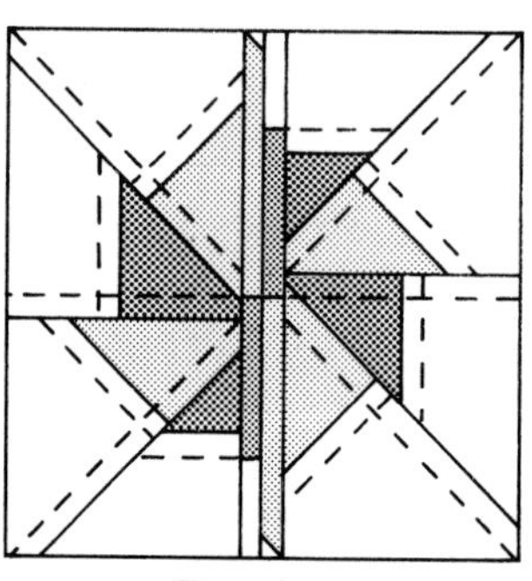

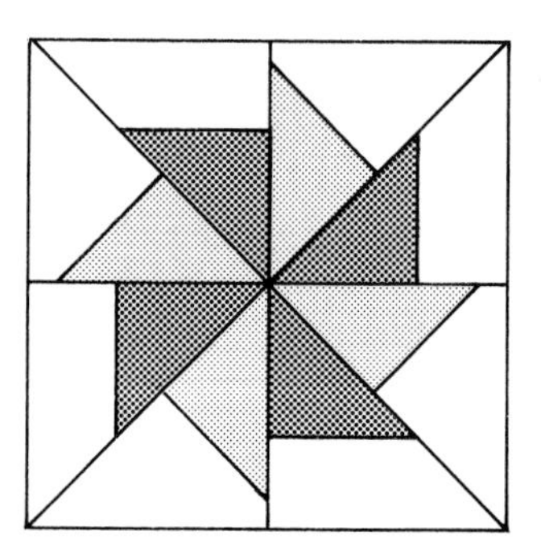

Pinwheel Quilt

Plate 7
Templates are on page 87.

Dimensions: $49\frac{1}{2}$" x 60"

Materials: (45" wide fabric)
Dark: $\frac{3}{4}$ yd. total assorted navy prints for piecing
Medium: $1\frac{1}{4}$ yds. blue print for set pieces
Light: 1 yd. total assorted light background prints with red and navy figures for piecing
Accent: 1 yd. total assorted red prints for piecing and inner and third borders
Outer and second borders: $1\frac{7}{8}$ yds. dark print
Backing: 3 yds.
Batting, binding, and thread to finish

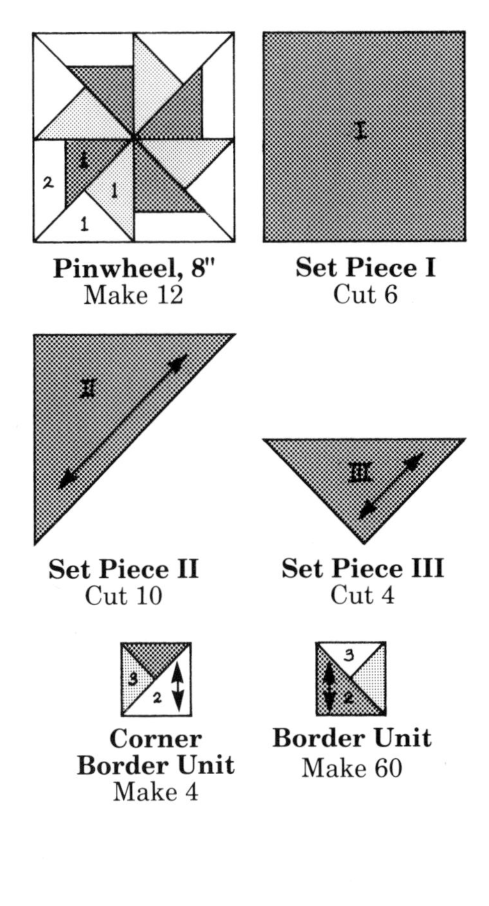

Pinwheel, 8" Make 12
Set Piece I Cut 6
Set Piece II Cut 10
Set Piece III Cut 4
Corner Border Unit Make 4
Border Unit Make 60

CUTTING

Borders

Cut the following border strips and set aside. Extra length will be trimmed later.

Hint: The width of the inner, second, and third borders can be adjusted to accommodate the actual sewn dimensions of the pieced border and the pieced center of the quilt. You may want to wait to cut and sew these "spacer" borders until the other piecing is completed. See Pieced Borders on page 94 for help in making pieced borders fit.

1. Inner border: From the crosswise grain of the accent fabric, cut enough 1" wide strips so that with seaming, you have 2 strips, 1" x 39", and 2 strips, 1" x 50".
2. Second border: From the lengthwise grain of the dark fabric, cut 2 strips, $1\frac{1}{2}$" x 39", and 2 strips, $1\frac{1}{2}$" x 50".
3. Third border: From the crosswise grain of the accent fabric, cut enough $1\frac{1}{2}$" wide strips so that with seaming, you have 2 strips, $1\frac{1}{2}$" x 45", and 2 strips, $1\frac{1}{2}$" x 56".
4. Outer border: From the lengthwise grain of the $1\frac{7}{8}$ yds. of dark fabric, cut 4 strips, 3" wide. Extra length will be trimmed later.

Pieced Borders

1. Cut 15 squares, $5\frac{1}{4}$" x $5\frac{1}{4}$", of assorted dark fabrics. Cut twice diagonally to yield 60 quarter-square triangles (Template #1).
2. Cut 16 squares, $4\frac{1}{16}$" x $4\frac{1}{16}$", of accent prints. Cut twice diagonally to yield 64 quarter-square triangles (Template #3).
3. Cut 15 squares, $4\frac{1}{16}$" x $4\frac{1}{16}$", of assorted light prints. Cut twice diagonally to yield 60 quarter-square triangles (Template #3).
4. Cut 1 square, $4\frac{1}{16}$" x $4\frac{1}{16}$", of a dark fabric. Cut twice diagonally to yield 4 quarter-square triangles (Template #3).

Pinwheel Blocks

1. Cut 12 squares, $5\frac{1}{4}$" x $5\frac{1}{4}$", of assorted accent fabrics. Cut twice diagonally to yield 48 quarter-square triangles (Template #1).
2. Cut 12 squares, $5\frac{1}{4}$" x $5\frac{1}{4}$", of assorted light fabrics. Cut twice diagonally to yield 48 quarter-square triangles (Template #1).
3. Cut 12 squares, $5\frac{1}{4}$" x $5\frac{1}{4}$", of assorted dark fabrics. Cut twice diagonally to yield 48 quarter-square triangles (Template #1).
4. Cut 48 pieces of assorted light prints (Template #2). Note that this is a directional template, so cut all pieces with the right side of the fabric up.

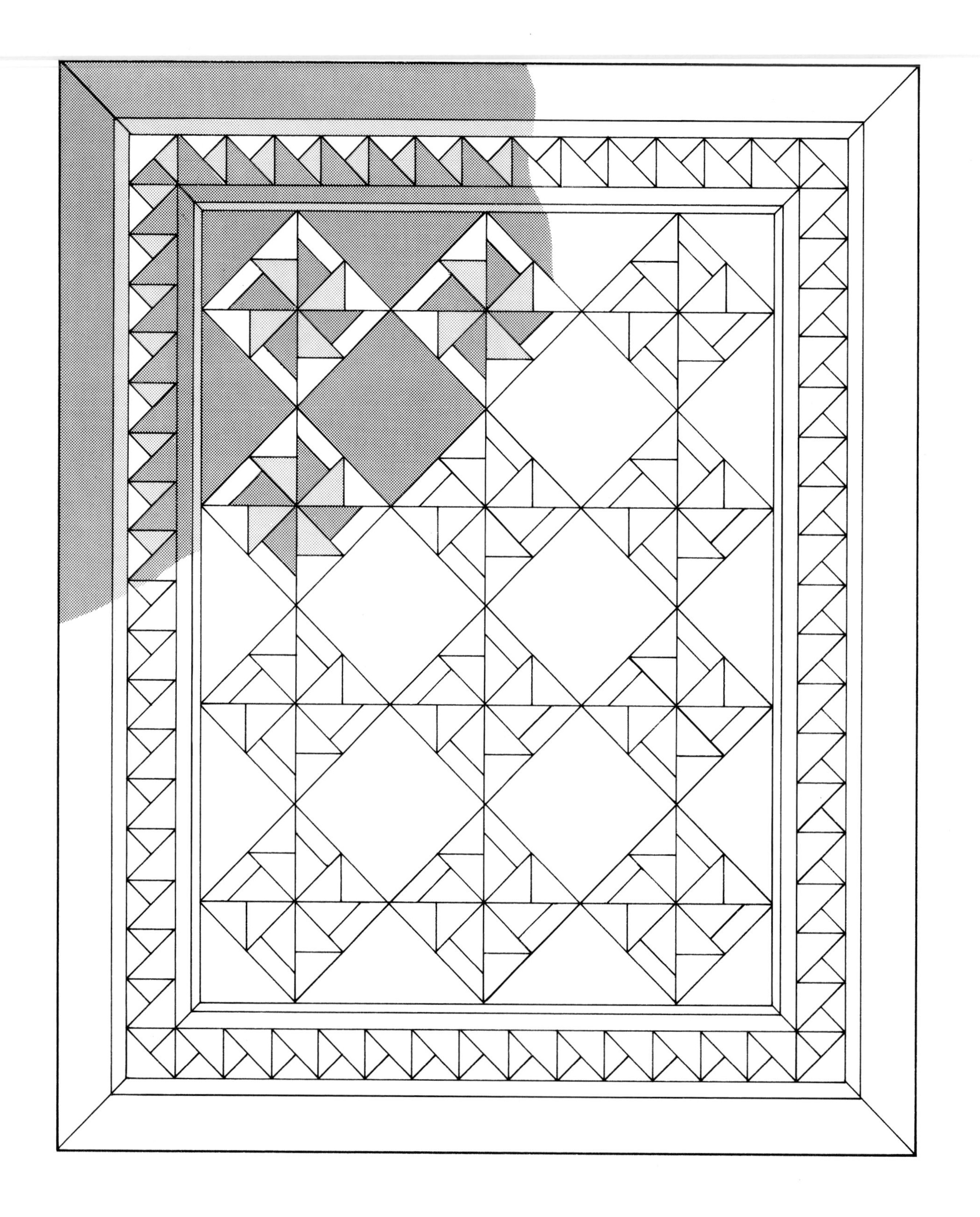

Set Pieces

1. Cut 6 squares, 8½" x 8½", of medium fabric for Set Piece I.
2. Cut 4 squares, 12½" x 12½", of medium fabric. Cut twice diagonally to yield 10 quarter-square triangles for Set Piece II.
3. Cut 2 squares, 6½" x 6½", of medium fabric. Cut diagonally to yield 4 half-square triangles for Set Piece III.

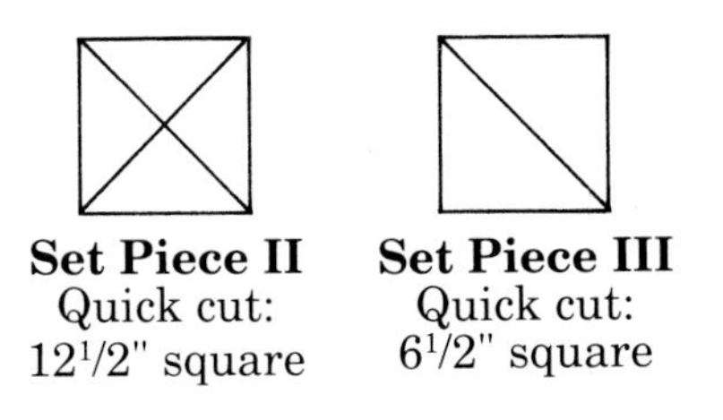

Set Piece II Quick cut: 12½" square

Set Piece III Quick cut: 6½" square

DIRECTIONS

1. Piece 12 Pinwheel blocks.
2. Sew blocks and appropriate set pieces together in diagonal rows, as shown. Sew rows together to complete center pieced section.
3. Stitch 1" wide accent fabric strips to 1½" wide dark strips to form inner border units. Add to center pieced section and miter corners.
4. Piece 60 border units and 4 corner border units. Make the 2 side pieced borders of 17 units each. Make the top and bottom pieced borders of 13 units each, plus 2 corner units, as shown. Sew pieced borders to center section.

5. Stitch 1½" wide accent fabric strips to 3" wide dark outer border strips. Sew to quilt center and miter corners.
6. Add batting and backing; quilt.
7. Finish edges with bias binding.

QUILT LESSON #8:

Darting Minnows

Darting Minnows contains a Square-within-a-Square, which is easy to piece accurately if the points on triangle templates are properly trimmed for easy matching. The block also has long skinny triangles, which are best handled by trimming points for easy matching. The other important element of the quilt pattern is that its construction is in rows (it is a bar quilt). Seams have been eliminated between adjacently set blocks to make the piecing easier.

Drafting category: nine-square grid
Preferred cutting: rotary techniques combined with paper templates
Sewing: straight seam, cut edge to cut edge
Matching concerns: trimming points on asymmetrical shapes for easy matching

DRAFTING

When I first drafted the Darting Minnows design, I wanted it to be an 8" block to fit with a series of other designs in the same size. The drafting is based on a nine-square grid. Divide the block size of 8" by 3 divisions on each side and the result is 2⅔", the size of the grid square. A dimension ending in thirds cannot be drawn on ¼" graph paper but can be managed easily on ⅙" graph paper. If ⅙" graph paper is not available, an alternative would be to change the block size to 9". 9" ÷ 3 = 3". The 3" grid squares can easily be drawn on ¼" graph paper.

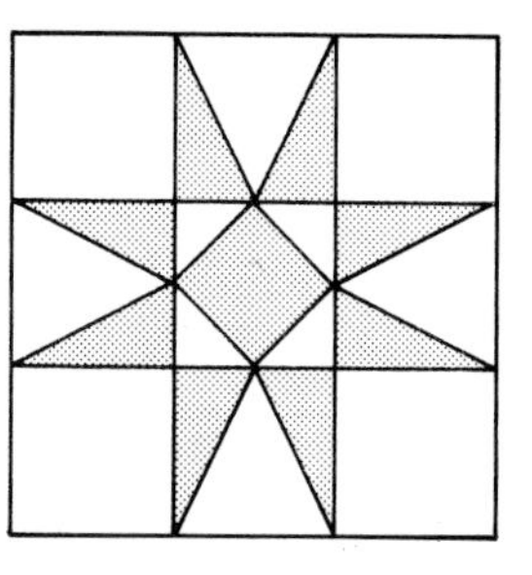

1. Draw an 8" square on ⅙" graph paper.
2. Draw a grid of nine 2⅔" squares in the 8" square.
3. In each of the middle side squares, draw two lines that connect the outer corners to the midpoint of the center square to create three triangles in the space. There will be two skinny triangles that are mirror images and one fatter triangle.
4. In the center square, draw a Square-within-a-Square by connecting midpoints of the sides of the center square with diagonal lines.
5. Identify the five shapes that are needed as templates and color them in. There are three triangles, a corner square, and a center square.
6. Add a consistent ¼" seam allowance around each shape. Refer to page 18 to trim points for easy matching, and to Making Templates on pages 10–13. Compare your templates with those found on pages 88 and 89 for accuracy.

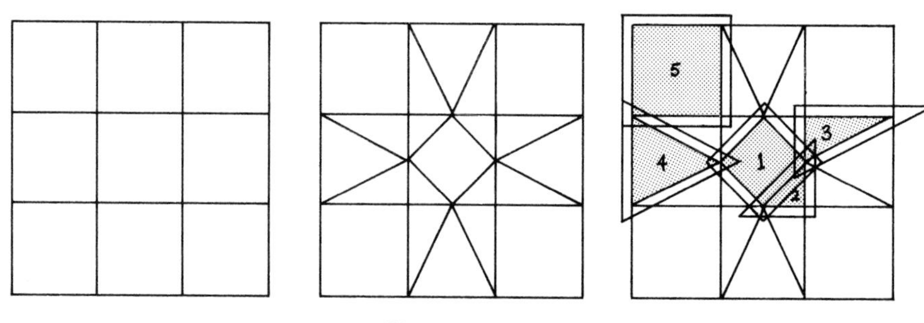

CUTTING

This Darting Minnows block has two colors: a light and a dark. Because the template shapes are odd, and the measurements don't necessarily correspond with markings on rotary cutting guides, a template method or template-plus-rotary cutter technique can be used to cut the shapes.

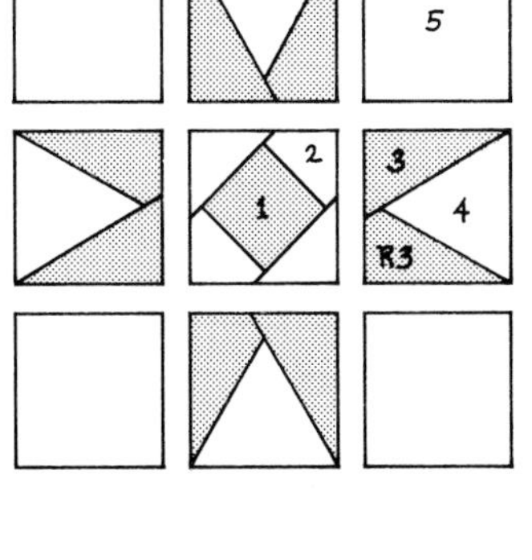

For one Darting Minnows block:
Template #1: Cut one dark.
Template #2: Cut four light.
Template #3: Cut four, plus four reversed dark.
Template #4: Cut four light.
Template #5: Cut four light.

PIECING

1. Lay the cut patches on the table to determine which pieces to sew together first. Begin by stitching the four three-triangle units, as shown. Notice that the points of the long skinny triangles are cut off for easy matching and that they must be cut as mirror images (four one way, four reversed).

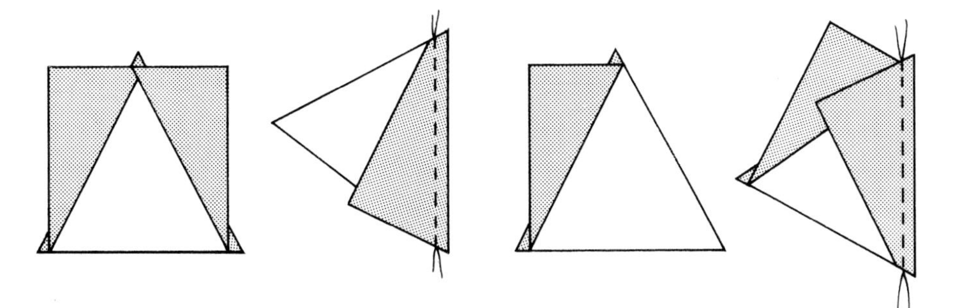

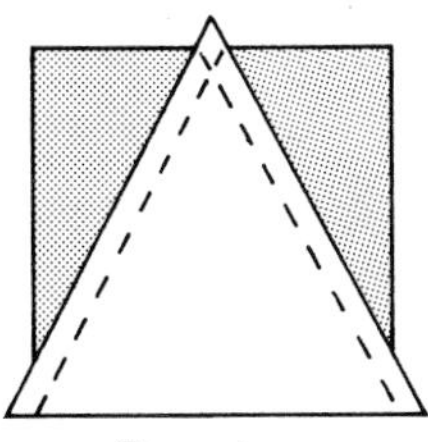

Pressing

Note: Long skinny triangles have a lot of stretch to them. A tip to keep the biases from stretching is to treat the fabric with spray starch before cutting. This stabilization with spray starch is also good for fabrics with low thread count.

2. Make one center Square-within-a-Square section, sewing four #2 triangles to the #1 square, in the order shown.

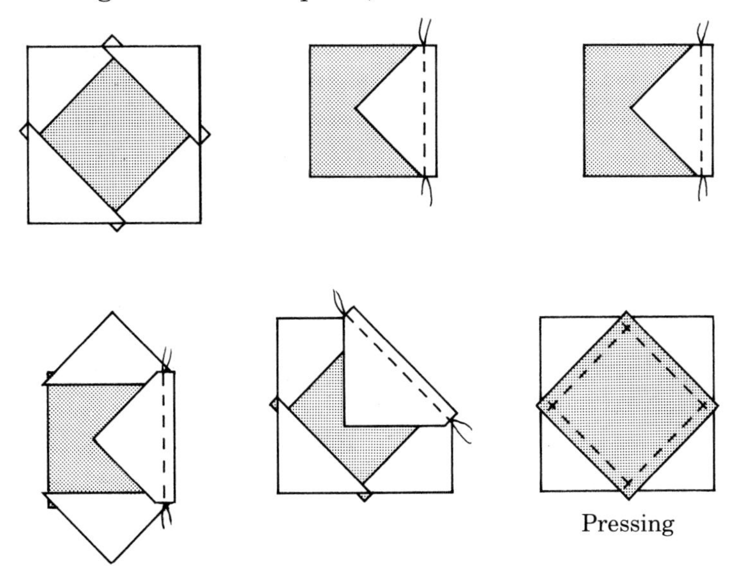

Pressing

3. Use chain piecing to sew side units together with the corner squares and center Square-within-a-Square in three rows. Use a positioning pin to match the midpoints of the side units to the center square.

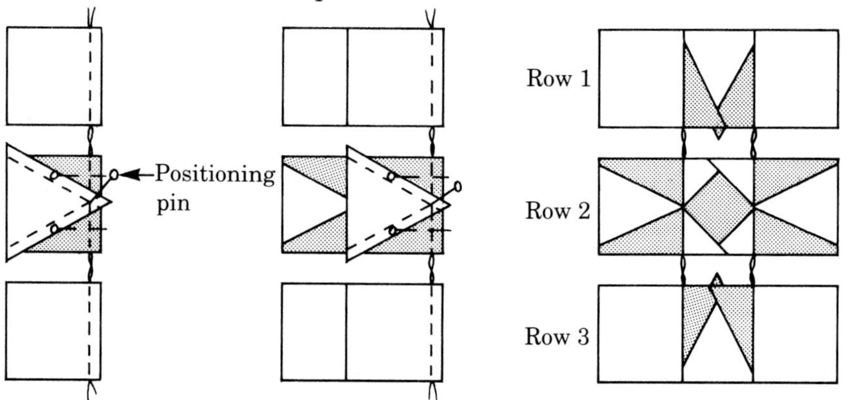

4. Pressing to take advantage of opposing seams, pin Row 1 and Row 2 together, as shown, and stitch the long seam. Join Row 3 to Row 2 in the same manner. Press, as shown.

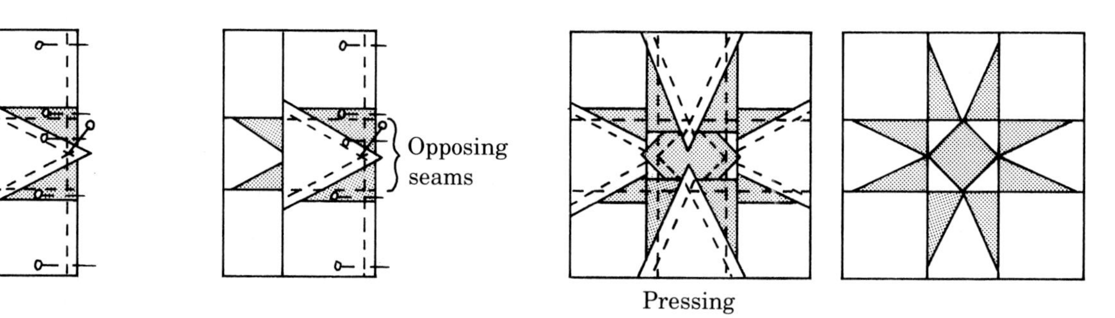

Pressing

Note: To change Darting Minnows to the bar quilt construction used in the quilt pattern on page 71, draw four blocks together and erase the appropriate block outlines. Essentially, the side triangle doubles to become a diamond, and the corner square quadruples to become a much larger square. Templates for these shapes are found on pages 88–89.

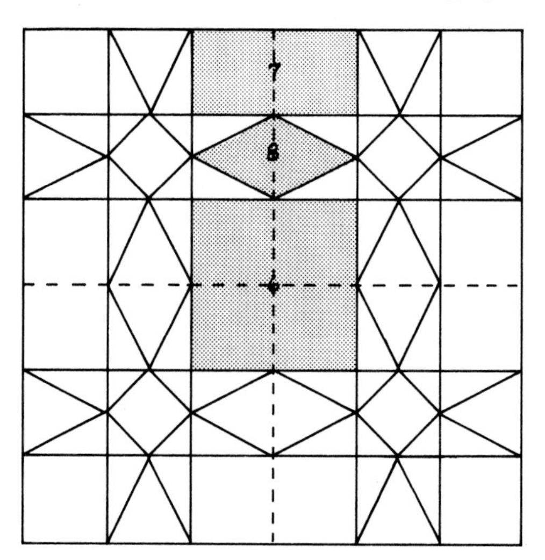

Darting Minnows Quilt

Plate 9
Templates are on pages 88–89.

Dimensions: 41" x 49"

Materials: (45" wide fabric)
First light: 1 yd. muslin for piecing
Second light: 1½ yds. stripe for large set squares and border
Dark: ¾ yd. total assorted yellow prints for stars
Backing: 1½ yds.
Batting, binding, and thread to finish

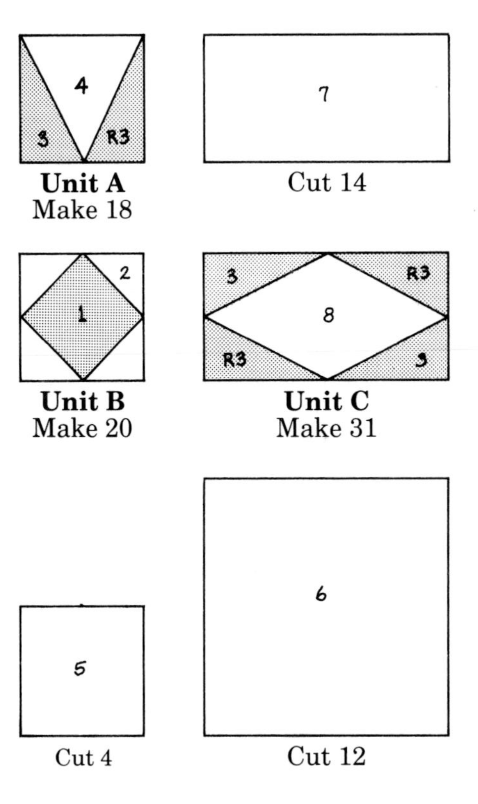

Unit A Make 18 · Cut 14 · Unit B Make 20 · Unit C Make 31 · Cut 4 · Cut 12

Cutting

Borders

1. From the lengthwise grain of the second light fabric, cut 4 strips, 5" wide, and set them aside. Extra length will be trimmed later.

Pieces

1. Cut 20 squares, 2⅜" x 2⅜", of assorted dark fabrics (Template #1).
2. Cut 40 squares, 2¼" x 2¼", of first light fabric. Cut diagonally to yield 80 half-square triangles (Template #2). Use template to trim points for easy matching.
3. Using Template #3, cut 80 triangles, plus 80 reversed, of dark fabric. Notice that the skinny triangles that are sewn to the #6 diamond have points trimmed for easy matching one way, while those that are sewn to the #4 triangle are trimmed differently, so you will need to make 2 templates of this shape.
4. Cut 18 triangles of first light fabric (Template #4).
5. Cut 4 squares, 3³⁄₁₆" x 3³⁄₁₆", from first light (Template #5).
6. Cut 12 squares, 5⅞" x 5⅞", from second light (Template #6).
7. Cut 14 rectangles, 3⅛" x 5⅞", of first light (Template #7).
8. Cut 31 diamonds of first light (Template #8).

Directions

Darting Minnows is pieced in sections and then in rows or bars. The star design is created when the rows of sections are sewn together. To get each star motif to consist of the same dark fabrics, the quilt pieces have to be cut, laid out, and then sewn in order.

1. Make 18 of Unit A. Each unit consists of a first light triangle (Template #4) and two long skinny dark triangles that are reversals or mirror images.
2. Make 20 of Unit B, the Square-within-a-Square star center, using the light #2 triangles and dark #1 squares.
3. Make 31 Unit C. Each unit consists of a #8 diamond and four #3 triangles cut as mirror images.
4. Lay the A, B, and C units out in rows with the #6 squares, #5 squares, and #7 rectangles, as shown. Make two Row 1, five Row 2, and four Row 3. Sew the rows together in order to complete the quilt top.

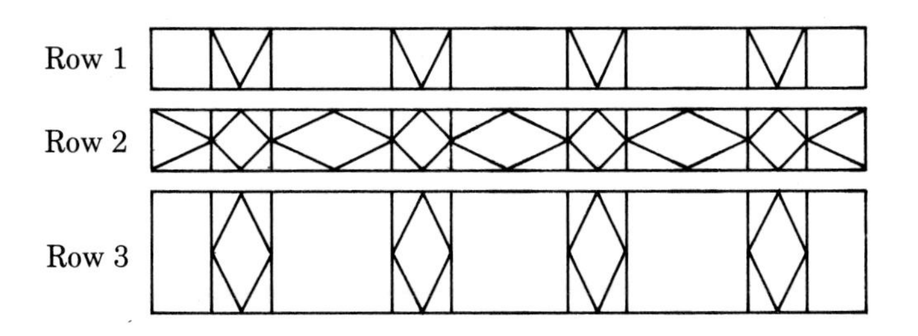

5. Add 5" wide border strips and miter the corners.
6. Add batting and backing; quilt.
7. Finish edges with bias binding.

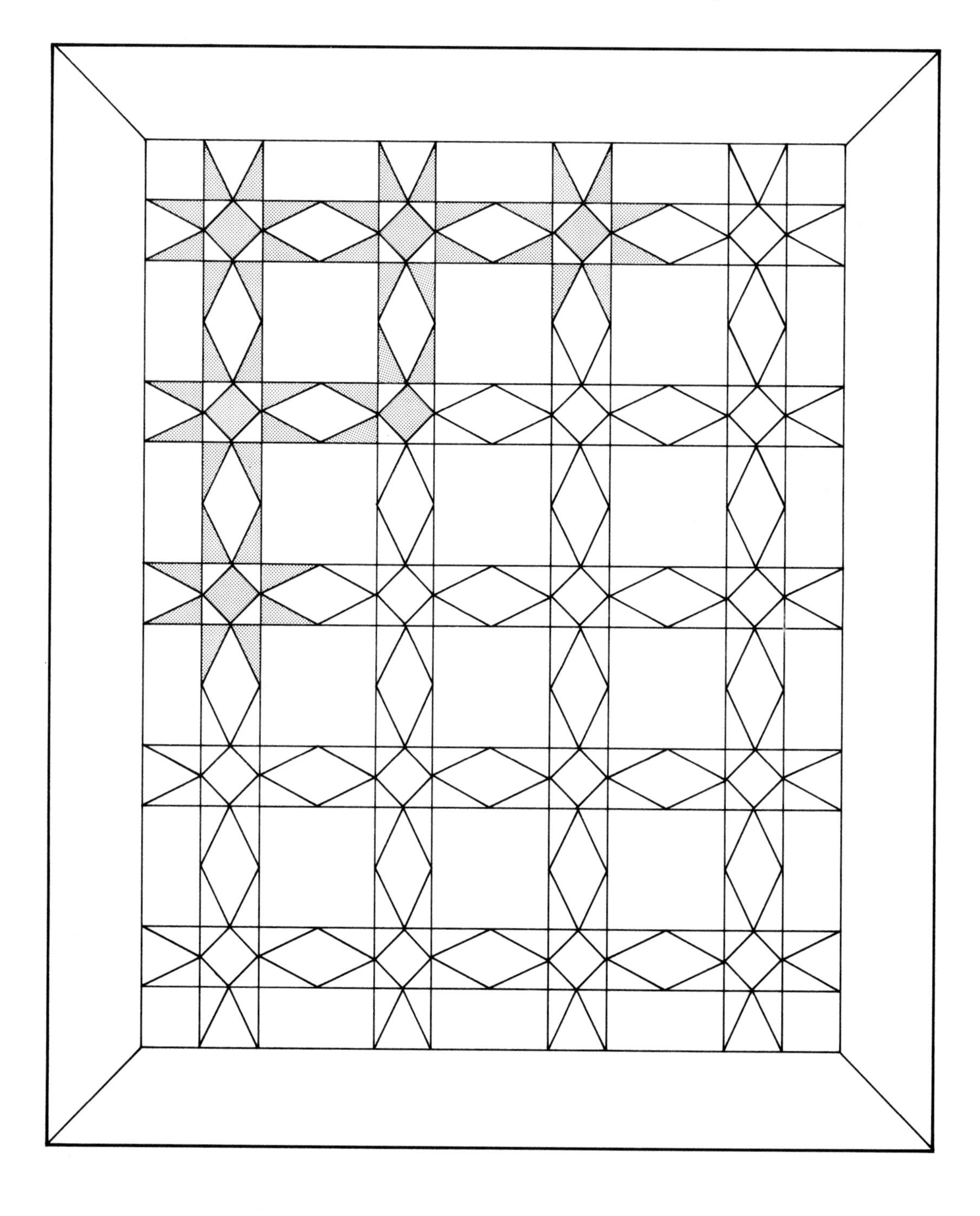

Quilt Lesson #9:

Dolly Madison's Workbox

The Dolly Madison's Workbox design, which is also known as Robbing Peter to Pay Paul, and the Pinwheel Daisy, which is Quilt Lesson #10, are both based on squares with curved seam elements. The draftings are important because they show how to find compass points for certain shapes and how to add seam allowances to curved edges.

Drafting category: single square with curved elements, compass needed
Preferred cutting: stiffened templates, cut with scissors
Sewing: straight seam and curved seam, cut edge to cut edge
Matching concerns: positioning pins where curves meet

Drafting

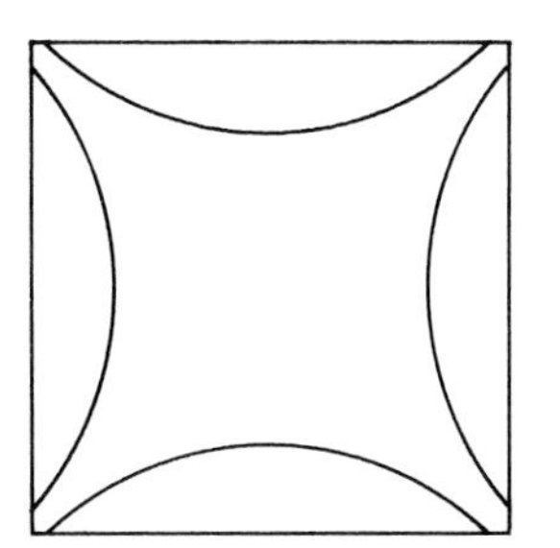

1. In the center of a large piece of graph paper, draw a 6" square.
2. To find the compass points necessary to draw the curves in the design, draw two 12" lines that bisect each other at the center of the 6" square, as shown.
3. To draw the curves, take a compass setting from the end of a 12" line to the side of the square, 1/4" from a corner, as shown. Draw four curves with the same setting, moving the compass point to each of the end points on the 12" lines.

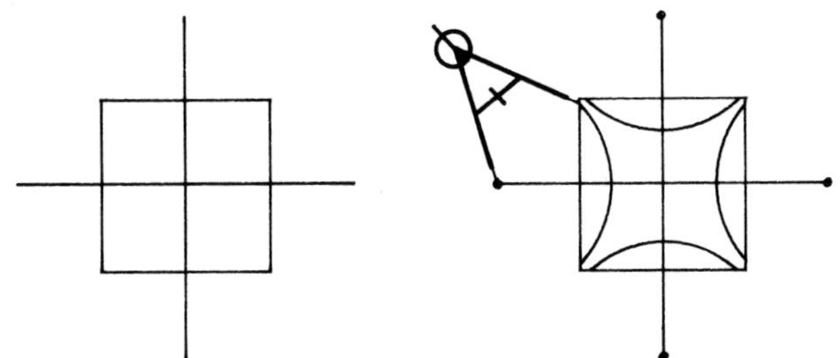

4. Repeat steps 1–3 to make a second drawing.
5. In the first 6" square, color in the large Template #1. In the second square, color in the small Template #2.
6. Draw seam allowances around Template #1 by reducing the original compass setting by 1/4". From the end points of the 12" lines, draw four curves. Add 1/4" corner seam allowances with a ruler.
7. Draw seam allowances around Template #2 by increasing the original compass setting by 1/4". From the end point of the 12" line, draw one curve. Add seam allowance to the straight side with a ruler. Trim points for easy matching. Compare your templates to those on page 90 for accuracy.

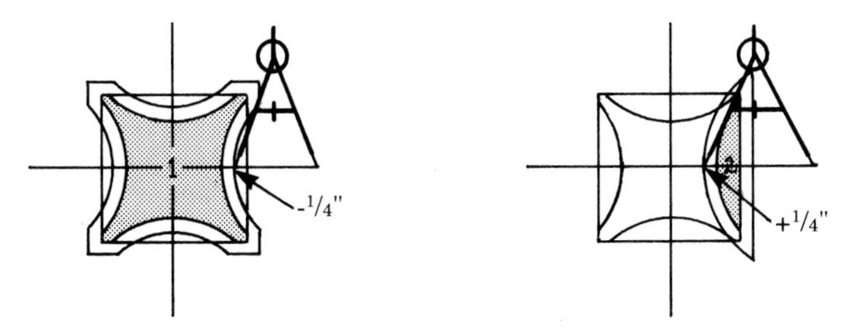

Cutting

For me, the most accurate method for cutting curved pieces is to make a stiffened template of each shape, trace around it onto the fabric, and cut carefully with scissors.

Dolly Madison's Workbox is basically a two-color pattern, requiring only a light and a dark fabric. Each 6" block will be a color reversal of the one next to it, and the curves will make large circles in the overall quilt design. To really learn how to piece the pattern, you will need to make four blocks.

For four 6" Madison's Workbox blocks:
Template #1: Cut two of dark fabric and two of light fabric.
Template #2: Cut eight of dark fabric and eight of light fabric.

Piecing

1. Sew four Template #2 pieces to each Template #1 piece (see Curved Seams on page 26).
   a. Find the center of each piece by folding it in half and making a crease.
   b. Match the centers of the pieces and pin.
   c. Utilizing points trimmed for easy matching, pin the two ends.
   d. With the convex curved piece (Template #2) underneath and the concave piece (Template #1) on top, carefully stitch the $\frac{1}{4}$" seam, matching the fabric edges along the curve as you go.
   e. After sewing all four seams, press them away from the center.

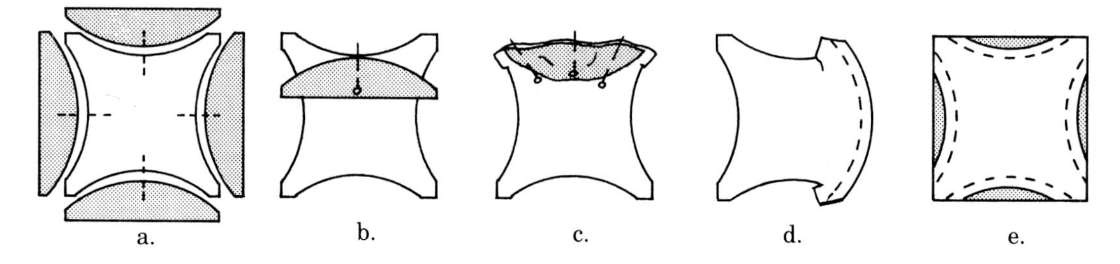

2. Sew a light and a dark complete 6" square together, using positioning pins to match the curved seams at the $\frac{1}{4}$" seam line. Repeat to make two sections. Press center joining seams open.

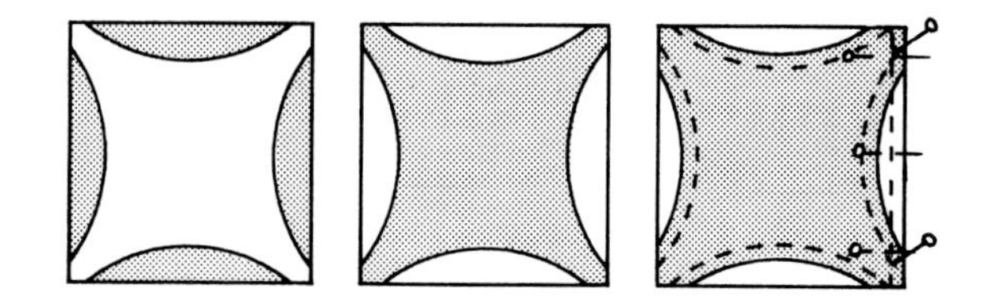

3. Sew the two sections together, using positioning pins to match the center and curved seams at the 1/4" seam line. Press the long seam open.

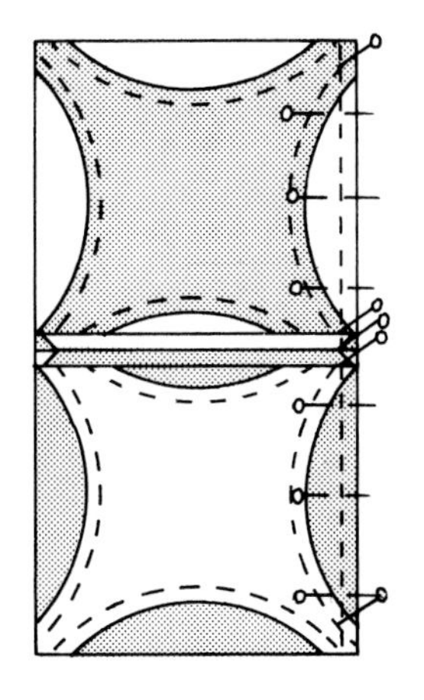

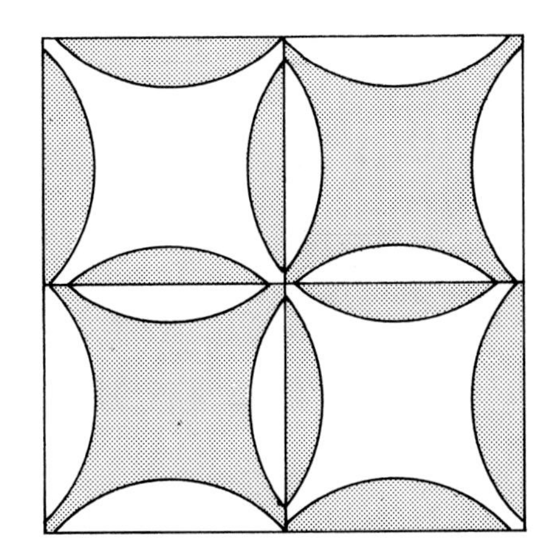

Dolly Madison's Workbox Quilt

Plate 8

Templates are on page 90.

Dimensions: 40" x 52"

Materials: (45" wide fabric)

Dark: 1 1/8 yds. total assorted dark blue prints for piecing

Light: 1 1/8 yds. total assorted light blue prints for piecing

Inner border: 1/4 yd. pink print

Outer border: 1 5/8 yds. blue plaid

Backing: 1 5/8 yds.

Batting, binding, and thread to finish

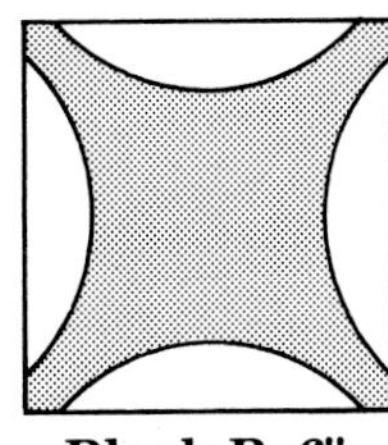

Block B, 6"
Make 17

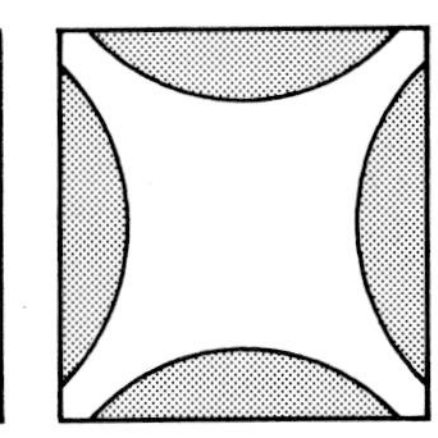

Block A, 6"
Make 18

Cutting

Borders

1. Inner border: Cut enough 1" wide strips from crosswise grain, so that with seams, you will have 2 strips, 1" x 42", and 2 strips, 1" x 54". Extra length will be trimmed when borders are sewn to quilt.
2. Outer border: Cut 5" wide strips from the lengthwise grain. Extra length will be trimmed later.

Dolly Madison's Workbox Blocks

1. Using Template #1, cut 18 of light fabric and 17 of dark fabric.
2. Using Template #2, cut 72 of dark fabric and 68 of light fabric.

Directions

1. Piece 18 Block A and 17 Block B.
2. Sew the A and B blocks together in rows, as shown. Pay close attention to the color order in each row.
3. Sew the rows together alternately in order to complete the center pieced section of the quilt.
4. Add the inner and outer borders, using either mitered or blunt-sewn corners.
5. Add backing and batting; quilt.
6. Finish edges with bias binding.

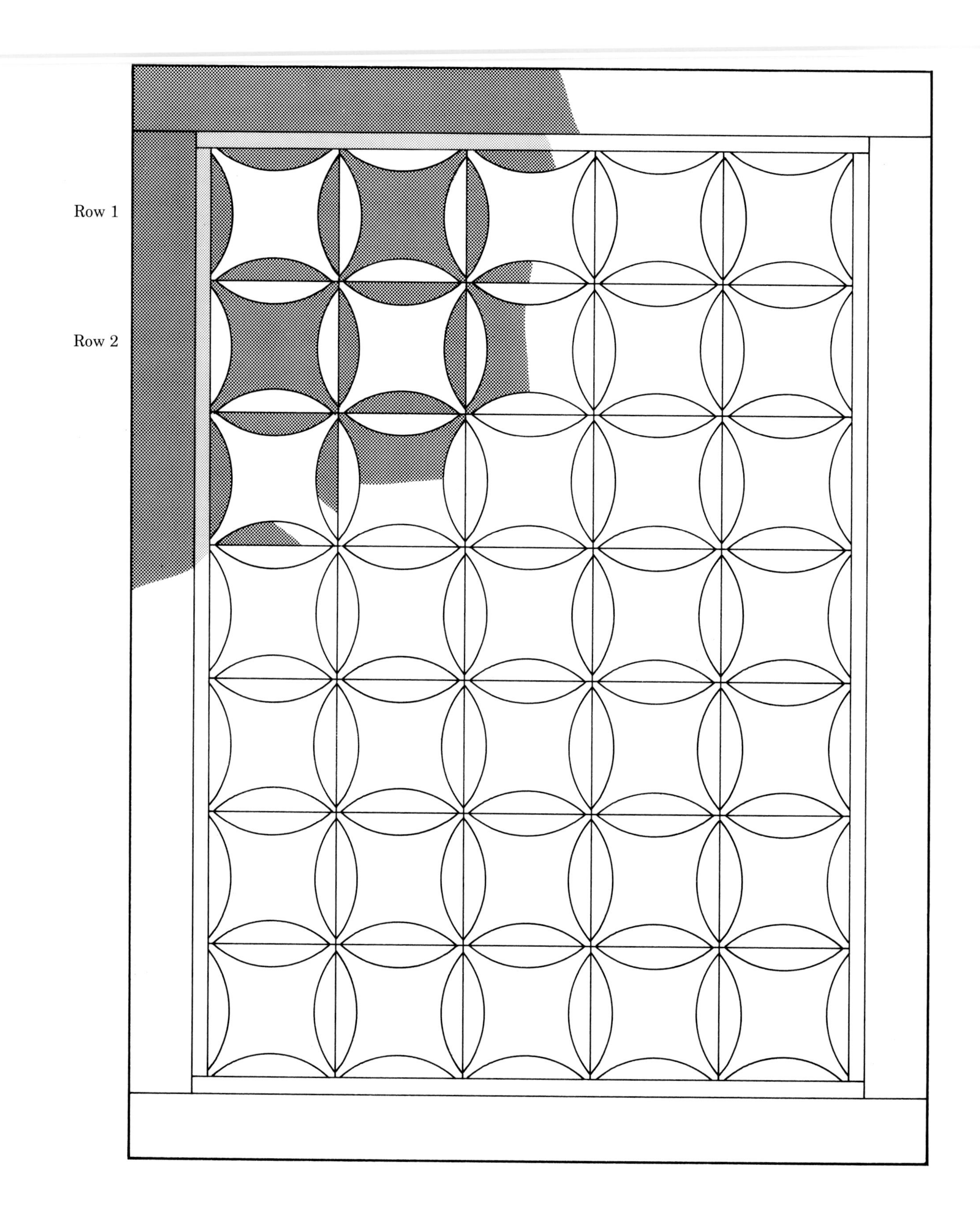
Row 1
Row 2

Quilt Lesson #10:
Pinwheel Daisy

Pinwheel Daisy is a pattern from the 1930s. The small quilt, shown in color (Plate 10), was made from 1930s fabrics. The design has gentle pieced curves and an appliqued circle in the center (so you don't have to make the eight points match!).

Drafting category: four-square grid with curved seams, compass needed
Preferred cutting: stiffened templates, cut with scissors
Sewing: straight seam and curved seam, cut edge to cut edge; center circle is appliqued
Matching concerns: very few

Drafting

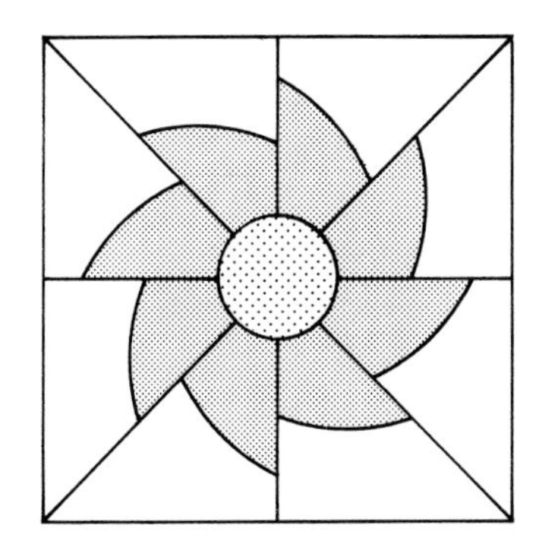

1. Draw an 8" square on 1/4" graph paper.
2. Draw a grid of four 4" squares.
3. Draw two opposing diagonal lines corner to corner across the 8" square to create eight large triangles.
4. With a compass, draw a circle with a 2" radius in the center of the square. This is a guideline for locating the compass points needed to draw the curves in the large triangles and will not be a seam line.
5. To draw the first curved seam line, set the compass from point #1 on the circle to a point on the center line 3 1/2" from the block center. Draw the curved line that divides the large triangle. Without changing the compass setting, move the point to point #2 on the circle and draw another curved line in the next triangle. Continue in this manner until all eight triangles contain curves.
6. Identify the three shapes that will be templates and color them in.
7. Add a consistent 1/4" seam allowance around each piece. Use a ruler to draw the seam allowance on all straight sides. To add seam allowances to the curves, either increase or decrease the setting used to draw the curves by 1/4" and use the same compass points to add the seam allowances (see page 9). Trim points for easy matching.
8. To draw the template for the appliqued circle in the center of the design, set your compass at 1" (the radius) and draw a 2" circle. Do not add seam allowance.

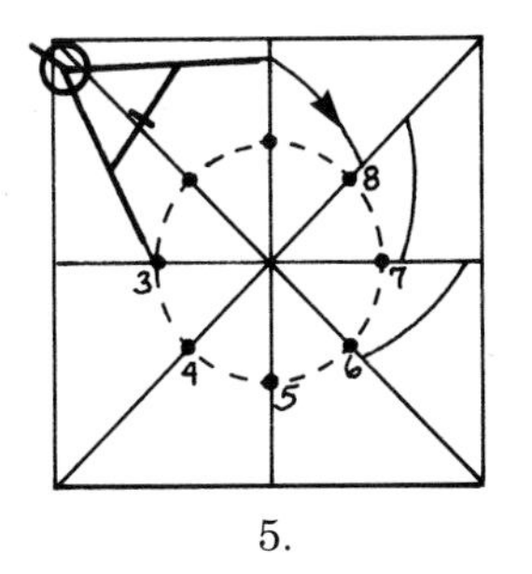

5.

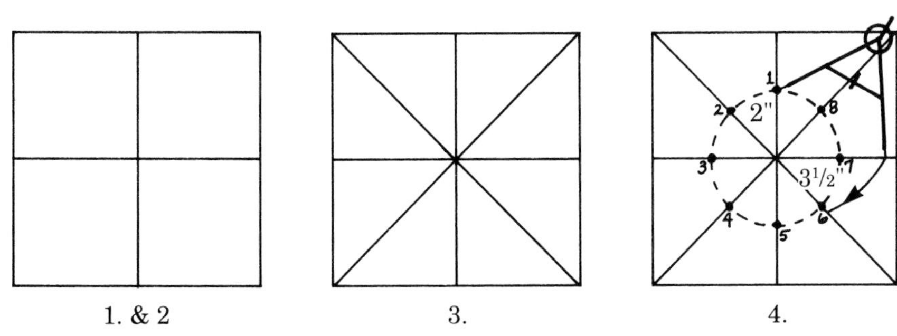

1. & 2 3. 4.

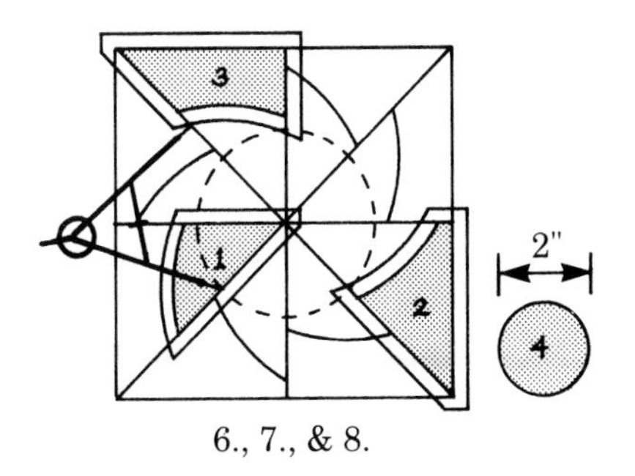

6., 7., & 8.

Cutting

Pinwheel Daisy is delightful done in brightly colored scraps on a muslin background. It really needs three kinds of colors: print scraps for the petals, a plain light for the background, and an accent fabric for the center circle.

Note that templates 1, 2, and 3 are asymmetrical shapes that must be cut with the template face up on the right side of the fabric. Be careful not to cut mirror image pieces. Make a stiffened template of each shape and compare with the templates on page 89 for accuracy.

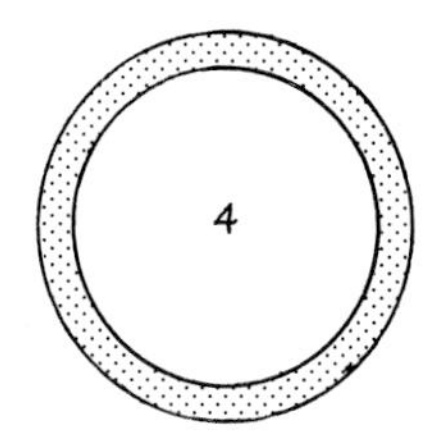

For one Pinwheel Daisy block:
Template #1: Cut eight, each from a different print.
Template #2: Cut four from muslin.
Template #3: Cut four from muslin.
Template #4: Make a 2" circle of paper. Pin it to the wrong side of the accent fabric and add a 1/4" seam allowance as you cut around it. Cut one.

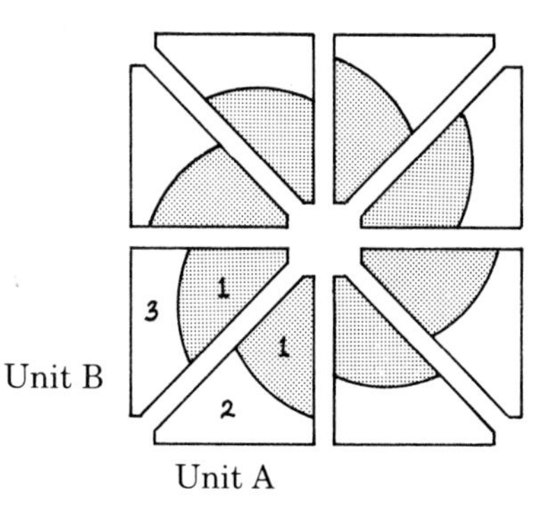

Piecing

1. Lay the pieces out to determine which to sew together first. To begin, make four Unit A and four Unit B. Because all the shapes here are asymmetrical, it is hard to find and match centers on the curved seams. So, in this pattern, match the ends of the seams. As you sew, match the edges of the fabric and ease in fullness. On these short, gentle curves, this method works fine.
   a. Make four Unit A. With Template #2 on top, match the starting edge for stitching with the trimmed points. Begin stitching slowly, pausing every 4-5 stitches to match fabric edges along the curve as you go. There is enough stretch in the top piece to accommodate the convex shape of the curve underneath. Press the seam allowance toward Template #1.

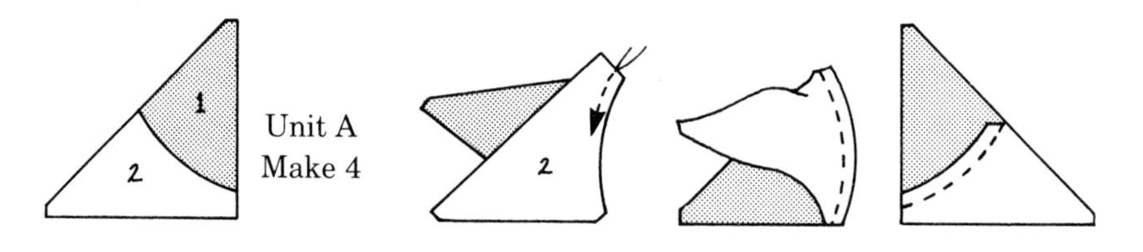

   b. Make four Unit B. This unit is pieced essentially the same way as Unit A.

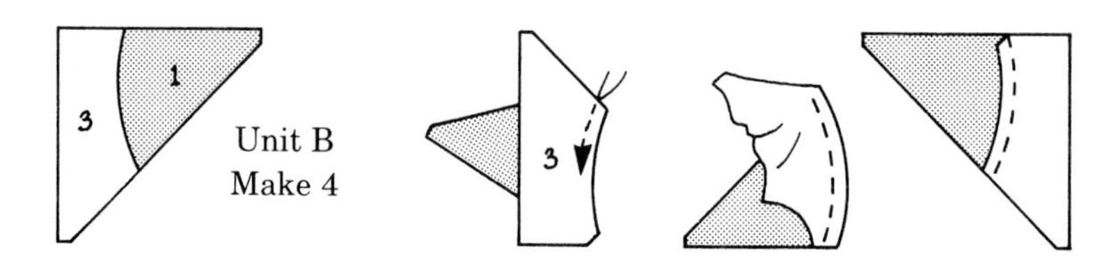

2. Join the four A units to the four B units to make four square C units. Press seams toward A units.

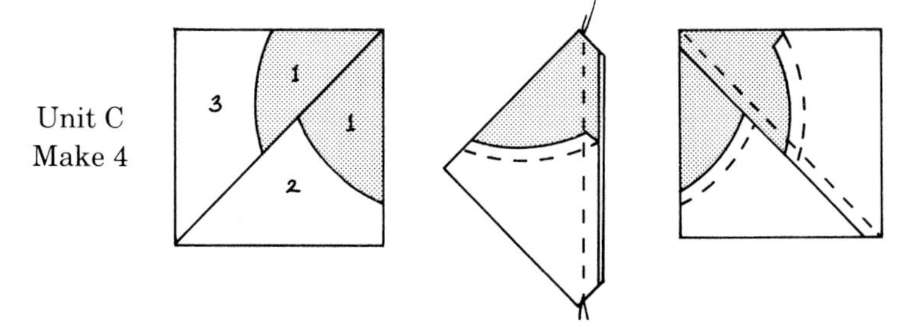

3. Matching diagonal opposing seams, sew the C units together to make two block halves. Matching at the center need not be terribly precise, as the center circle will be appliqued over it. Press center seams to the left.

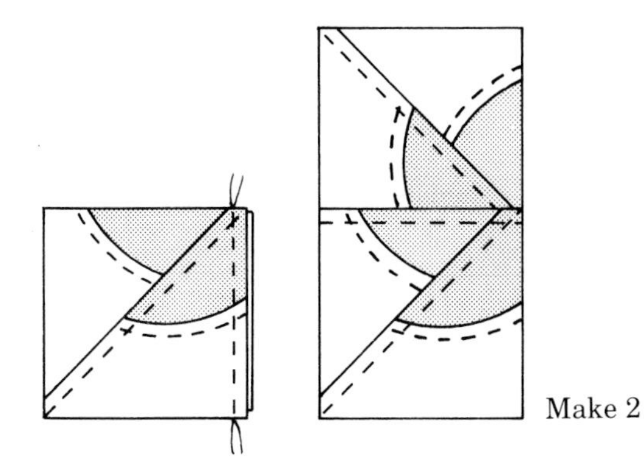

4. Match the centers of the block halves. Opposing vertical and diagonal seams will "nest." Pin, as shown. Stitch center seam through the X. Press seam to one side.

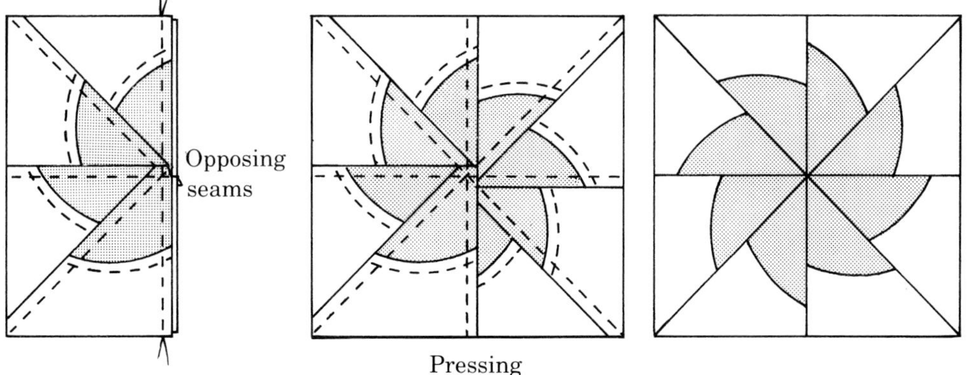

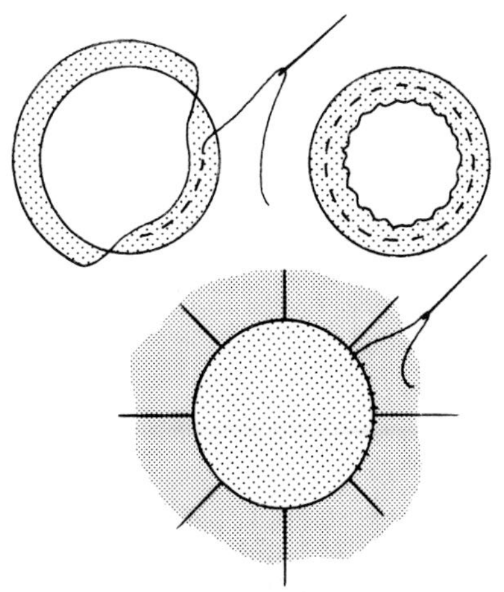

5. To prepare the center circle for applique, turn the seam allowance over the paper's edge and baste the fabric to the paper. Ease fullness on the curve with a small running stitch. Press.
6. Leaving the paper in, applique the circle to the center of the pieced Pinwheel Daisy, using a blind stitch and the same color thread as the circle.

7. To remove the paper, turn the block to the wrong side and carefully cut away the pieced area behind the appliquéd circle, leaving ¼" seam allowance. Remove the basting stitches and pull out the paper from the back.

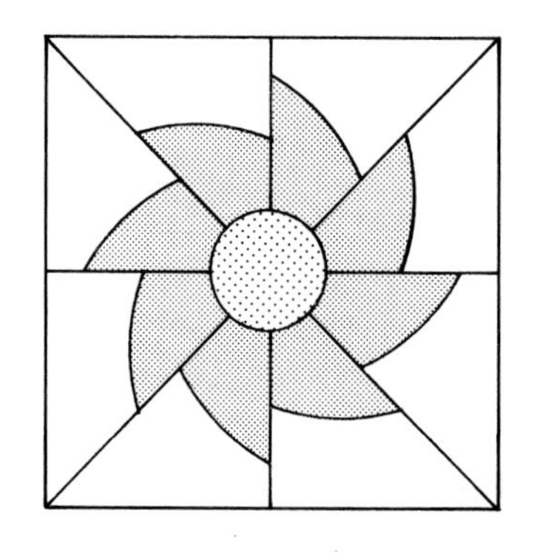

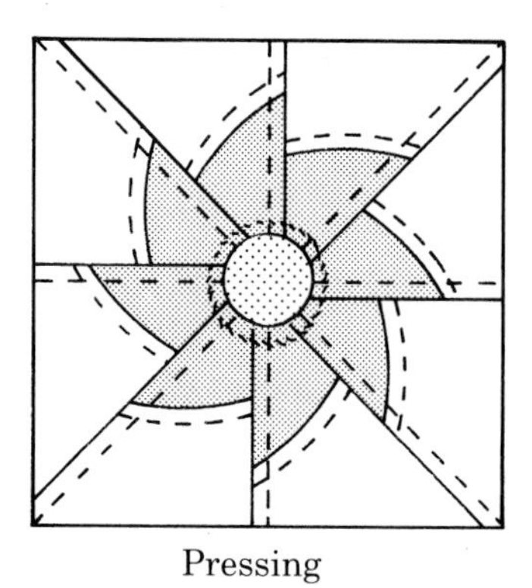

Pressing

Pinwheel Daisy Quilt

Plate 10

Templates are on page 89.

Dimensions: 44" x 55"

Materials: (45" wide fabric)

Dark: 1 yd. total assorted bright prints or scraps for the daisy petals, lattices, and Four Patches

Light: 1 yd. unbleached muslin for block backgrounds

Accent: ⅛ yd. red print for daisy centers

Borders: 1⅝ yds. pink print

Backing: 1⅝ yds.

Batting, binding, and thread to finish

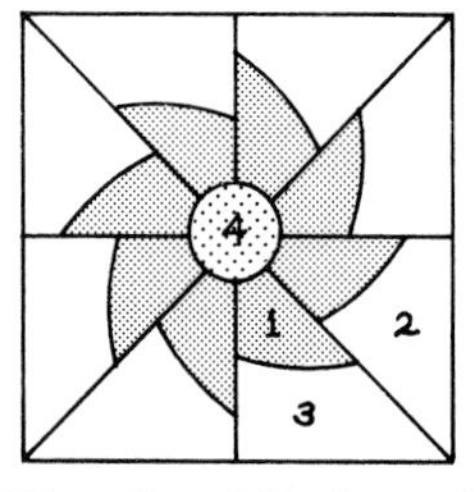

Pinwheel Daisy, 8"
Make 12

Lattice
Make 31

Four Patch
Make 20

CUTTING

Borders

1. Cut 4 strips, 4½" wide, from the length of the border fabric. Extra length will be trimmed when the borders are sewn to the quilt.

Pinwheel Daisy Blocks

1. Using Template #1, cut 96 pieces from assorted bright color prints for daisy petals.
2. Using Template #2, cut 48 pieces from muslin for block backgrounds.
3. Using Template #3, cut 48 pieces from muslin for block backgrounds.
4. Using paper pieces of Template #4, cut 12 circles of accent fabric for appliquéing to center of each block.

Set Pieces

1. Cut 62 rectangles, 2" x 8½", from assorted bright prints for lattice sections.
2. Cut 80 squares, 2" x 2", from assorted bright prints for Four Patches.

Directions

1. Make 12 Pinwheel Daisy blocks.
2. Make 31 lattice sections, each consisting of two 2" x 8½" rectangles.
3. Make 20 Four Patches, each consisting of four 2" squares.
4. Arrange the finished blocks, lattices, and Four Patches in rows, as shown in the quilt diagram.
5. Sew the rows together in order to finish the center section of the quilt.
6. Add the 4½" wide border strips, using either blunt-sewn or mitered corners.
7. Add backing and batting; quilt.
8. Finish edges with bias binding.

Templates

The templates in this section are provided for your convenience, so you can check the templates you have drafted in the Lessons for accuracy. They also make it possible to skip the drafting part of each lesson and go straight to the piecing of the blocks.

In order to accommodate the work methods of as many quilters as possible, templates in this section are offered in a multiuse form. Each shape has a number, which is referenced in the quilt directions. The inner dashed line is the sewing line; the outer solid line is the cutting line and includes the 1/4" seam allowance. Essential finished or sewn dimensions are indicated just inside the sewing line; cutting dimensions are indicated just outside the cutting line. Quick-cutting configurations and dimensions are given for all half-square and quarter-square triangles.

Triangle points have been left on to aid in measuring for rotary cutting, but lines show where to cut off the points for easiest matching.

If you prefer using a ruler and rotary cutter, use the measurements provided with each shape for cutting, and compare your patches to the templates in the book to check for accuracy. You can also use these measurements for strip piecing squares and rectangles (see page 27).

Grain lines are for lengthwise or crosswise grain and are shown with an arrow on each piece. Detailed directions for using templates are on page 15.

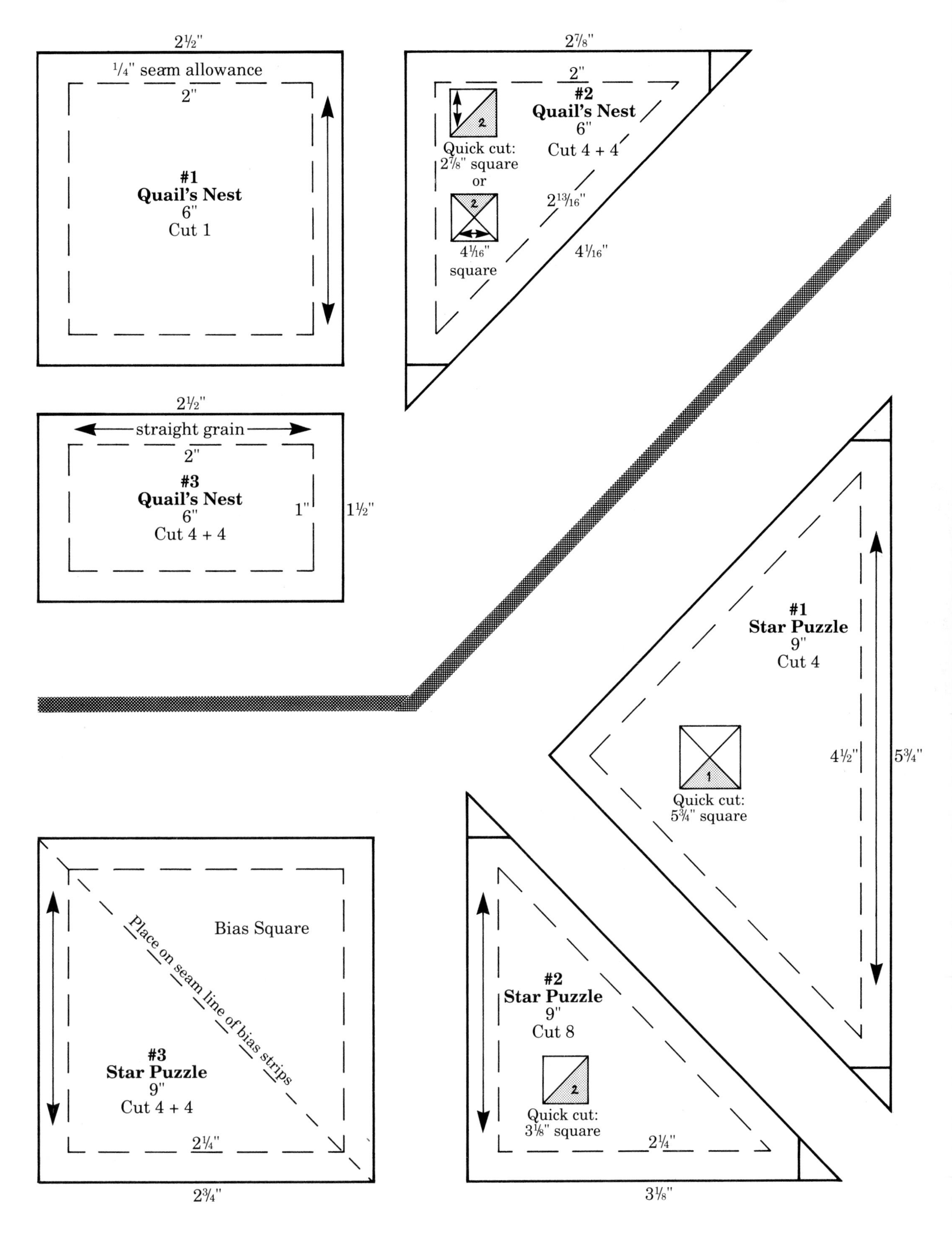

2½"
¼" seam allowance
2"
#1
Quail's Nest
6"
Cut 1
2⅞"
2"
#2
Quail's Nest
6"
Cut 4 + 4
Quick cut:
2⅞" square
or
2
2
4 1/16"
square
2 13/16"
4 1/16"
2½"
straight grain
2"
#3
Quail's Nest
6"
Cut 4 + 4
1"
1½"
#1
Star Puzzle
9"
Cut 4
1
Quick cut:
5¾" square
4½"
5¾"
Bias Square
Place on seam line of bias strips
#3
Star Puzzle
9"
Cut 4 + 4
2¼"
2¾"
#2
Star Puzzle
9"
Cut 8
2
Quick cut:
3⅛" square
2¼"
3⅛"

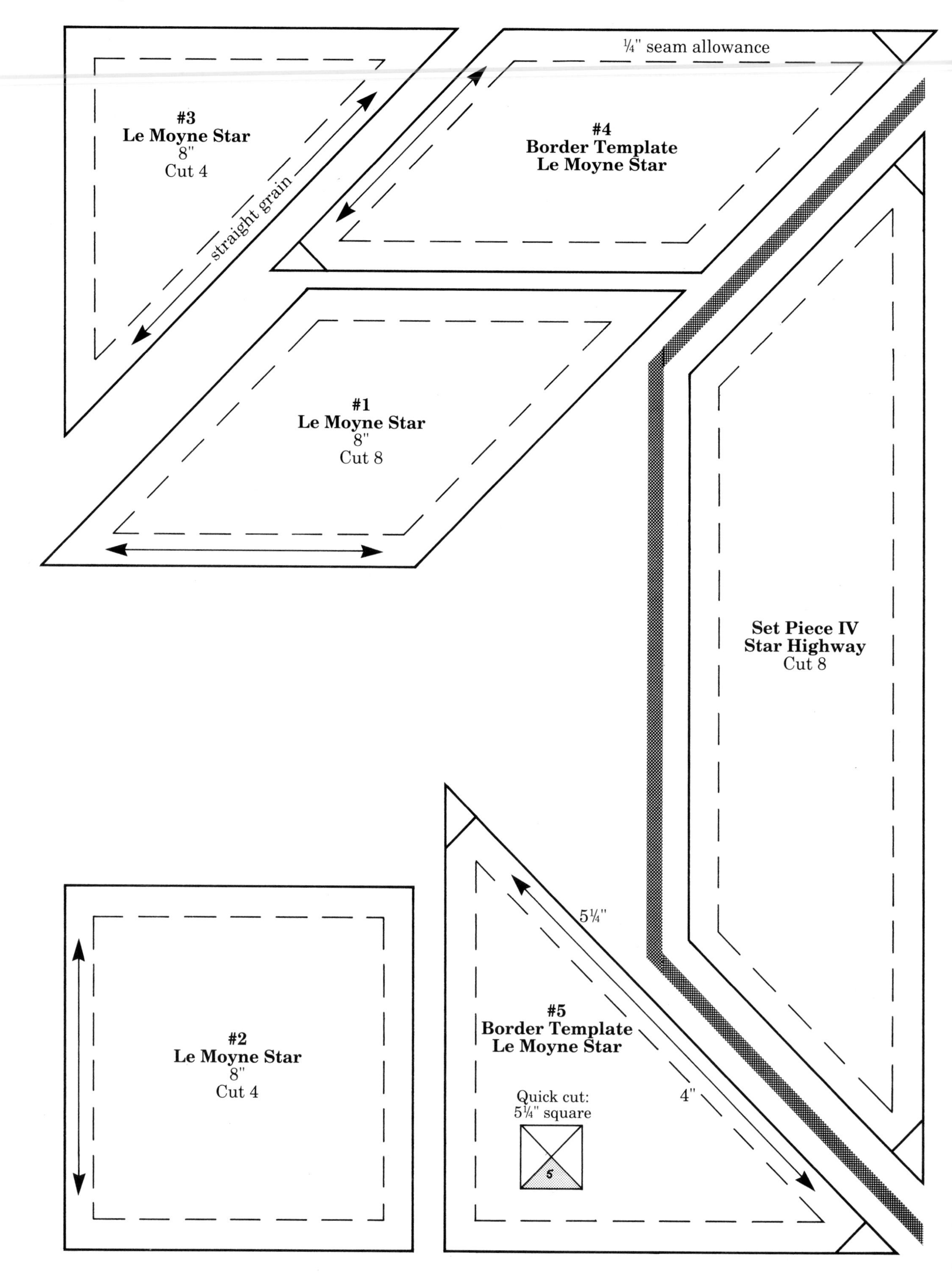

¼" seam allowance
#3
Le Moyne Star
8"
Cut 4
straight grain
#4
Border Template
Le Moyne Star
#1
Le Moyne Star
8"
Cut 8
Set Piece IV
Star Highway
Cut 8
5¼"
#5
Border Template
Le Moyne Star
Quick cut:
5¼" square
5
4"
#2
Le Moyne Star
8"
Cut 4

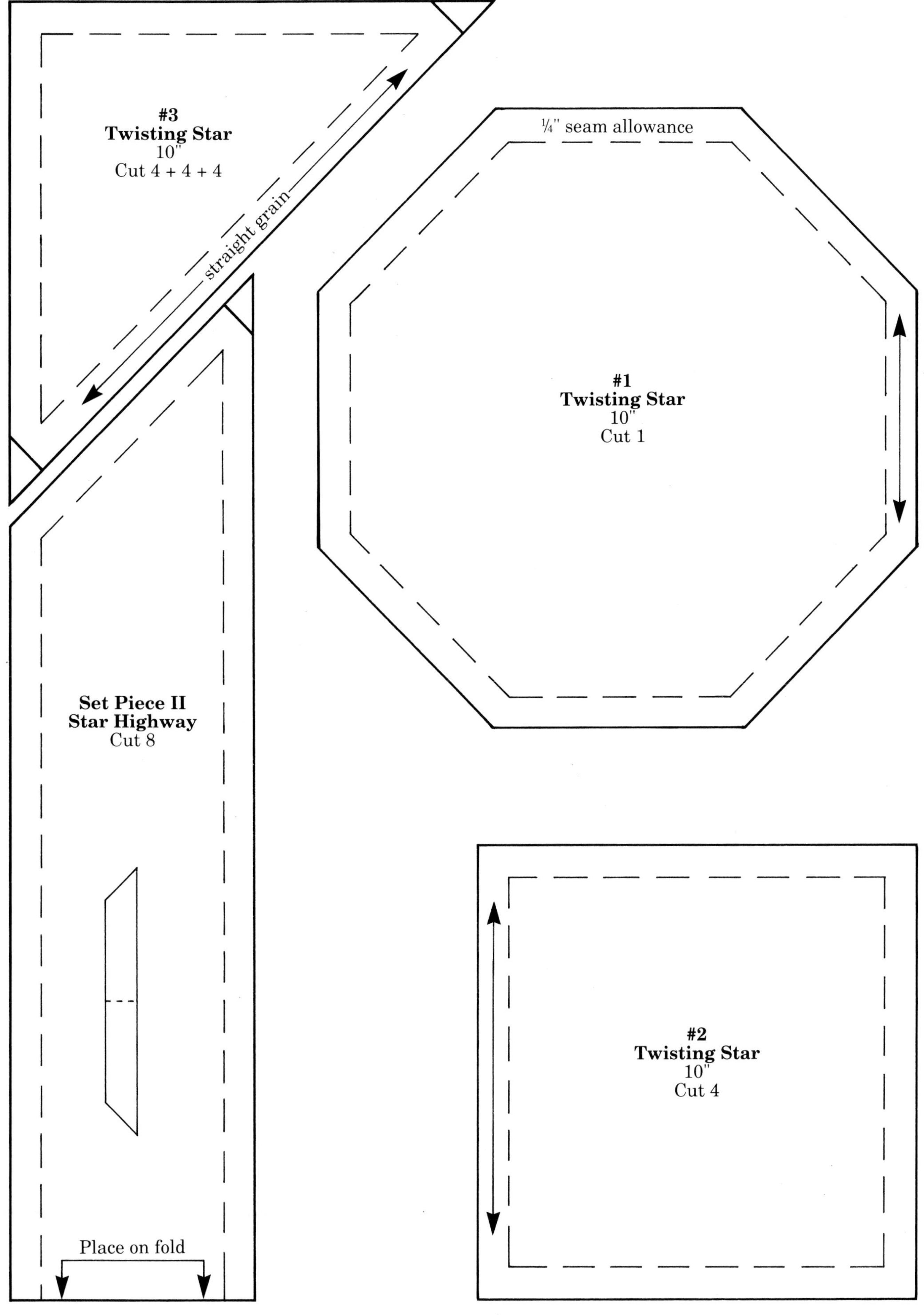
#3
Twisting Star
10"
Cut 4 + 4 + 4
straight grain
¼" seam allowance
#1
Twisting Star
10"
Cut 1
Set Piece II
Star Highway
Cut 8
#2
Twisting Star
10"
Cut 4
Place on fold

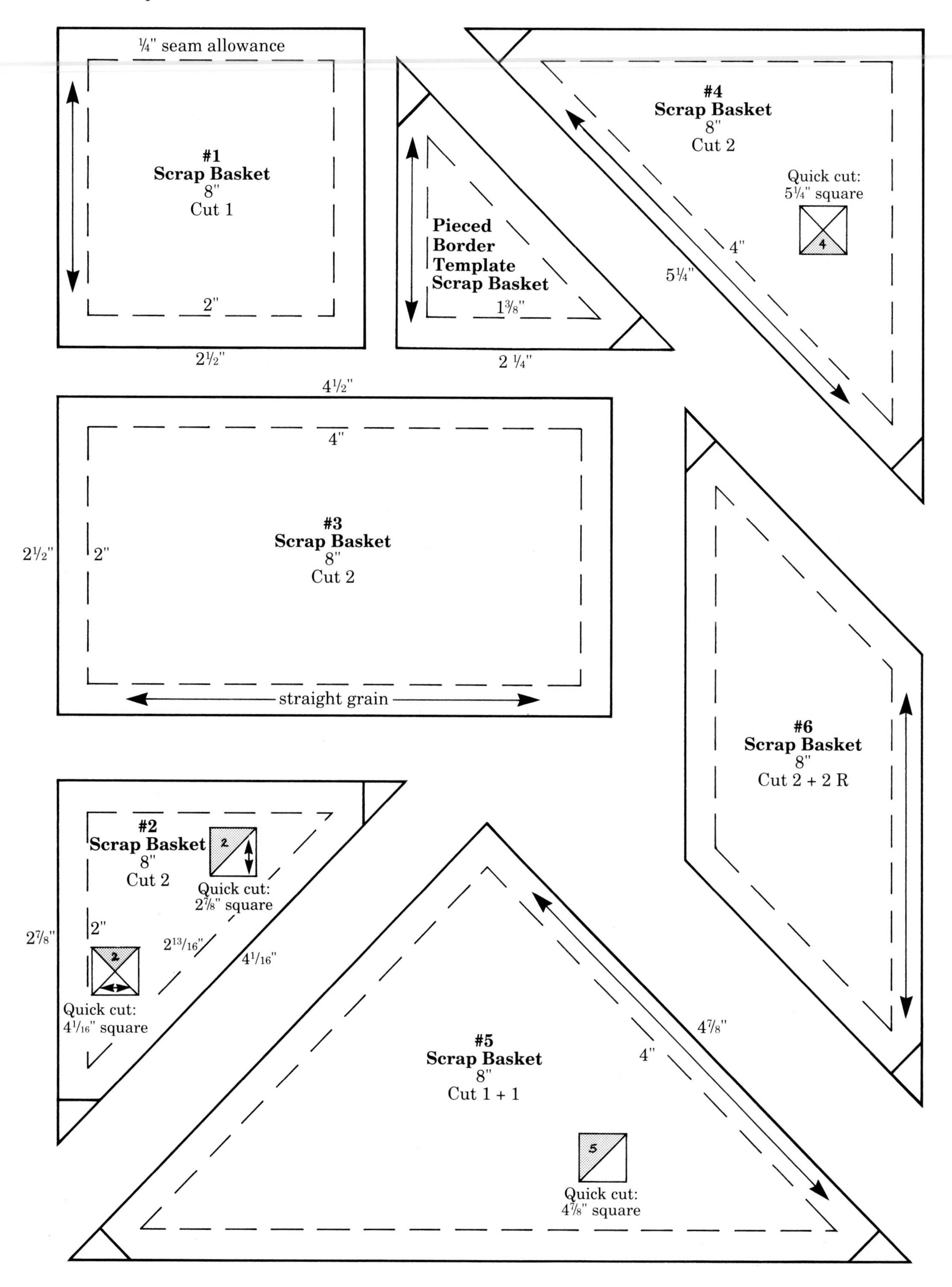

¼" seam allowance
#1
Scrap Basket
8"
Cut 1
2"
2½"
Pieced
Border
Template
Scrap Basket
1⅜"
2 ¼"
#4
Scrap Basket
8"
Cut 2
Quick cut:
5¼" square
4"
5¼"
4½"
4"
#3
Scrap Basket
8"
Cut 2
2½"
2"
straight grain
#6
Scrap Basket
8"
Cut 2 + 2 R
#2
Scrap Basket
8"
Cut 2
Quick cut:
2⅞" square
2⅞"
2"
2 13/16"
4 1/16"
Quick cut:
4 1/16" square
#5
Scrap Basket
8"
Cut 1 + 1
4⅞"
4"
Quick cut:
4⅞" square

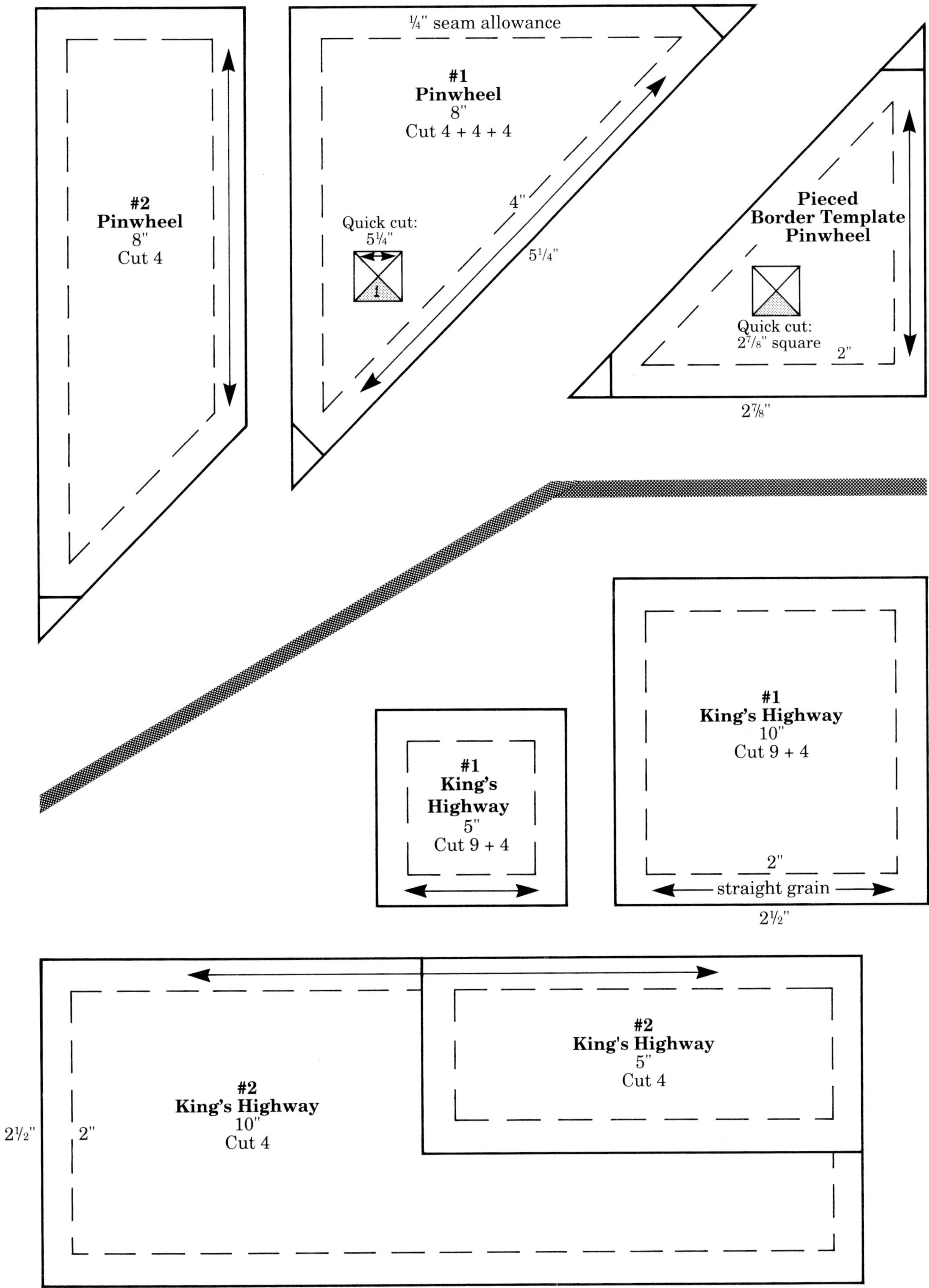

¼" seam allowance
#1
Pinwheel
8"
Cut 4 + 4 + 4
Quick cut:
5¼"
4"
5¼"
#2
Pinwheel
8"
Cut 4
Pieced
Border Template
Pinwheel
Quick cut:
2⅞" square
2"
2⅞"
#1
King's Highway
10"
Cut 9 + 4
2"
straight grain
2½"
#1
King's
Highway
5"
Cut 9 + 4
#2
King's Highway
5"
Cut 4
#2
King's Highway
10"
Cut 4
2½"
2"
6½"

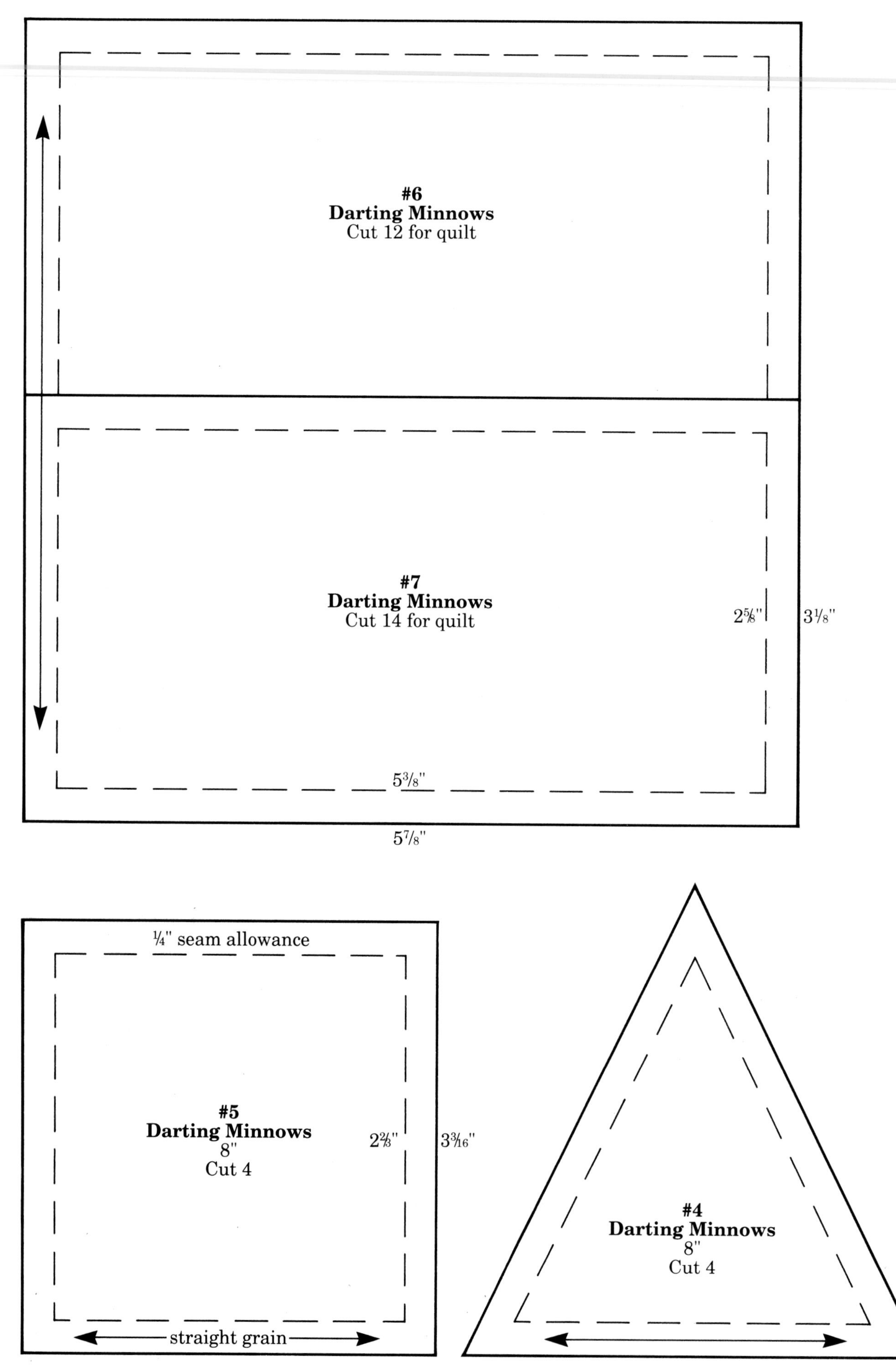
#6
Darting Minnows
Cut 12 for quilt
#7
Darting Minnows
Cut 14 for quilt
2⅝"
3⅛"
5⅜"
5⅞"
¼" seam allowance
#5
Darting Minnows
8"
Cut 4
2⅔"
3³⁄₁₆"
straight grain
#4
Darting Minnows
8"
Cut 4

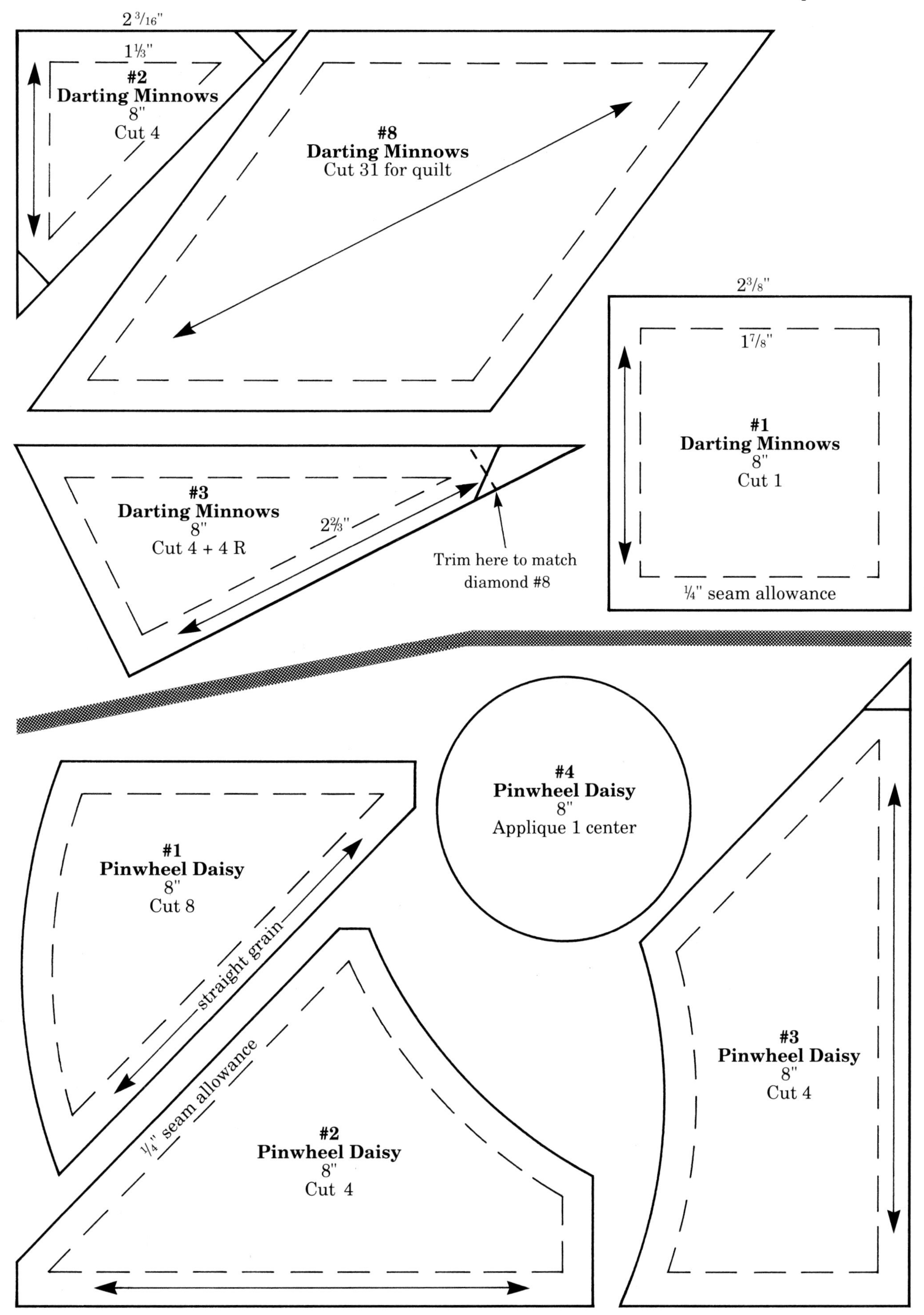
2 3/16"
1⅓"
#2
Darting Minnows
8"
Cut 4
#8
Darting Minnows
Cut 31 for quilt
2³/₈"
1⁷/₈"
#1
Darting Minnows
8"
Cut 1
¼" seam allowance
#3
Darting Minnows
8"
Cut 4 + 4 R
2⅔"
Trim here to match
diamond #8
#4
Pinwheel Daisy
8"
Applique 1 center
#1
Pinwheel Daisy
8"
Cut 8
straight grain
¼" seam allowance
#2
Pinwheel Daisy
8"
Cut 4
#3
Pinwheel Daisy
8"
Cut 4

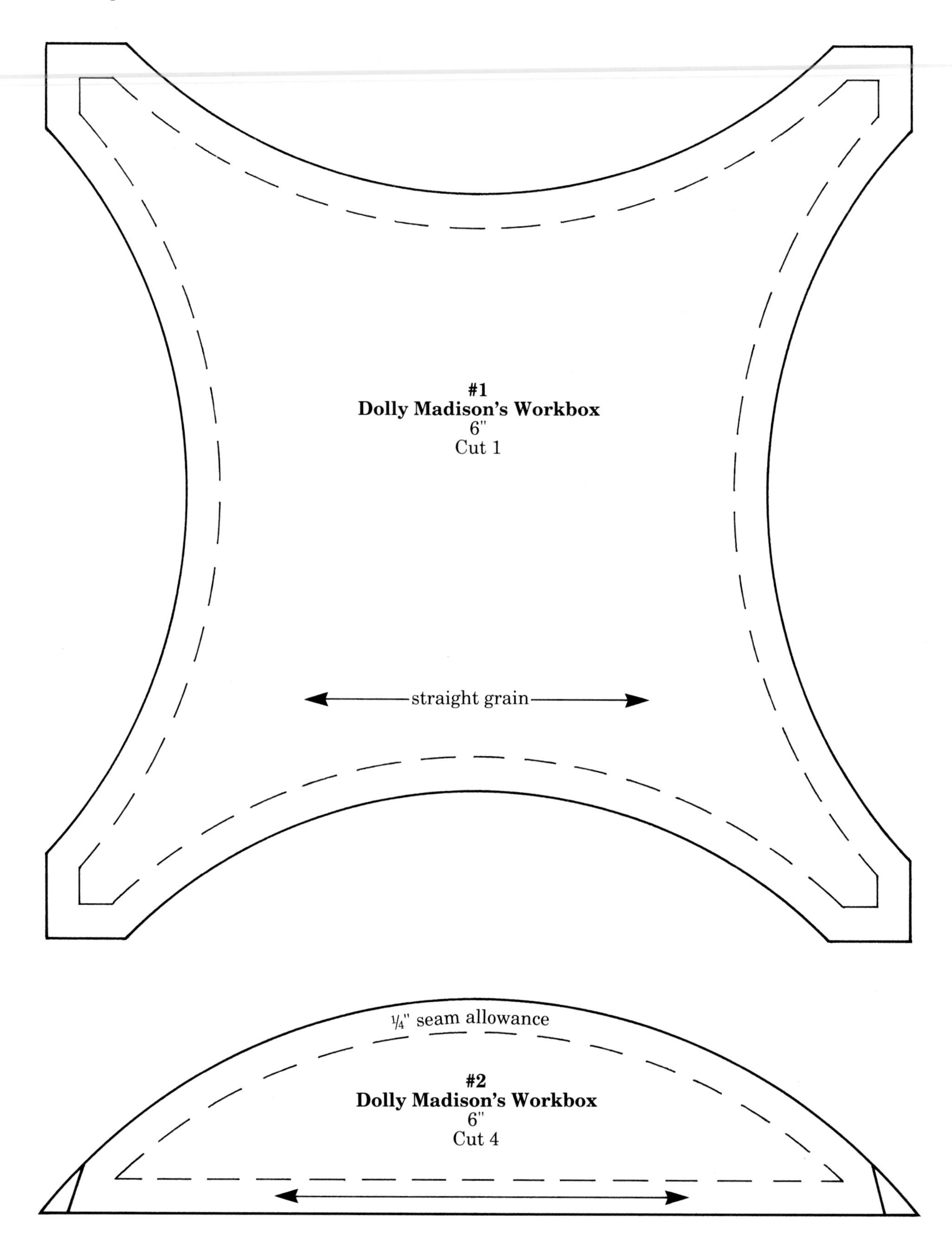
#1
Dolly Madison's Workbox
6"
Cut 1
straight grain
¼" seam allowance
#2
Dolly Madison's Workbox
6"
Cut 4

Glossary of Techniques

Setting the Quilt Together

When unit blocks are sewn together to make a quilt top, it is called the "set." Though there are literally thousands of unit block designs, there are relatively few basic ways to put them together. However, an amazing number of quilt top designs can be achieved by using and combining these few basic variations.

One way to "set" design blocks is to sew them together side by side (adjacently). In other sets, design blocks can be separated by set pieces, which can be unpieced squares, rectangles, or triangles. Sets can be straight or diagonal. Alternate block sets the same size as the design blocks can be placed between them in checkerboard fashion. Diagonal sets using alternate blocks require side triangles to complete the set. Strips of fabric, called lattices, can also be used to separate the unit blocks.

Set pieces need not be plain squares or lattice strips. They can be pieced in different ways to add to the overall quilt design.

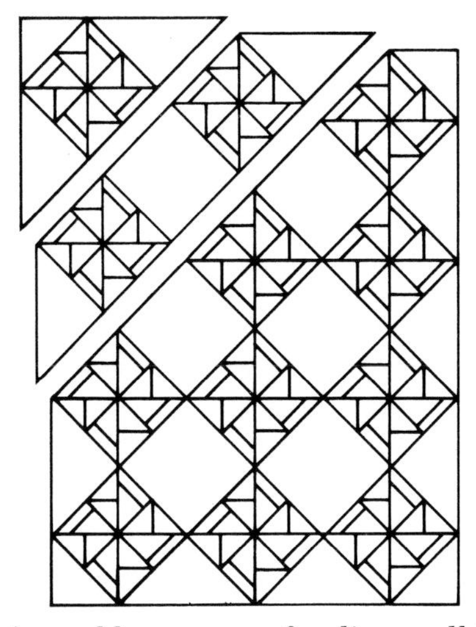

Assembly sequence for diagonally set quilt

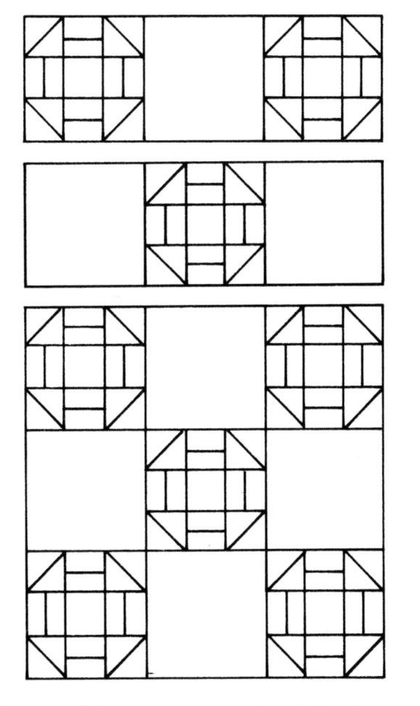

Assembly sequence for blocks set straight-on with alternate unpieced squares

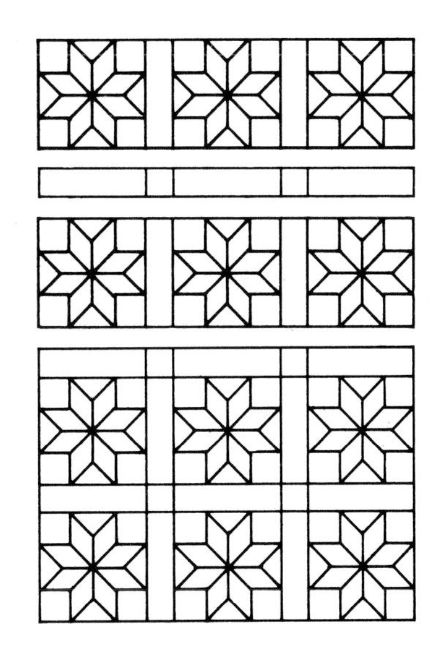

Assembly sequence for straight-set quilt with lattice strips and square set pieces

Feel free to experiment with different sets. Remain open to new possibilities. Although I usually have a quilt plan in mind when I make a group of unit blocks, I like to play a bit to see how they look in various arrangements after they are finished. Allow time for this important part of the quilt design process. Discovering a better quilt plan to suit the blocks after they are made is an exciting part of quiltmaking. Often, the blocks appear quite different made up in fabric from the way they looked drawn on paper, and the original quilt design will need adjustments. Lay the blocks out on the floor or bed. Try diagonal and straight-on sets. Vary spatial arrangements and try to think ahead to appropriate border treatments.

It may be wise to put off buying fabric for alternate blocks or lattices until part or all of the unit blocks are finished. To find the best fabric for the set pieces, lay the blocks out on a few different lengths of uncut fabric that you are considering. When these fabric possibilities are in front of you, the best choice often becomes obvious.

Whatever set you choose for your quilt, the general construction rules for sewing unit blocks still apply.

1. Sew exact 1/4" seams edge to edge.
2. Look for the longest seams to establish piecing units.
3. Keep straight grain on the outside edges of the quilt sections.
4. Press for opposing seams.
5. Pin all points of matching.

Preparing the Blocks

All the blocks in your quilt need to be the same size (if that is the way it was planned). Anyone who has made a sampler quilt (one that includes many block designs) or worked on a group quilt (where each block was made by a different person) knows that if the size of the design blocks varies by more than 1/8" or so, it can be extremely difficult to sew the blocks together.

So, as you piece your blocks, measure them to make sure they are all the proper size. Proper size is the finished dimension of the block as drafted, plus 1/2" for seam allowances. If your blocks are not coming out to proper size, they should at least be all the same size. With experience, you will learn how much variance is acceptable. I find I can work with blocks that vary in size from 1/8" to 3/16", but when the size difference is more than that, I either don't use the most extreme blocks or design the quilt set to correct for the varying sizes of the blocks.

Some quilters "true up" (trim) or "block" their sewn blocks to the proper size. With my piecing technique, I have never found it necessary. If templates, cutting, and 1/4" seams are precise, the blocks will just naturally be the right size.

Cutting Set Pieces

Set pieces are cut just like those in the design block, but larger. If your pieced blocks are slightly too small or too large for the set pieces that were cut, the set pieces should be cut to fit with the design blocks. Measure your blocks before cutting set pieces and make necessary adjustments to measurements so they will all fit together.

Alternate squares and rectangles for lattices are cut with the straight grain along the straight sides. If the set is diagonal, the straight grain on side triangles should fall on the long side or along the outside edge of the quilt top. If the fabric pattern requires a bias edge in this position, stay-stitch 1/8" from the edge to keep the bias from stretching out of shape.

Setting the Quilt

In preparation for sewing blocks and set pieces together, lay them out on the floor or up on a design wall. Look for the longest seams to determine construction rows. For straight sets, some quilters prefer to keep the longest seams going the length of the quilt for strength. Sew vertical rows of blocks together and then join the rows.

Diagonal sets are made up of diagonal rows of blocks and set pieces that are different lengths. Laying the whole top out will help you see which pieces go in each row.

Pressing

To achieve crisp points and corners and to avoid excessive seam allowance bulk when sewing blocks together, plan your pressing of blocks and set pieces for opposing seams. In quilts with lattices or alternate blocks, this usually means pressing away from the pieced block.

When pieced blocks are set side by side, pressing can be a little more complex, and you need to think about how the blocks will be joined as they are being pieced and pressed. Plan a piecing and pressing order that includes as many opposing seams, where blocks meet, as possible to evenly distribute bulky seam allowances and aid in precise piecing.

In some designs, identical blocks can be pressed all the same way and then rotated alternately to match opposing seams.

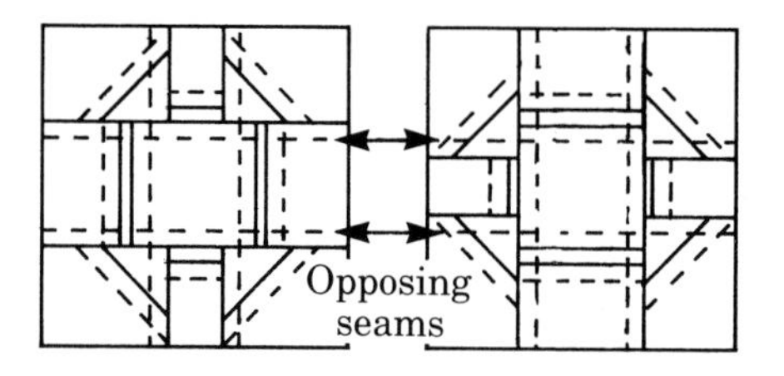

I find that I do a lot more pinning while setting a quilt top than I do in normal piecing. Pin to establish points of matching and where easing will be needed. Easing blocks to set pieces and vice versa is fairly normal. I find it helps to pin and match seams on the ironing board. A shot of steam here and there seems to help the rows fit together and the sewing go more smoothly.

Adding Borders

Most quilts have borders of some kind. They visually contain the design and keep it from running off the edge. Borders emphasize and enhance the central quilt design, provided they relate to it properly in scale, motif, and color. Scale is the size of the pieces. Motif is the shape of the pieces. So, the sizes and shapes of border pieces should echo or be similar to those present in the quilt. The color of an outside border will bring out that color in the quilt design. For instance, if a quilt is rust, cream, and blue in about equal amounts, adding a blue border will emphasize the blue.

Borders can also be used to bring a quilt out to size without making more unit blocks. Be careful, though, not to make the borders so wide that they outweigh the quilt design in visual importance.

Borders can be:

1. Plain with straight-sewn corners
2. Plain with mitered corners
3. Multiple plain strips with mitered corners
4. Patchwork (pieced or appliqued)
5. Any combination of the above

Borders should be cut to fit the actual size of the quilt center. At first, cut border strips longer than you think you'll need, then trim them later to fit the quilt.

It is important that the quilt end up "square" (with 90° corners) and true. Top and bottom dimensions should be equal, and the two side dimensions should be equal. I once made a quilt with one side fully seven inches longer than the other. Needless to say, the quilt wouldn't lie flat and it surely couldn't have been hung on a wall.

To find the proper length of borders with blunt-sewn corners, first measure the length of the quilt through the center, edge to edge (including seam allowances). Cut both side strips this length and stitch them to the sides of the quilt. To measure for the top and bottom, take the dimension across the center of the quilt (including the side borders and seam allowances). Cut the borders this length and stitch. It is not uncommon to have to ease one side of a quilt to fit a border and stretch the opposite side slightly to fit the same dimension.

To measure the fit of mitered corners, you will need two sets of dimensions. First, determine the finished outside dimensions of the quilt. Cut the borders this length, plus two or three extra inches for seam allowances and ease of matching. Second, measure the width and

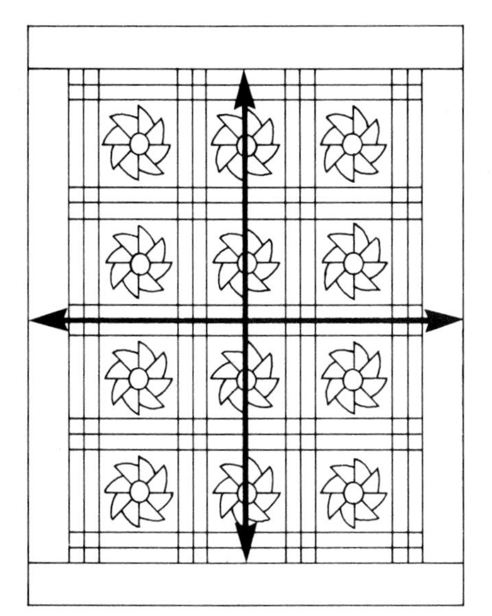

Measuring for borders with blunt-sewn corners

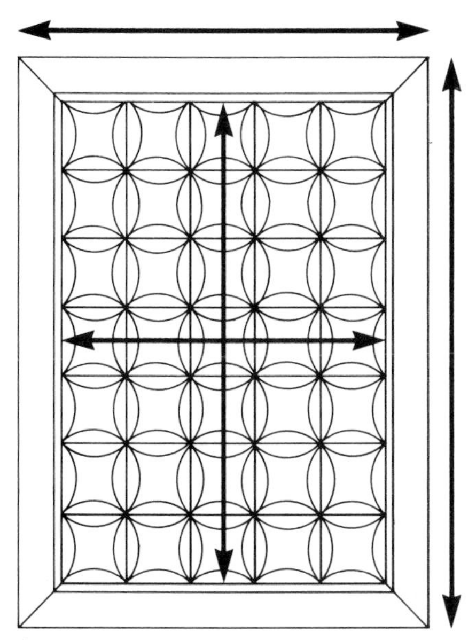

Measuring for borders with mitered corners

length of the quilt through the center, seam line to seam line (not including seam allowances). Find the center of the border section and mark the seam line measurements according to that center. Match these marks on the border to the appropriate edge of the quilt top and proceed as outlined below.

When pinning borders in place for sewing, I like to work at the ironing board. Pin the quilt to the board to keep it from slipping. Position the border on the quilt by matching centers, ends, and important points of matching. Ease and generously pin everything in between. Pressing the border to the quilt top with a steam iron at this point helps the two fit together and makes the sewing go more smoothly. Steam both shrinks and stretches fabric, allowing you to adjust the fit where it is needed.

Plain Borders

A plain border is simply one that is not a pieced design. If it is cut from a stripe or border print, it can look fancy but still be easy to construct.

A strip of fabric needs to be cut for each side of the quilt and for the top and bottom. The ideal method is to cut the strips from the length of the fabric, so you do not have to piece them. Lengthwise grain of the fabric is more stable than crosswise grain, so borders cut on the lengthwise grain will have less stretch.

Borders cut from the length of the fabric require continuous yardage, which can be expensive. As a result, I sometimes opt to buy less fabric, cut border strips from the width or crosswise grain, and sew them together to get the needed length. Seams should be pressed open and placed in the center of each side for minimum visibility. Crosswise grain does have some give to it, so I try not to use borders cut this way for outer quilt edges. However, I often use strips cut cross-grain and pieced for inner border strips.

If you choose plain borders with straight-sewn corners, first sew borders to the long sides of the quilt, then to the top and bottom. Striped fabrics make lovely quilt borders, but the corners must be mitered to make the design turn the corner gracefully. It is also important to miter corners when using multiple plain borders. Mitering corners is not difficult and worth the effort in many design situations.

Mitering Corners

1. Prepare the borders. Determine the finished outside dimension of your quilt. Cut the borders this length, plus 2" or 3" for seam allowances and ease of matching. When using a striped fabric for borders, make sure the design on all four sides is cut the same way. Multiple border strips should be sewn together and the resulting "striped" units treated as a single border for mitering.

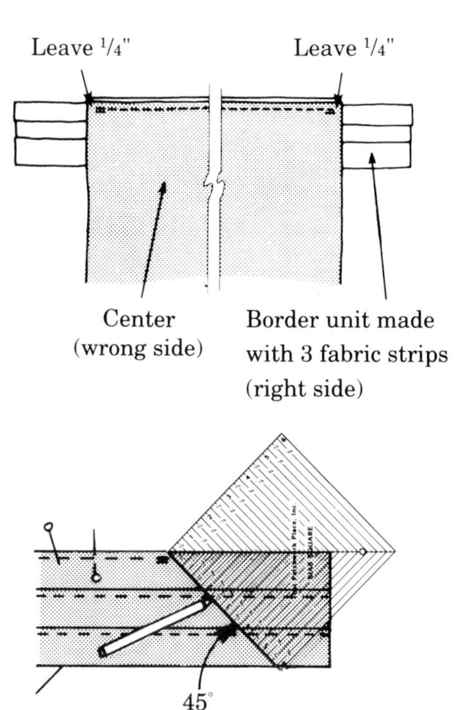

2. To attach the border to the center section of the quilt, center each border to a side, so the ends extend equally on either side of the center section. Beginning and ending with a backtack, sew the border to the center with a 1/4" seam; sew seam line to seam line, leaving 1/4" unsewn at the beginning and end. Press seam allowances toward the border.
3. Arrange the first corner to be mitered on the ironing board, as illustrated. Align the edges of the borders, pinning the center pieced section out of the way. Press the borders flat and straight. Pin the quilt to the ironing board to keep it from slipping.

   Using the Bias Square™, a 90/45° triangle, or other ruler with a 45° angle, draw a line that begins at the inside seam allowance, where the previous stitches stopped, and lies at a

45° angle to the outside edge of the borders. This is the sewing line. Pin in place.

4. Backtacking at the beginning, stitch on the drawn line from the inside ¼" seam line to outside edge. Trim excess fabric to ¼" along the mitered seam. Press this seam open. Press other seams to the outside.

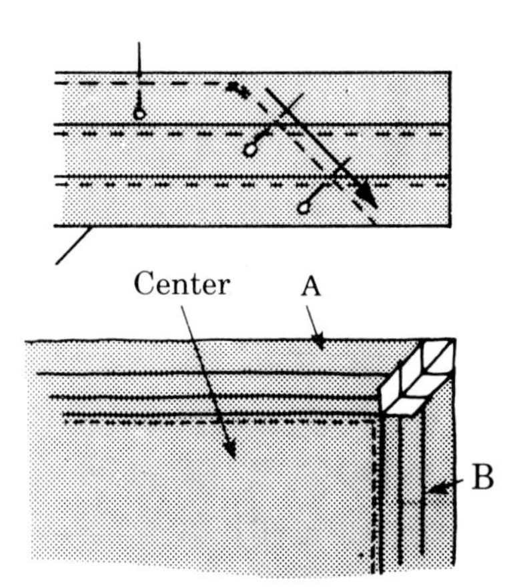

Pieced Borders

Pieced border designs are basically unit blocks or portions of unit blocks strung together in rows. Each design unit within a border design is called a repeat. A repeat can be simple or complex, square or oblong, pieced or appliqued. It can be set straight or on the diagonal.

For a pieced border to fit, the finished dimensions of the central patchwork design need to be equally divisible by the border repeat measurement. To use 2" repeats, for instance, the space in which the border is to fit needs to have a finished dimension divisible by 2". A 4" border repeat fits only measurements evenly divisible by 4", and so on.

Because fabric stretches and seams vary, no matter how well a border is planned, it rarely measures exactly what it should after the actual cutting and sewing is done. So, the challenge is to fit the pieced border to the pieced quilt center, even though the measurements often are not what you planned. The following strategies will help make the borders fit:

1. Try making a sample section of your pieced border and measure it to see if your cutting and sewing is yielding the proper dimensions. Adjustments can be made to achieve the desired results.
2. Plan your quilt design to include plain borders to separate the center of the quilt from the pieced border. This plain border is called a spacer strip because it can fill in whatever space you need. Wait to cut it until the center and border sections are complete. To arrive at a dimension for the spacer strip, measure the pieced sections. Do not include seam allowances in these calculations. Subtract the size of the quilt center from the length of the pieced border. Divide the resulting dimension by two and you'll have the finished width of the spacer strip. Add ½" for seam allowances before cutting strips.
3. Some quilters like to leave the outside edges of complex pieced borders on the bias, especially when there are critical matching points. Bias edges stretch but are also simple to ease in, if need be.

Preparing to Quilt

Marking

In most cases, the quilt top must be marked with lines to guide stitching, before you quilt. Where you place the quilting lines will depend on the patchwork design, the type of batting used, and how much quilting you want to do.

Try to avoid quilting too close to the seam lines, where the bulk of seam allowances might slow you down or make the stitches uneven. Also, keep in mind that the purpose of quilting, besides its aesthetic value, is to securely hold the three layers together. Don't leave large areas unquilted.

Thoroughly press the quilt top and mark it, before it is assembled with the batting and backing. You will need marking pencils; a long ruler or yardstick; stencils or templates for quilting motifs; and a smooth, clean, hard surface on which to work. Use a sharp marking pencil and lightly mark the quilting lines on the fabric. No matter what kind of marking tool you use, light lines will be easier to remove than heavy ones.

Backing

You often can use a single length of 45" wide fabric for backing small quilts. To be safe, plan on a usable width of only 42" after shrinkage and cutting of selvages. For larger quilts, you will have to sew two lengths of fabric together.

Cut the backing at least 1" larger than the quilt top, all the way around. Press thoroughly with seams open.

Batting

Batting is the filler in a quilt or comforter. Thick batting is used in comforters that are tied. If you plan to quilt, use thin batting and quilt by hand.

Thin batting comes in 100% polyester, 100% cotton, and a cotton-polyester (80%–20%) combination. All-cotton batting requires close quilting to prevent shifting and separating in the wash. Most old quilts have cotton batting and are rather flat. Cotton is a good natural fiber that lasts well and is compatible with cotton and cotton-blend fabrics.

Less quilting is required on 100% polyester batting. If polyester batting is glazed or bonded, it is easy to work with, won't pull apart, and has more loft than cotton. Some polyester batting, however, has a tendency to "beard" or "migrate" (the small white polyester fibers creep to the quilt's surface between the threads in the fabric). This migration most often occurs when polyester blends are used in the quilt top instead of 100% cotton fabrics. The cotton-polyester batting is said to combine the best features of the two fibers. You also can use a single layer of preshrunk cotton flannel for filler instead of batting. The quilt will be very flat, and quilting stitches highly visible.

Assembling the Layers

Lay the backing face down on a large, clean, flat surface. With masking tape, tape the backing down (without stretching) to keep it smooth and flat while you are working with the other layers.

Gently lay the batting on top of the backing, centering and smoothing it as you go. It is a good idea to let the batt "relax" for a few hours at this point, to ease out wrinkles. Trim batting to size of backing.

Center the freshly ironed and marked quilt top on top of the batting, right side up. Starting in the middle, pin baste the three layers together while gently smoothing out fullness to the sides and corners. Take care not to distort the straight lines of the quilt design and the borders.

After pinning, baste the layers together with needle and light-colored thread. Start in the middle and make a line of long stitches to each corner to form a large X. Continue basting in a grid of parallel lines 6"–8" apart. Finish with a row of basting around the outside edges. Quilts that are to be quilted with a hoop or on your lap will be handled more than those quilted on a frame; therefore, they will require more basting. After basting, remove the pins. Now you are ready to quilt.

Quilt top Batting Backing

Basting Masking tape

Hand Quilting

To quilt by hand, you will need quilting thread, quilting needles, small scissors, a thimble, and perhaps a balloon or large rubber band to help grasp the needle if it gets stuck. Quilt on a frame, a large hoop, or just on your lap or a table. Use a single strand of quilting thread not longer than 18". Make a small single knot in the end of the thread. The quilting stitch is a small running stitch that goes through all three layers of the quilt. Take two, three, or even four stitches at a time if you can keep them even. When crossing seams, you might find it necessary to "hunt and peck" one stitch at a time.

To begin, insert the needle in the top layer about ¾" from the point you want to start stitching. Pull the needle out at the starting point and gently tug at the knot until it pops through the fabric and is buried in the batting. Make a backstitch and begin quilting. Stitches should be tiny (8–10 per inch is good), even, and straight. At first, concentrate on even and straight; tiny will come with practice.

When you come almost to the end of the thread, make a single knot ¼" from the fabric. Take a backstitch to bury the knot in the batting. Run the thread off through the batting and out the quilt top; snip it off. The first and last stitches will look different from the running stitches in between. To make them less noticeable, start and stop where quilting lines cross each other or at seam joints.

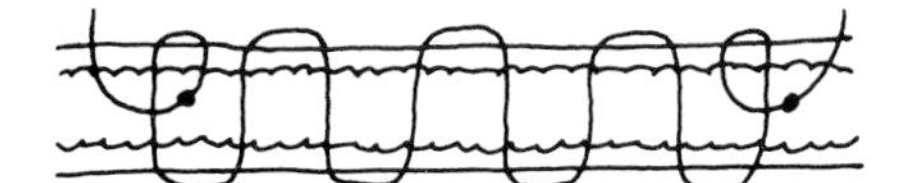

Hand quilting stitch

Binding

Bias Strips

Binding that will be used to finish the edges of a quilt is usually made from bias strips of fabric. To find the true bias, bring one side of fabric to the adjacent side and press, or use a ruler with a 45° angle marking. Using a rotary cutter and mat, cut 1½" wide strips along the bias. One-half yard of fabric will yield 5¼ yards of 1½" bias binding. Three-fourths yard of fabric will yield 12 yards of 1½" bias binding.

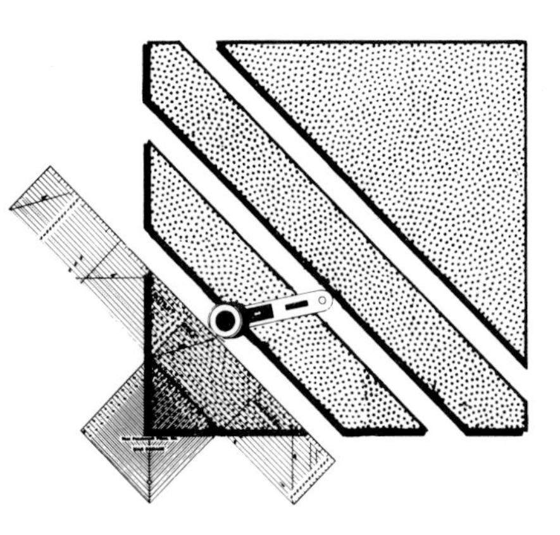

Seam ends together to make a continuous strip long enough to go around your quilt, with a few extra inches for joining.

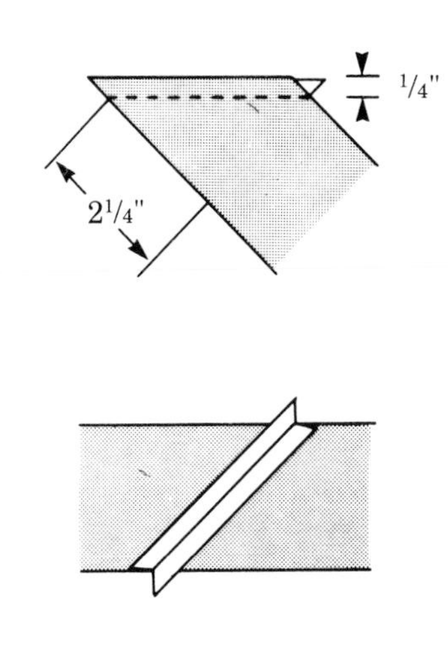

Binding the Edges

After quilting, trim excess batting and backing even with the edge of the quilt top. A rotary cutter and long ruler will ensure accurate straight edges. If basting is no longer in place, baste all three layers together.

1. Using a 1/4" seam allowance, sew the binding strips to the front of the quilt. Begin at the center of one side and sew through all layers. Be careful not to stretch the bias or the quilt edge as you sew. Stitch until you reach the seam line point at the corner. Backstitch; cut threads.
2. Turn quilt to prepare for sewing along the next edge. Fold the binding away from the quilt, as shown, then fold again to place binding along edge of quilt. (This fold creates an angled pleat at the corner.)

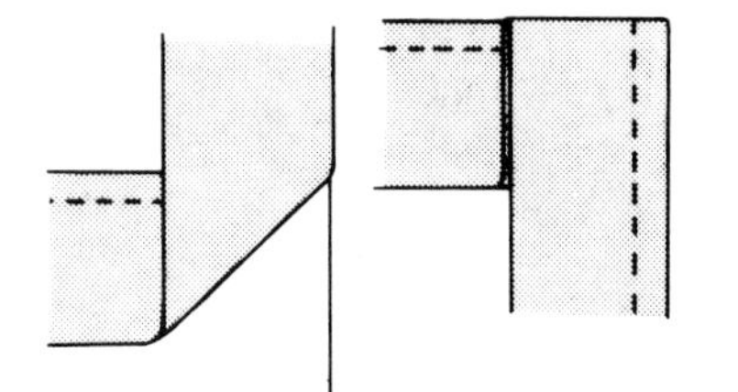

3. Stitch from the fold of the binding along the seam line to the seam-line point at the next corner. Backstitch; cut threads. Fold binding as in step 2 and continue around edge.
4. Join the beginning and ending of the binding strip, or plan to hand sew one end to overlap the other.
5. Turn binding to the back side, turning raw edge under, and blindstitch in place. At each corner, fold binding in the sequence shown to form a miter on back of quilt.

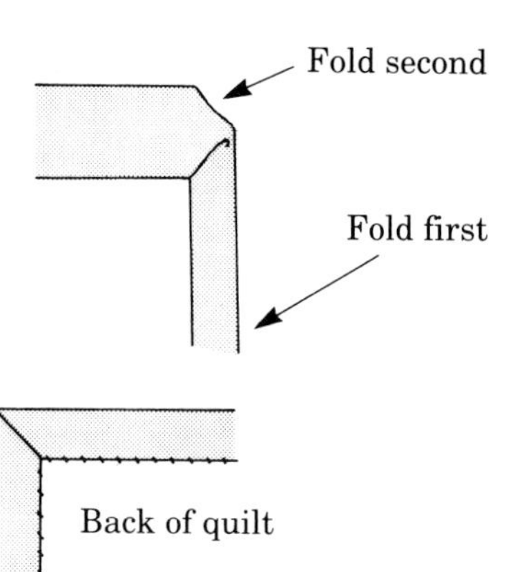